EIGHT WORDS
FOR THE STUDY OF
EXPRESSIVE CULTURE

Eight Words

for the Study of

Expressive Culture

EDITED BY BURT FEINTUCH

UNIVERSITY OF ILLINOIS PRESS

URBANA, CHICAGO, AND SPRINGFIELD

Library of Congress Cataloging-in-Publication Data
Eight words for the study of expressive culture /
edited by Burt Feintuch.
p.   cm.
Includes bibliographical references and index.
ISBN 978-0-252-02806-9 (cloth : alk. paper)
ISBN 978-0-252-07109-6 (pbk. : alk. paper)
1. Folklore—Terminology. 2. Folklore—Philosophy.
I. Feintuch, Burt, 1949– .
GR44.4.E44   2003
398'.01'4—dc21   2002008284

To the memory of my father, Stanley Feintuch,
who believed in using words well

Contents

Acknowledgments

An earlier version of *Eight Words* appeared in 1995 as the final issue of the *Journal of American Folklore*, at the end of my five-year term as that publication's editor. After that issue, which was titled *Common Ground: Keywords for the Study of Expressive Culture*, came out, I began hearing from friends and colleagues, some of whom I knew, others who were new to me. All said in one fashion or another that we had created an important and useful collection of essays, and that led to the idea of a book version. This is a significantly different publication from that special issue of a journal. *Identity* didn't figure at all in the 1995 version. Two of the other essays here are entirely different from their predecessors, and the authors of several others have edited or significantly revised their original contributions. I've enjoyed having a second chance to get it right.

Quite a number of colleagues helped me choose my words. The conversation began in *Journal of American Folklore* editorial board meetings, and it moved outward from those sessions. I would like to thank Barbara Babcock, Richard Bauman, Charles Briggs, the late Gerald Davis, Linda Dégh, Mary Hufford, Barbara Kirshenblatt-Gimblett, Henry Glassie, Thomas Green, Elliott Oring, Gerald Pocius, Neil Rosenberg, Jack Santino, Amy Shuman, and Jeff Titon for their help. Thanks, too, to Judith McCulloh, Jeff Titon, Joanne Sacco, and Max Feintuch for their comments on earlier versions of this introduction, to Barbara Ward for her editorial assistance in shaping this volume the first time around, and to Jennifer Beard for her help in bringing this volume to press. Joan Howard provided a kind of editorial expertise I don't have, for which I am very grateful. At the University of New Hampshire, the College of Liberal Arts and the Department of English provided funding, and I thank Marilyn Hoskin and Shelly Lieber for that support. Finally, I am very grateful to John Bealle of John Bealle Indexing Services for his excellent work in creating the index for this volume.

BURT FEINTUCH

Introduction:
Eight Words

Group, art, text, genre, performance, context, tradition, identity. No matter where we are—in academic institutions, in cultural agencies, surrendering to the lure of the local—these are words we use when we talk about creative expression in its social contexts. We think with them. We teach with them. Much scholarship rests on them. They form a significant part of a set of conversations extending through centuries of thought about creativity, meaning, beauty, local knowledge, values, and community. If words have natural habitats, the environments for these range across scholarly disciplines and other fields of practice. On their own and in various combinations these eight words stand for much of what is good and enduring in being human. Together, they constitute a common ground for talking about expressive culture.

"Common ground" is a familiar rubric, implying shared space—physical, emotional, conceptual, social, political, symbolic. I use it here to refer to the symbolic and the conceptual. Eight authors examine a set of words that are at the heart of conversations about expressive culture. I've called these *keywords,* following Raymond Williams's magisterial 1976 book *Keywords: A Vocabulary of Culture and Society.* There Williams offers broad essays on words, such as *culture,* that in his view are at the foundation of the study of humankind. On that model this book presents essays on another set of keywords. These are words we need when we talk about culture's expressive realms—the forms, processes, emotions, and ideas bound up in the social production of what Robert Plant Armstrong

1

has called "affecting presences," aesthetic forms and performances in everyday life—music, verbal art, play, material culture, celebration, ritual, and display. The notion of *key* has several facets that apply here. It implies centrality, importance; these words are key in discussions ranging across many constituencies. No matter whether you are an anthropologist, an arts administrator, a literary critic, or a museumgoer, these are likely to be among the words you use most as you ponder aesthetic expression. *Keys* open; I hope that this book will open new discussions of fundamental concepts. *Key* implies tone or pitch, and the eight authors here, all folklorists, share a certain inflection or attitude coming from our discipline. Although a *key* can also be the code or the answer, *Eight Words* stops short of making such a claim. But in a certain sense, the authors and I hope it contributes to cracking a code, laying open the ways in which common terms have come to be especially meaningful.

Group, art, text, genre, performance, context, tradition, identity. Deeply nuanced and always inflected by the moment, these are sonorous words. This book's eight essays attempt what most of the authors would finally admit is impossible: to define words that are notoriously slippery. Each essay begins by offering a succinct characterization, an attempt to fix for a moment a useful, or "operational," definition, all the while understanding that meaning is always circumstantial, not likely to be crystallized for more than a flash. Then the essays delve deeper, grounding those definitions in ways of knowing, histories of interpretation, and the authors' own points of view, simultaneously examining their word's ambiguities, abstruseness, and other contingencies, locating them in the conversations that produced them, and, at times, suggesting useful ways of employing them. If this book is really about shared conceptual spaces, each space is a point of departure or a reference point. It's not a final destination.

When I began this project, I had two seemingly contradictory goals. One has to do with interdisciplinary value. The other has to do with a single discipline. I wanted to create a lexicon with only a few entries—a fundamental stock of words, each with thoughtful exegesis, and I wanted it to appeal across disciplinary boundaries. For me, a frequently cited statement from Dell Hymes captures the essence of *expressive culture.* Hymes writes that "the capacity for aesthetic experience, for shaping of deeply felt values into meaningful, apposite form, is present in all communities" (1975:346). The very idea of *expressive culture* sweeps across scholarly disciplines and fields of criticism, as it stands for ways of thinking about how culture is expressed in artistic action and aesthetic medium. Go to the library catalog or search the Web, and you will find that discussions in many of the fields of the humanities and social sciences use the inventory of words in this book. These eight words really are, I am convinced, at the center of many conversations about socially based creativity, about the ways in which individual aesthetic and symbolic action is grounded in that hazy realm we term "culture." That's the first goal, the desire to make a book that speaks beyond disciplinary provincialism.

But inevitably my disciplinary orientation comes into play: I thought it was time for folklorists to offer their take on these fundamental concepts. Why folklorists? Usually attending to forms and practices of human expression that have until recently existed far from the centers of other disciplines, folklorists have a distinguished history of work with aspects of culture traditionally not part of the canons of Western academic thought. To be a folklorist has nearly always been to hold an expansive view of human expression and to have particular interest in the local, the noncanonical, the vernacular. From long before it was fashionable, folklorists claimed that culture is plural. Our gaze tends to rest on cultural continuities, and it seems that we are advocates for creativity wherever it happens. The folklorist's work is an antidote to parochial notions that would limit meaningful aesthetic action to more rarefied sites and contexts. I remember being at a conference years ago when Imamu Amiri Baraka characterized folklorists as academic outlaws, renegades. He may have been right then, even if his language was dramatic. It did seem for a very long time that folklorists worked in quiet opposition to the historically canonical disciplines—art history, musicology, literary criticism, and other endeavors that favored culture with a capital *C*. Of course, these days canons hold much less authority, and in some fields it seems that nearly anything goes when it comes to subject. But in many cases, it was folklorists who first traversed the ground, or were, at least, there early, in realms ranging from material culture to African American verbal art to ethnographic studies of the suspect or marginal, long before other scholarly fields began addressing them.

As a result, folklorists stand at a peculiar sort of crossroads. We were early on the scene, working to document and understand the astonishingly plural nature of human expression. We have a long history of contemplating the extraordinary embedded in the ordinary, the artistic partially obscured in the quotidian. At the same time, we share and use the fundamental word-stock of more traditionally canonical disciplines. We use a broad, humanistic vocabulary to talk about historically unorthodox sites and subjects. For decades much of our work has implicitly argued for an opening up of that terminology. These days, it seems that history is on our side, as the academy, critics, and other cultural specialists attempt to do a better job of comprehending, and serving, the world beyond the canons. Meanwhile, potters throw their clay, communities mark and celebrate what they value, people get in the groove to an incredible array of local musics, and narrators tell their stories. Our subject is in the bedrock of the soul. It is the sinew of community. And no matter what field we're in, most of us realize the futility of talking only to ourselves.

Group, art, text, genre, performance, context, tradition, identity. Together, they stand for expressive culture's social base, its aesthetic nature, its categories, and its relationship to time. Nearly all of these essays are ethnographically based. That is, their authors have wrestled with abstract concepts such as these in the very real circumstances of the everyday lives of people in an array of social settings. All would agree that an understanding of these concepts must be grounded in everyday life, in knowing that real people create, reenact, reframe, and reconstitute culture in social life. Dorothy Noyes's essay on *group* gets at expressive culture's social base. Noyes points out that *group* is a simple term for complicated connections. She worries about the comforting and familiar term *community,* using social network theory as a way to think about the ways in which people affiliate and make meaning together. Folklorists have centered their interest in groups. Opening with a very evocative example of Italian Americans, African Americans, and a Southeast Asian interacting in the context of an Italian street festival, Noyes helps us think about how not to oversimplify the human relationships at the foundation of our research.

Only lately have many scholars come to the folklorists' and anthropologists' understanding that *art* is a term that describes aspects of everyday life, folding into itself notions of product, behavior, and performance. Gerald Pocius has done significant research in Newfoundland communities, ranging from the ways in which making hooked rugs makes meaning to the ways in which people artfully embellish their part of the landscape to the subject of professional wrestling. *Art,* he tells us, has to do with a community's sense of excellence. It seems to be a universal, although not all societies categorize the products of creativity as Western elites do.

A *text,* Jeff Todd Titon writes, is any object of interpretation. In its most conventional use, *text* connotes words on paper, words given a kind of authority—a work of literature, a narrative transcribed for study or publication. The model of the text—the authoritative written version— permeates the study of expressive culture, but at the same time, that study has radically expanded the term. Titon, whose work has ranged widely over vernacular musics and sacred speech, proposes the notion of "knowing texts," self-conscious creations mediating between the experience of the ethnographic research and authorial point of view, cognizant of issues of representation and authority that shape texts, written or not. We build *genres*, terminologies and hierarchies of those objects of interpretation. Trudier Harris-Lopez discusses *genre* as a set of categories or system of classification. Creating terms such as *narrative* and imbuing them with authority is itself an act of interpretation, and genre is an attempt to give order to a great diversity of forms. As a way of naming forms, genre is never finished; it is always changing, as ways of knowing shift. For critics and scholars, genre is a convenience, a set of keywords that allow conversation. The term shifts dramatically if we take it to mean local ways of naming art, the terms members of cultural communities use to describe performances and products of cultural creativity.

If expressive culture has a social base in particular groups, it is also based in social acts. Expressive culture is performed. Deborah Kapchan writes about *performance* as aesthetic action in social life, different every time—sometimes frozen when scholars translate from social act to text. From Kenneth Burke to Roger Abrahams and Richard Bauman, *performance* has become a prominent word in folklorists' lexicon, and it has recently achieved currency in many other fields, from literary studies to education theory. Here, Kapchan connects performance to history, locality, and individual creativity, helping us understand how performance, contexts, and texts are linked. Her research in Moroccan markets, especially with women performers in those markets, animates her essay.

Performances and texts are inextricably bound up with *contexts*. Mary Hufford begins by pointing out that the word *context* contains the word *text*. In fact, the two words share the same root, *tek*, implying weaving together. "At close range," Hufford writes, "a context is any frame of reference created in order to constitute and interpret an object of attention. Viewed more broadly, contexts model the master frameworks that relate the world's disparate elements, holding some together and pushing others apart." The model isn't one of nested boxes, texts inside contexts, she points out; it's something far more complicated. There are "contexts of situation," which are more immediate, whereas "contexts of culture" are the broadest frameworks for establishing shared meaning. Hufford's discussion begins close to home, as she watches children model culture in play, and it moves to larger frames as she discusses ways in which contextual frameworks lead to divergent ways of understanding heritage in the context of contested ground in Appalachian West Virginia.

Tradition is a powerful word, standing for perhaps the broadest form of context. Sitting at the hearth and listening to old men and women in a small community in Northern Ireland, immersing himself in the lives of artisans in Turkey and Bangladesh, and talking with people about artistic transformations of wood, clay, metal, and fiber gives a certain kind of authority and point of view to Henry Glassie's take on *tradition*. For Glassie, tradition represents a relationship between past and future, and it contrasts with history as another way of understanding a dynamic that links continuity, creativity, and the future's possibilities.

And on *identity*, Roger D. Abrahams writes, there "is no more important keyword in the vocabulary of cultural discussions." Because of its familiarity, it is a comforting term for many. But at the same time, it's a highly politicized word. Abrahams follows the traces of the word in history, in its transformation from a way of thinking about individuals to a set of ways of thinking about groups, and ultimately to the end of its usefulness. Perhaps the most loaded word of any in *Eight Words*, *identity*, Abrahams suggests, is also both vacuous and dangerous.

In editing this collection, I asked the contributors to explore their words broadly, to stake a claim to them. By *claim* I don't mean to imply ownership. But I did want to encourage folklorists to participate in fundamental discussions of large cultural issues and consequences. Examining our words is one way to do that. It is also a way to reflect on how our unique disciplinary experiences contribute to larger conversations across fields of knowledge. I hope this volume will be useful to readers who come to it in the expansive spirit in which we offer it. Here, then, are eight words for the study of expressive culture. Grounded in the field as we have made it, they offer the possibility of a common ground for an enduring conversation.

References Cited

Armstrong, Robert Plant. 1971. *The Affecting Presence: An Essay in Humanistic Anthropology*. Urbana: University of Illinois Press.

Hymes, Dell. 1975. "Folklore's Nature and the Sun's Myth." *Journal of American Folklore* 88:345–69.

Williams, Raymond. 1976. *Keywords: A Vocabulary of Culture and Society*. New York: Oxford University Press.

I Group

Ideas about group are the most powerful and the most dangerous in folklore studies. Our influence as a discipline has often come from
arguing for small groups against big groups. Against imperialism, we argue for the nation-state; denying the homogeneity of the nation-state, we
argue for the ethnic group or the social class; at last, wary of the dangers
of essentialism at any level, we turn to the face-to-face community.

It is less comfortable to recall that we have also argued for big groups
against small groups: for the historical and racial unity of a nation against
the diversity within it, for example. Today, on the left, we often participate in efforts to redefine and organize stigmatized social categories as
"communities." On the right, we cringe as we see our abandoned struc-
tural-functionalist models reborn in claims for "community values."
Applying for grants, we know we'll do better if we can frame our project
around a "community"—that is, a viable political constituency—instead
of a practice.

We prove the reality of a group by demonstrating that it has a culture, unified within and differentiable without (Handler 1988). In documenting, "preserving," and synthesizing this culture into canonical
forms—the Kalevala, the *Kinder- und Hausmärchen*, the Catalan sardana,
the open-air museum, the American ethnic festival—we diffuse and gen-
eralize it among that group's potential members, thus improving the iso-
morphy of group and culture (Klusen 1986 [1967]).

And yet, working ethnographically, we are aware of the fragility of the
group concept put to the test. We learn in interaction of the status differences within a group that may make men public, and women private, per-

formers; we discover the creative individual whose influence galvanizes and directs performance in a particular milieu; we find that a festival declared by all to be a celebration of unity is in fact animated by vigorous factionalism; we discover the complex networks of contacts and influences feeding into and emerging from an apparently bounded community.

The impossibility of a neat definition of the group became clear to me one day in 1988 when, as part of fieldwork for the Philadelphia Folklore Project, I was visiting Italian Market Days, the autumn festival that promotes the market to the rest of the city. With a photographer, I had come to rest in front of the greased pole, a New World reflex of the *albero di cuccagna*. The Tree of Cockayne, a common feature of European carnivals, promises infinite satisfaction if only you can get to the top of it. Here it was, a twenty-five-foot metal pole planted by the city on the base of a streetlamp; from a little platform on the top there hung lengths of salami, whole legs of prosciutto, balls of cheese, and an envelope of money. The length of the pole had been generously rubbed with bacon fat.

A group of teenage boys clustered around the pole, trying to get up. By their looks they were working-class Italian Americans, the kids who work in the market. They had come up with a collaborative strategy, forming a tight circle of bodies at the base and a second layer of lighter boys on their shoulders. They had to decide on the best way of linking arms and scrambling up backs, and they tumbled down several times before getting it right. Then a few boys tried for the top, inching up with their knees, sometimes wiping the fat off with a towel, always sliding back down at the end. At one point a girl came in and climbed up to the second layer, but the hands and the jokes of the boys became too much, and she soon retreated. Later we were agreeably surprised to see an African American boy stepping in; he was dressed like the others and seemed to be a friend, remaining part of the group until the end. Exhibition label text began composing itself in my head: here was the freedom of the marketplace fostering multiethnic collaboration for the common prize. I checked myself—was my subconscious turning Republican on me?— and the boys also decided to take a rest. We and a large crowd had been watching them, rapt, for a good hour and a half.

The advent of a Southeast Asian man prevented that text from ever being written. Perhaps from the new Vietnamese neighborhood adjacent to the market, the man looked thirty; he was wearing nothing but a brief pair of white shorts, and he strode straight to the pole through the gap made by the relaxing boys. Then, with no help whatsoever, he started up, using his feet instead of his knees. On his second try he had reached the top and grasped the leg of prosciutto, grinning hugely.

The boys on the ground, who had been frozen with surprise, now began to stir. They shouted at him, struck at the low part of the pole. One, then another, threw a sneaker at him, narrowly missing. Then they began to shake the pole from side to side. The man decided to come down before the shoes became stones and, trying to treat it as a joke, smiled and walked away rather quickly.

As we caught our breath—imagining the consequences if there had been a larger Vietnamese presence in the crowd—the boys started up at the pole again. This time, galvanized by the competition and having observed the Asian man's technique, they made it up within a quarter of an hour. The boy on top scrambled onto the platform, enjoying his triumph, and gestured to the crowd, tossing small toys down to them and waving his clasped hands in victory. Eventually he took the envelope of money and slid down to the cheers of his companions.

The photographer approached him and asked what we were both wondering: "What happened? That black kid was with you, and that was okay. Why couldn't the Asian guy get it?"

He was not at all embarrassed. "We know that kid," he said. "We go to school together, he works in the market with us, he's a friend. But this Chinese guy—" ("Chinese! I hate Chinese!" interjected one of his friends) "—just came out of nowhere. This is an Italian festival, an Italian should get it. He's got his own festival to win at." Then he excused himself: he was ready for a beer.

The first time I told this story in class I learned that the incident was not unique: a student interrupted my recital to say that he had seen an Asian shaken off the pole that year. The story highlights many of the familiar contradictions of contemporary American identity politics.

— "Italian Market" is in fact an outsider's term, a tourist label. Locals call it the Ninth Street Market and are aware that it used to be Jewish and that its clientele is increasingly African American. Nonetheless, the market sells itself to the city at large as Italian. And the Asian man, though a neighbor, was clearly not a member.
— Ethnic and racial prejudice diminishes with frequency of interaction and—crucially—with common economic interests. The Italian owners of Ninth Street businesses depend on African American labor and customers. The Vietnamese, however, shop in their own stores and compete in the restaurant business. They have only been around for fifteen years or so, having "come out of nowhere" and been resettled in this depopulating neighborhood. To most Italian Americans in the neighborhood, they are still strangers.
— As we know from the theorists of creolization, childhood is the key

moment of mixing: those you grow up with are Americans, the ones who come after are strangers.

— Festival politics in Philadelphia today territorializes, essentializes, and compartmentalizes ethnicity. Each group that has arrived at political representation has its "own" festival, in which others are invited as spectators and consumers, but in which the "insiders" alone have the right to participate. Ideally, festivals are located in centers of historical settlement that still retain a high residential concentration of the group celebrated. The miniaturization of the ideology of the bounded nation-state in the urban village can be seen in the T-shirts, sold during Italian Market Days, that layer the map of Italy over the map of South Philadelphia. In contrast, the pan-African diaspora celebration of Odunde has suffered continual harassment from claiming a site on South Street, a historical center of African American culture but now the border of a gentrified area. Odunde has repeatedly been treated by the city as requiring containment, and the city has sponsored alternative festivals in more clearly African American and less "central" locations, such as North Philadelphia.[1] Alternatively—and better yet from the city's point of view—festivals are put in the neutral spaces of Penn's Landing and the Parkway, each group getting its turn at these barren sites devoid of everyday resonances. Here one finds the ethnic festival at its most formulaic: only the colors of the flag and the spice in the sausage change from Sunday to Sunday.

— White people cannot tell Asians apart: hence, to obtain civic recognition and civil rights, such historical enemies as the Vietnamese and the Cambodians, both possibly seen as "Chinese," are obliged to form Asian American Associations and work together as a bloc. The same goes for Latinos; the diverse Africans brought to these shores by slave traders went through the process long ago, and new African and Caribbean immigrants are confronting the issue of "blackness" as a social category that erases their own distinctiveness.

— The most spectacular performance genres of such festivals are marked explicitly as ethnic but might just as well be labeled by gender. The exclusion of the Asian man was breathtakingly visible; the exclusion of the Italian-American girl was effected by a quieter and more intimate transgression of her person to inform her that she was transgressing male space. This level of "intimate difference" (Mills 1993) easily goes unnoticed in larger political-economic debates.

Several definitions of collectivity are at play (at war?) in this incident. The group created in everyday interaction, the group united by common interest, the group made by exoteric ascription, the bounded descent group, the group defined by territory, the gendered peer group, the group as a category of political and touristic representation, and the group emerging from performance all make their cases here.

But perhaps we may simplify the problem. At bottom, folklorists have been interested in the group as the locus of culture and as the focus of identity. Our difficulties with such concepts as "folk," "nation," "race," and so on may be seen as resulting from the confusion of the two. Starting from the formulations of the "Toward New Perspectives" paradigm, we can distinguish between the empirical network of interactions in which culture is created and moves, and the community of the social imaginary that occasionally emerges in performance. Our everyday word *group* might best serve as shorthand for the dialogue between the two.

Toward New Perspectives on the Folk: Small Groups and Differential Identities

The essentialism and othering inherent in the word *folk* are now such commonplaces of our discipline that I need not discuss them here: it is for this reason, I am sure, that I was assigned the less loaded term *group* for this volume. Certainly the prestige of Dan Ben-Amos's definition of folklore was another reason. When, as part of the would-be scientific revolution that culminated in the publication of *Towards New Perspectives in Folklore*, Ben-Amos defined folklore as "artistic communication in small groups" (1972), he intended the sociological conception of small group to overcome some of the difficulties inherent in the notion of *folk*.[2] The classist, racist, and antimodern connotations of *folk* were all problematic in an American context; moreover, the word was tied to an old paradigm that understood the people as bearers, not makers, of tradition. Following Alan Dundes's assertion that a folk group could be "*any group of people whatsoever* who share at least one common factor" (1965:2), Ben-Amos identified two conditions that must hold "for the folkloric act to happen": "both the performers and the audience have to be in the same situation and be part of the same reference group" (1972:12). The face-to-face criterion of the sociologists focused attention on the interactions of the performance situation and the shaping role of audience; the notion of reference group carried this concern with audience into the interpretive realm, implying the specificity of meaning to a particular group with shared codes and values, a common identity.

For different historical reasons, German Volkskunde also found itself uncomfortable with the *Volk* in this period. Klusen, in his article "The Group Song as Group Object" (1986 [1967]) proposed the same terminological shift as Ben-Amos: he would use the social-science notion of the primary or face-to-face group. Group, he declared, is more objective a conception than "community"—like "folk," an idealization of a more complex reality. Instead, group "defines an exact unity of people who interact" (1986 [1967]:186). It can be ad hoc or short-lived and need not be grounded in a historical identity. "It must be guaranteed that they all know each other, that all can communicate directly with each other and that they can interact directly, i.e., from two to a few dozen people. It is necessary that every group have at least one dominant element in its make-up and function, what folklorists have called the 'creative thought'" (1986 [1967]:187)—that is, Dundes's common factor or the unity of Ben-Amos's reference group.

Like Ben-Amos, Klusen begins to suggest a redefinition of the group in his critique of the notion of community. He insists that the community sought by folklorists is not a vanishing survival, but a project for the future, and likewise, that the national song did not exist until Herder created it. The diffusion through print of the songs collected by early folklorists turned them into national culture (Klusen 1986 [1967]:198–99).

Intimations that the group is a product of interaction rather than its precondition were followed up by the Texas school. The Texas approach emerged from the quiet insistence of Américo Paredes on the role of cross-border gazing in both performance and scholarship and from the awareness of folklorists (themselves often African American or Latino) doing fieldwork on the borders that the face-to-face group is by no means the only and certainly not the most dangerous locus of performance (see Kodish 1993). The Texas concern with "neighborly names" and interethnic performance both hostile and hospitable, culminating in Abrahams's concept of the display event (1981), called on an implicit network model of interaction between different social positions. Bauman pointed out that scholars had previously tended to conceptualize the folklore-bearing group as a social category, that is, as people sharing a given status or label. Instead, the sociological idea of group proposed by Ben-Amos depended not on shared identity but on the fact of regular interaction (1972). As Bauman demonstrated, much folklore in fact takes place in regular interaction between people belonging to different social categories and plays upon this very fact of difference. Boasting, competition, denigration, hospitality, teasing: all depend on and highlight the difference in social location between performer and addressee. The large-scale display events that have become characteristic of plural societies draw boundaries as loci of political, economic, and cultural conflict.

The Texas approach lets us see how, in the greased-pole contest, the category of "Italian" is situationally invoked as a boundary device: it quietly encompassed the African American male, silently excluded the Italian American female, and noisily expelled the Asian. The genre of display event, or, more specifically, ethnic festival allows us to understand the rules unwittingly—or deliberately?—breached by the stranger. There at the "traditional" core of the festival, the part most highly marked as esoteric, instead of watching and admiring as his role called for, he showed the Italians up on their own turf. In punishing this serious breach of display event etiquette, one of the boys proffered the culturally sanctioned alternative: "He's got his own festival to win at."

The display event model presumes a larger society of complex linkages within which boundaries are regularly drawn and redrawn. Performance, sanctioned and unsanctioned, becomes a key means of boundary construction and maintenance, each festival or demonstration declaring difference between copresent individuals.

Network, Transmission, Boundary Drawing

That groups are not homogeneous is the first realization of any scholar doing fieldwork. The first stages of fieldwork are a trajectory through a social network, from the margins toward the center.[3] Initially we are often sent to the high-status marginals of a network: its "brokers," those accustomed to dealing with outsiders and representing the inside to them. If we show ourselves to be at all open, the low-status marginals also gravitate to us—eccentrics, alcoholics, "street-corner philosophers." All of these, high and low, transform their enforced social distance into critical distance: attempting to defend their distinction, their exclusion, or their chosen exile from a group and its habits, they think a great deal about the group and develop a discourse that sounds rather close to our own theory. Initially, at least, we may find them the most articulate consultants. From us, bearers of alternate and sometimes more prestigious values, they in turn seek validation for their own distance.

But our object is to get to the center: the best singers, the men who dress the devils, the healers. For this we have to rely on introductions, connections, friends of friends. If, after long and patient self-insinuation, we do reach the center, we learn that we can no longer simply depart. Our entry has changed the shape of the network, and we are part of it. Not that we have assimilated, become like them; on the contrary, our difference is often what makes us valuable. The important thing is that we have contracted ties through the hospitality shown us. Our physical departure from the group does nothing to change this; indeed, it may heighten our usefulness. When we return to our own land of business schools, Rockies to be climbed, and Timberland boots, we are called upon to reciprocate.

The riddle is a genre particularly dependent on network structure and has led more than one folklorist to propose a network model. As new fieldworkers in small-scale communities, Roger D. Abrahams and Alessandro Falassi both found themselves targets of riddling, in part out of hostility toward outsiders, in part because they provided a new audience or butt for the good old jokes (Abrahams 1983; Falassi 1980:92–93). Honorio Velasco found that riddles were differentially distributed in a Spanish village among networks of family, neighbors, or friends, and that they were habitually directed out from the center of these networks toward newcomers and children for the obvious reason that everyone else knew them already. He concluded that "the real social locus of oral tradition (at least of riddles) is not the local community, but social networks. . . . The intervention of specific ties is differential, or can be, for the different genres of oral tradition. In the case of riddles, the diversity of ties is greater than in that of proverbs. The amplitude, density, and openness of a social network are factors determining the availability of texts and their renewal" (Velasco 1986:172–73, translation mine).

Kenneth S. Goldstein had made the same discovery in the northeast of Scotland more than twenty years before. Observing that riddling was a marginal activity among the adult settled rural population, he asked why it continued to be vital among the travelers, a formerly itinerant population of peddlers. He concluded that the energetic visiting practices of the travelers—a relic of the solidarity of their wandering days—gave them the opportunity to learn new riddles, while the settled population, whose social circle was limited to immediate neighbors, knew all its riddles already and found no amusement in telling them. This analysis was confirmed by the fact that children, who because of the geographic scope of rural schools had a larger acquaintance than either adult group, were the most enthusiastic riddlers of all. "It follows that in those societies in which the network of outside contacts is large there will be a more vital riddling tradition than in those societies with a more limited series of outside contacts" (Goldstein 1963:333).

Goldstein's interest in the traveler population and his use of an implicit network model grow out of the northern European folkloristic tradition of transmission studies. Ever since Benfey's hypothesis of Indian origins for folktales, folklorists have been considering the role of migrant populations and professional itinerants such as gypsies, colporteurs, and journeyman artisans in the diffusion of oral tradition. Carl W. von Sydow came to a sophisticated view of the process in his critique of the superorganicism and mechanicism of the Finnish model (1948). Rejecting the theory of the automigration of tales, von Sydow emphasized the move-

ment of people, in both permanent migrations and the temporary movements of work, military service, and visits to kin, markets, and festivals.
He spoke not only of mass migrations but of the movement of individuals and how their formation of new relations facilitates the exchange of
tradition. He recognized a differential diffusion based on the channels and
barriers of economic and political relationships. Still more important, he
noted the uneven distribution of tradition within apparently homogeneous communities, depending on differential experience resulting from
occupation, gender, age, and social position, and from such different contexts as the ritual, the familial, and the casual.

Even the "oicotype," a concept suggesting belief in a bounded homogeneous community, is more flexible than von Sydow has generally been
given credit for. The development of a marked oicotype depends on how
isolated and how integrated an area is; to use Benedict Anderson's term,
it depends on the "limited pilgrimages" of residents (1983). "The narrower
the cultural area is, the more uniform will be the development and the
more distinct the oicotypifications" (von Sydow 1948:16).

Von Sydow's insights have led to a large body of subsequent work:
studies of active and passive tradition bearers (e.g., Goldstein 1972); public
and private traditions and gendered performance (e.g., Mathias and Raspa
1985; Thomas 1983); individual makers of songs (e.g., Abrahams 1970;
Ives 1964); and new channels of transmission such as the telephone and
the mass media (e.g., Dégh 1994). Dégh's work on legend transmission
(notably in Dégh and Vászonyi 1975) explicitly builds on von Sydow's
program, and in turn the sociologically networked folklorist Gary Alan
Fine integrates social network theory into this "multi-conduit" model
(Fine 1979, 1980).

Despite the declaration of differential identity made by Bauman
(1972:34),[4] we can also see the concerns in performance theory and the
ethnography of communication with authority, rights to performance,
disclaimers, reported speech, and so forth as having deep roots in this
tradition. The return to a newly formulated textuality (see Bauman and
Briggs 1990) has brought these continuities to the forefront.

We should recall that our comparative tradition compares texts, not
national or local "cultures." Turning from evolutionism to diffusionism,
this kind of comparativism retains no necessary link to a nationalist or
racist agenda and indeed precludes an understanding of the group as bounded. Rather, it presupposes a network model, with individuals and geographic communities as nexuses in a variety of relationships and social ties,
some intimate and long-lasting, others temporary but influential.

Folklorists have a long tradition of using the network as both field method and theoretical model. The more formal development of the network idea in sociology and social anthropology can enrich this usage and facilitate a more fine-grained analysis of the social base of cultural practices.

Social Network Theory

According to Jeremy Boissevain, the notion of social network was initially broached by Radcliffe-Brown in 1940 as a means of testing empirically the assumptions of structural functionalism: that is, it was a means of understanding the group and particularly the notion of social control at the experiential level (Boissevain 1989:557).[5]

Methodologically, we construct a network by placing an individual at the center and charting all of his or her social relationships, then tracing the relationships between all of his or her connections and adding in all of their connections. The resulting structure of linked individuals will have certain obvious features:

— Greater or lesser size of the first-order zone (immediate acquaintances) and the second-order zone (acquaintances of acquaintances, including the eminently useful friend of a friend). The role of culture "brokers" between social groups enters here, as a single tie in the first-order zone can open up a large number of ties in the outer zone.

— Greater or lesser density: "the ratio of actual to potential contacts" (Milroy 1987:46). Socially mobile individuals tend to have sparse networks, knowing many individuals who are not known to each other. In more stable situations, dense networks in which everyone knows everyone else are likely to emerge. Typically, "mobile" and "stable" have been interpreted literally, with proximity and longevity of residence taken as predictive of a dense network. However, a dense network may well be global, as long as it comprises regular interactants: one may think of such specialized occupational groups as international bankers, opera singers, royalty, and folklorists.

— Centrality and peripherality. An individual may be central to a network—that is, known personally to everyone in it—or peripheral, dependent for access on a few intermediaries (the typical situation of the newcomer or the fieldworker).

— Clustering. Within a large network dense clusters emerge—nuclear families, small bands of close friends, cabals, and so on.

Less easily read but equally important to network description are its interactive aspects—that is, the specific qualities of its individual ties. These include:

— Multiplexity or single-stranded relationship may be based on only one factor: working together, for example. A multiplex relationship is one in which my sister-in-law works with me, lives in the house down the block, and spends her free time in my kitchen chatting.
— The content of a relationship: occupational, familial, neighborly, sociable, erotic, political, commercial, and so on.
— The frequency of a tie: daily meetings versus yearly Christmas cards.
— The duration of a tie: casual affair versus a lifelong partnership. The tie acquires a history, with periods of greater or lesser intensity, variety in the content of the relationship, and so forth.
— Affective intensity: the father-daughter tie is usually more important than the worker-worker tie, for example. A short-lived tie may rank high in intensity: if once I met Miles Davis or was presented to the Queen of England, this tie may figure more significantly in my personal identity and my conversation than its duration alone would warrant.
— Exchange rights and obligations. The directional flow of goods and services in the relationship. Depending on status and power differentials, one party may be defined as patron and one client; one provider, the other customer; one teacher, the other student.

Structural and interactional characteristics of networks affect each other: in particular, a dense network tends also to be multiplex. This kind of network has been the most studied, in part because it fits our classic notion of community, in part for obvious methodological reasons. In such situations, to make one acquaintance is to make several, and a friend of a friend is easily pulled into the everyday round of interactions. Thus the working-class neighborhood, the "urban village," has been the key site of sociological fieldwork, just as folklorists have found their work most satisfying in African American churches, Newfoundland outports, Turkish villages, or Maine lumber camps.

The dense multiplex network is also likely to be the repository of conservative vernacular culture. Characterized by frequent interaction, a high degree of solidarity, and an equally high degree of social control effected by mutual observation and gossip, this sort of network has sufficient integrity to resist the pressure of hegemonic norms. Sociolinguistic change has been understood to depend on second-order ties and peripheral network members (Milroy and Milroy 1992, following Granovetter 1982). It is these weak ties that connect networks to the larger society and create what integrity a society has. New forms enter networks through the observation of colleagues, employers, or neighbors from other ethnic groups. The innovations introduced by these boundary encounters are most often taken up by the peripheral network members least subject to social control. Once a critical mass of peripheral members have adopted an innovation, central members incur less risk in taking it up; their influence then quickly causes the innovation to become general (Milroy 1987).

Paradoxically, then, the weak ties are culturally powerful, a fact folklorists have also long recognized in studying not only the center of the community but its marginals: the gypsies, the drunks, the migrants, the peddlers, the colporteurs. Walter Benjamin recognized the two poles of cultural transmission when he defined his two archetypal storytellers. One is the long-time member of the village community: the oldest inhabitant, we might say, recalling the procedures for the legal ascertainment of local custom in medieval Europe (Thompson 1993). His (or her) tales are those of the founding struggles, the exemplars, the external threats vanquished. The other is the traveler who tells the news: the bizarre, the marvelous, the unimagined. The two figures and the two kinds of narration merge into the same life cycle, Benjamin notes, in the journeyman artisan, whose *Wanderjahre* end in a triumphant return to the point of origin (1969:85). Therefore it is not so much a question of different sorts of community members, but of the multiple interactive worlds of individuals.

Ulf Hannerz, also following Granovetter, follows up this interest in the weak ties that provide access to new models and alternative norms. He suggests the network metaphor as the most suitable way of understanding the "global ecumene," a world interconnected by migrations, marketplaces, and media. In the latter connection he adds that we need not think of all ties as face to face, for some are made through the mass media, and many more are made through limited-circulation media like the professional journal, small-scale media like the cassette tape and home video camera, and interpersonal media like the telephone, the Internet, and the old-fashioned letter. The postmodern world, then, is not a collection of bounded nation-states, but a "network of networks" (Hannerz 1992).

Density and multiplexity, or the lack thereof, must be understood as strategic rather than natural to a given situation. Network ties, being defined by interaction, disappear with disuse: they are not like the apparently eternal ties of shared identity. Here we need to remember that unhappy verb, "to network," which figures so largely in the lives of new Ph.D.s and other mobile individuals seeking stability. For precariously situated individuals, it is advantageous not only to make numerous contacts but to intensify existing ones with affective content and material obligation: to make friends of the neighbors, to suggest a useful resource to a senior colleague, to fix up a brother with a best friend, to find a job for a cousin newly arrived from the old country. Mobile individuals, however, tend to network upward, with those who have more resources than they do, and to let downward ties lapse.

Characteristically, according to Lesley Milroy, middle-class people have the least incentive and opportunity to form dense multiplex networks. These, rather, are characteristic of traditional working classes and of elites—contexts of comparative equality and stability. The rich need to defend their position by a solidary distribution of rewards and the exclusion of intruders, and the poor need to pool scarce resources in order to use them effectively. A shared territory is crucial to working-class community, however, for it allows the frequent interaction and mutual observation that the rich can maintain through airplane tickets and fax machines. The disruption of working-class neighborhoods, as during urban renewal, breaks up networks. Denied their accustomed occasions of personal respect and recognition, relocated people are inclined to become more interested in impersonal respect and recognition through the signs of status—education and consumer goods (Milroy 1987).

Hannerz broadens this picture of network strategies, proposing a model of three (1992:44–45). "Segregativity" is the tendency to maintain the distance between one's divergent contacts, compartmentalizing one's activities. "Integrativity" is a strategy of drawing links between one's disparate connections, attempting to bridge the gaps but maintain diversity. "Encapsulation" is the cultivation of maximum cohesiveness through a dense multiplex network in which all the meaningful contacts of life occur. This tripartite distinction provides a useful framework for discussing the cultural implications of network strategies.

Segregativity

Segregativity may offer the pleasures of a double life, but usually it emerges from societal pressures and is more appropriately tied to double consciousness. I suspect that segregativity most often takes the form of a boundary drawn between "public" and "private" behavior, with the drawing of the line dependent on power differentials. Lesley Milroy found that working-class people in Belfast drew the boundary at the physical border of their neighborhood: within that "private" context, one was free to enter any kitchen one pleased and stay as long as one liked (1987). James Scott offers a more general theory of "public" and "hidden transcripts" (1990), suggesting that the space of the hidden transcript of subordinate populations varies with the intensity of elite surveillance. Not all dominators have studied Foucault: some leave untouched large spaces of everyday life, in which resistance can take shape. Others effectively isolate individuals and colonize their psyches to the extent that resistance remains, barely articulable, within the self.

Stigmatized social categories recently granted civil rights are generally admitted to the hegemonic realm on the condition that their cultural difference remain invisible. Their behavior must display the desire and the ability to assimilate to apparently unmarked, culture-free organizational norms. Michael Bell's account of a middle-class African American bar in the early 1970s demonstrates the intensity of private play that can result from self-repression in the workplace and the consequent fear of inauthenticity in the self (1983). Joelle Bahloul examines the elaboration of a traditional means of expression into a complex segregative mechanism in her study of the foodways of Algerian Jews in Paris (1983). Strictly kosher and Algerian at home in food items and methods of preparation, this group reproduces its separateness in the private sphere. But because an important part of its identity, not to mention its income, comes from cosmopolitan ties, group members regularly go out to eat with Gentile colleagues; even when by themselves at restaurants, they make a point of eating shellfish. The non-Jewish food serves to incorporate an important aspect of their self-concept, but the occasions are kept strictly distinct, so that they can participate fully in both worlds. Cleanliness has been reinterpreted as separation rather than exclusion.

The "intimate difference" of gender falls here also. Early network studies of working-class communities in Britain showed that strong norms of gender difference were maintained by the largely separate networks of husband and wife: these networks preceded marriage and were maintained alongside it, imposing separate norms of conduct and reinforcing traditional gender roles (Bott 1971). Turning this around, one can see that a societal division of labor by gender fosters the separation of networks. Where men work and women stay at home, men socialize with their workmates; women's networks are made of kin and neighbors. Women have thus a context of performance that has generally been described as "private," the term "public" being reserved for mixed-gender or all-male gatherings (see Thomas 1983 and various essays in Jordan and Kalcik 1985).[6]

In Western societies where women also work, network and cultural differences may become even stronger. As several sociolinguists have noted, working-class men tend to work in large-scale occupations where they associate with each other, such as mining or construction. Women working as domestics, in shops, or in offices are more isolated from their cohort and more exposed to prestige norms, and these contacts in fact offer them opportunities for an ascent in status. Consequently their speech and sometimes even their political attitudes come closer to prestige norms (Downes 1984:178–83). Exposed to a wider variety of material culture and custom than men, they are more disposed to experimentation and innovation. Their cultural repertoires in the presence of their husbands can thus differ considerably from those invoked in the workplace, in their own socializing, and with their children.

Integrativity

Integrativity at the level of network parallels hybridity at the level of culture. Deborah Kapchan describes a Moroccan market woman who demands of her male customers, "Aren't we all Muslims?" At the cultural level, the vendor is dialogizing a cliché generally used between Berbers and Arabs. Socially, she is claiming the right to be integrated into this larger category of mutual acceptance (Kapchan 1993). Examining these two levels together lets Kapchan make concrete the marketplace metaphor so popular since Bakhtin as a shorthand for the process of cultural mixing (see also Abrahams n.d.).

Hybridization and integrativity are often a consequence of migration, as is evident in the earlier concept "creolization," rooted in the large-scale movements effected by European imperialism. Today we are equally likely to find our mixing in the spatial juxtapositions of urban immigrants. Hannerz redefines the "cultural role of cities" as that of a kind of switchboard between messages and communicators of widely distant points of origin (1992:51).

Migrants who use their culture of origin as an economic resource are key to the transnationalization of culture and the growth of a cosmopolitan urban sensibility. To return to Philadelphia's Ninth Street Market, we may consider the fate of the "decorated palm," an Italian American art form used in Philadelphia to adorn family graves on Palm Sunday (Noyes 1989:60–65; Philadelphia Folklore Project n.d.). Some such palms are made for domestic consumption; others are made by church groups for the congregation. But some are sold in the market, and these, to the knowledge of the vendor, have gone on Protestant altars, yuppie door knockers, and even Passover dinner tables. In yet another context of exchange, the public-sector folklore workshop, exhibition, and artist's market, the decorated palms have become "folk art" and entered both a museum and private collections.

Based on the nature of the network ties, we can see differing constraints on the recontextualization of these objects. When transmission takes place within multiplex and dense bonds of kinship, religion, neighborhood, and ethnicity, there is by definition no recontextualization. The

situation being constant, so are use and meaning: the baggage of obligations and resonances does not have far to travel.

Of course the situation is never wholly constant or the network
wholly isolated: consequently we see the gradual formal differentiation
of the palms in, for example, church congregations concerned to encompass the full range of community preferences and economic possibilities
in a parish comprising several generations. Differentiation allows the
maintenance of a network, though a looser one, and of a cultural norm,
though a more flexible one.

The public marketplace offers still fewer constraints. While Ninth
Street is in part a neighborhood market, whose customers consider long-
standing relationships and local knowledge as assurances of quality, it also
depends on patrons from outside who value the market's apparent pre-
modernity. These are tourists, and what they do with their purchases will
have as much to do with their own assumptions about tradition and ethnicity as with any communication from the source.

The public-sector folklife festival or exhibition foregrounds this communication, since the tie between maker and audience is now defined
as educational rather than commercial. However, while contextual information is transmitted, contextual obligation is not. The object ob-
tained in this kind of exchange is often reborn from its first life of use in
the community to a second life as "triumphant object" (Klusen 1986
[1967]), displayed in a collection with a narrative of its original use.

Of course such contacts can also create new relationships, with the
practitioner acquiring a powerful identity as "artist." In this case the aesthetic and monetary value placed on the object in its new set of relationships will feed back to the network of origin, and here too the object may
gain new prestige and receive new elaboration. Given the lability of any
kind of display event and the increasing skill of public-sector presenters
at creating participation instead of spectacle, it is not unheard of that the
audience may be converted, consumed rather than consuming. Sometimes
the audience accommodates to the practitioner instead of vice versa.

In considering Bauman and Briggs's model of the making and remak-
ing of texts (1990), which does not stress the sources of constraints on
recontextualization, the network metaphor can help us think about
mediation. A text that moves from one location to another through several contacts has undergone several recontextualizations and is transformed to a much greater degree than one that moves from one network
point to the next. We can see the implications of the network for many
situations in which an exchange of expressive forms is not accompanied
by the sharing of everyday-life relations; and commodification may be

defined as the degree to which the expressive form can move without interaction between the points on the network.

Commodification can be mitigated and concealed by the entextualization of context. Increasingly, "folk art" is sold with a narrative attached. I have a beautiful skirt decorated with small bells and fragments of mirrors, bought by my mother on a vacation in Rajasthan. She was told that the skirt was so adorned so that the girls herding goats in the mountains could be seen from the village when they got lost. The girl whose skirt I wear is well and truly lost now: a pity, for I would certainly like to hear her version of this absurd story. But it seems unfair that I should be able to buy her story as well as her skirt, while my mother's money gives her nothing of mine. And although she has been so transparently presented to me, I feel safe in assuming that she is a fiction. However, when we receive the lies of cultural commodity in return for the opacity of money, it is still not an even exchange.

So I am not ready to abandon the idea that power is lost with mediation. If the fictional girl and I met face to face, not only my invisibility but her visibility would be compromised. To her face I do not think I could ask her such silly questions about her private life; it would be rude. At this distance, far behind her back, I can say whatever I like about her. Indeed, I can assert that I have nothing to do with her and forget all about her.

When Union Carbide did this to Bhopal, the consequences were rather more serious. We are familiar with the smooth disclaimers of relationship when the North is called upon to account for the economic, ecological, and political disarray of the South. The denials of responsibility are made possible by the attenuation of commodity networks across complex and many-pointed paths of transmission (see Wallerstein 1983). I like to think, in contrast, of the early medieval preference for gift and theft over trade (Geary 1986). The former were valued because they established a relationship between origin and destination. The condescension of the giver and the thirst for revenge of the robbed were both preferred to indifference.

Encapsulation

We have tended to view the dense multiplex network and its conservative culture as historically prior to other kinds of networks and cultures. We might turn the problem around, however, and instead of defining this network type as the structure of the traditional community, define it as the product of a desire for tradition, a closing of ranks in conditions of threat. Threats to network may be cultural and work in two directions of exchange. Authorities in the network may attempt to exclude innovations they consider threatening; or a group in a disadvantaged position may wish to control the commodification of forms that have emerged from within its ranks. In each case, network position has an influence: those who draw boundaries are those whose strength comes from their centrality.

Arjun Appadurai observes a conflict of interest between merchants and rulers, whom we might see as peripheral and central elites: "Whereas merchants tend to be the social representatives of unfettered equivalence, new commodities, and strange tastes, political elites tend to be the custodians of restricted exchange, fixed commodity systems, and established tastes and sumptuary customs" (1986:33). Political elites fear contact and incipient hybridity, for it presents the possibility and perhaps the attractiveness of alternative social arrangements.

This is true of the smallest networks as well as the larger society. There too central members, often senior men, both bear the responsibility for and benefit from the reproduction of existing assumptions and structures. So, for example, in the rural family of Catalonia, eldest sons consistently think and vote more conservatively than their brothers and sisters, whom they attempt to dominate through invocations of traditional authority. The eldest inherits the farm—a dubious advantage in the present economy—and needs as much of the traditional support system of unmarried siblings as he can muster. This dense family network is sustained by values of self-sacrifice for the continuity of the whole, symbolized in the house and its name. Without such sacrifice, a small farm cannot be maintained. However, the younger children have powerful reasons to leave home. They will inherit only a share of the movable property and can expect to prosper to the degree that they embrace individualist, innovative, capitalist values (Barrera González 1990; see also Streicker 1995 on the cultural conservatism of senior men). As peripheral members of the farm-based network, they have little material interest in its maintenance.

Resistance to the exit of expressive forms from the network is easily understood as a protection of cultural capital, the appropriation of which robs the network of a resource.[7] When I did fieldwork on the Patum of Berga, a Catalan Corpus Christi festival unique in the region for its historical continuity and present intensity, I was surprised to find both the senior political elite and the senior working-class men who control access to festival participation united in their rejection of more mobility for the festival (Noyes 1992). These two groups, who disagree in most other matters, together refuse invitations for the Patum and its elements to travel or to be performed out of season for touristic or honorific purposes—practices with, respectively, one hundred years and perhaps four hundred years of local precedent. They ridicule the "copies" of the Patum that have arisen throughout Catalonia since the death of Franco. "The Patum is for Berga, for Corpus; that's it," both groups say, to the endless frustration of a young, middle-class intelligentsia that sees the economic salvation of the town in the cultivation of wider network ties.

But the contestation is not merely political: much as the young people would like to wrest some control from the older generation of politicians and *patumaires,* they too are ambivalent about the former and future commodification of the Patum: "If the tour buses start coming, the Patum will be ours no longer." They compare its intimacy, the familiarity of its gestures, the security of its dense crowd of participants with the alienation of the Running of the Bulls at Pamplona since Hemingway brought it to international notice.

The most militant Berguedans, sometimes called the *integristes,*[8] not only insist on the immutability and incommensurability of the Patum (they kindly observe to me that although my scholarly efforts are welcome as bringing another member to the community, they will be worthless in explaining anything of the Patum to anybody), but have a utopian vision of total encapsulation. When they drink, they talk about closing the town off at the borders for Corpus Christi, of an "anarchism properly understood" with no institutions but the Patum and the sanctuary of the local Madonna, of a Berga sufficient unto itself: quite the opposite of this industrial town's long history of economic dependence and violent engagement in larger political projects. Authenticity, as they use the word, is what emerges from the local; the alienation they know and fear is that of their situation's being defined for them from above. The Patum, their most valued possession and all they have to make them unique, is uniquely vulnerable to such alienation.

Instead, they make the Patum a shibboleth to mark off Berga from the world. Outsiders are recognized by their failure to master certain gestures, exclamations, or nuances of dress, insignificant except as they testify to long familiarity with the festival. Such boundary mechanisms are familiar in many cultural forms, often linguistic, as the word *shibboleth* reminds us. Lesley Milroy notes the resistance of certain phonetic realizations to change: they have become signs of network loyalty (1987:194–97). Tongue twisters can be used to spot foreigners: Castilian immigrants in Catalonia were once asked to pronounce "Setze jutges d'un jutjat mengen fetge d'un penjat,"[9] which calls for the rapid alternation of voiced dental fricatives, alveolar fricatives, and alveolar affricates, none of which exist in Spanish. Other cultural shibboleths are less demanding, calling for a possible but still effortful act of mastering the culture. In Catalonia at large, the ability to dance the sardana is one; in the Bar

La Barana of Berga, where the central *patumaires* congregate, it is the willingness to eat low-status foods like lentils and to drink cognac with Pepito. This sort of shibboleth demands less competence than volition, and the newcomer's agreement to make this declaration of allegiance earns him or her a place in the network. Indeed, a number of Catalans consider allegiance to the shibboleths more important than birth in the ascription of identity: I and many other outsiders have often been told approvingly, "You are more Catalan than many Catalans are."

Shibboleths become emblems of identity, the most conservative elements of the culture, and may be frozen while other elements are changing rapidly. Parody of them is treated as desecration (Ayats n.d.). The deepest insiders, however, may break this rule and joke with the sacrality they create and sustain. The dancing eagle of the Patum of Berga, an official symbol of the city to which outsiders and ordinary citizens are expected to pay the most rigorous respect, is referred to as "the old magpie" by central *patumaires* in the heat of action.

"As long as we have the Patum we'll have Berga," they say. The shibboleth attests to the power of the network and ensures its continuity. Controlling the access of outsiders, it also creates feelings of community within.

The network as both field procedure and organizing metaphor is better adapted than more bounded notions of group to get at the social grounding of expressive practices. Using the network lets us get rid of those boundaries, so theoretically troublesome, and gives us a structure for talking about long-distance and mediated relationships. It addresses our concerns with multivocality and complexity by understanding actors as interrelated and uniquely positioned agents; it prevents us from making a priori assumptions about meaning or origins by demanding that we examine the content and character of any given set of relationships. It might even let us ground the split postmodern subject in some social reality, helping us trace, in Bakhtinian fashion, the dialogue of influences at play in an individual.

Community, Imagined and Performed

In proposing the network as our analytic metaphor for talking about the social location of culture, I do not want to throw out the notion of group altogether: First of all, because the establishment of shibboleths is obviously a crucial aspect of network practice. And, more generally, because the body of theory that has destroyed the group as a natural object has simultaneously resurrected it to abundant life as a cultural creation. The group—which in this context I will give the more affectively charged name "community"—is an "invention" in the historical materialist world of Hobsbawm and Ranger (1983); an "imagining" in the more post-modern discursive realm of Benedict Anderson and assorted French theorists (Anderson 1983; Miami Theory Collective 1991); and, we may argue from our own pragmatic tradition of Kenneth Burke and Dell Hymes, "the naming of a situation" (Burke 1957). Finally, calling on the phenomenological-experiential tradition of Victor Turner, community is a felt reality (see Mills 1993:185).

A felt reality is quite real enough. By declaring the community to be a product of the social imaginary, I by no means intend to consign it to insignificance. We must still deal with that problem, raised but never quite addressed by Benedict Anderson, of how an "imagined community" can be worth dying for; unhappily, we must also understand how it can be worth killing for. Colonial inventions have given birth to imagined nations as well as empirical states. New namings of situations can contest all-too-real hegemonic definitions and sometimes lead to the abolition of quite material injustices.

Moreover, imaginings are not limited to their first imaginers. Like texts, ideas once propounded live in the world and travel long distances from their points of origin. Still more, if we adopt the French agenda of a history of images rather than one of ideas (Le Goff 1988), we can see ideas as living in concrete realizations: texts, performances, and objects, all transmissible and open to recontextualization. The traces left by these realizations in social memory—what Le Goff calls the "imaginary"—sediment around the first irritant of an act of naming like the nacreous coverings of a pearl. This object builds up in the social imaginary, ever larger, ever more real, until at last it is as big, as dense, and as difficult to deconstruct as "race" or "Germany."

As is now well known, folklorists have been particularly active in defining and objectifying the culture of imagined communities in such genres as the museum, the dictionary, the national epic, the collection of tales, the preserved site, and other *lieux de mémoire* (Nora 1984).[10] The prestige of objective reality—if not as a political entity, at least as a culture—gives a well-known boost to the position of a group in the imaginary. And, of course, it makes the culture negotiable as commodity in the material realm. As we know, there is nothing new about these acts of reification for economic purposes, from below or from above: Philip II of Spain, to whom we owe the first folk-cultural questionnaire I know of, seems basically to have been interested in finding things he could tax (see Abrahams 1993).

But communities are not just reified representations, and ideological claims are not convincing without experiential confirmation. The New Perspectives turn focused and advanced earlier insights that identification with a community is effected in performance.

That identity is a performance was entirely clear to early modern Europeans, with their manuals of conduct for courtiers and the tensions between appearances and reality in their theater, which regularly pointed out that "all the world's a stage." Other parts of the world, notably the Indonesian islands as described by Geertz (1980) and Keeler (1987), seem to find this insight equally obvious. The naturalization of identity into biology is, as we now realize, an ideological concomitant of European imperialism. Twentieth-century phenomenological sociology rediscovered the role of performance. Erving Goffman showed us how individuals and teams stage themselves for an audience (1959), and Harold Garfinkel delved deeper into microanalysis of the performance of "normal" gender roles (1967).

Judith Butler's recent synthesis argues that such apparently natural categories as gender are reproduced through repeated individual performances. The heavy social sanctions on deviant gender performance imply a deep-seated recognition of gender's constructed status: it must be constantly policed and reinforced to maintain itself. "Gender reality is performative which means, quite simply, that it is real only to the extent that it is performed" (Butler 1988:527).

Folklorists have long been aware that certain kinds of identity are derived from performance, most obviously in the case of professional performers where such performance is stigmatized: female dancers, bluesmen, con men, gypsies, and so on. We have also realized the frequent basis of stereotypes in misunderstandings of exoteric norms of interaction and thus performance: Anglo-Americans accustomed to looking one another straight in the eye understand the respectful averted gaze of Asians as "shifty-eyed," or WASPs accustomed to wider interactive distance and more monophonic turn-taking complain of "pushy Jews." But the richest work on the ascription of identity from performance has perhaps been done in the Caribbean, where available social identities are, for historical reasons, exceptionally fluid and multiple. In the West Indian dichotomy of "reputation" and "respectability," performance itself is the basis of social identity (see Abrahams 1983). More complexly, racial identity in many Caribbean and Latin American societies is ascribed less on the basis of physical features than on behavior, both everyday performances of self and more framed performances of music, dance, religion, or sport (e.g., Streicker 1995). Linguistic performance is also central to such ascriptions. In their work on Belize, Le Page and Tabouret-Keller propose that, given the multiple codes available to speakers and their fuzzy boundaries, any utterance is an "act of identity," as much constitutive of as constituted by social namings (1985).

If individual acts of identification create the reality of social categories, the reality of a community with which to identify comes from collective acts. Le Page and Tabouret-Keller note that different social or historical conditions facilitate the "focusing" or "diffusion" of a linguistic norm. We may say of collective identities generally that although they are often reactive, responding to external ascriptions and oppression, they become realities with the taking of collective action. This, James Scott notes, is why dominant populations so often regulate the assembly of subordinates: even the most innocent social gathering, even a collective act of respectful submission, is dangerous if it is not dictated from above. Any such act creates a collective out of an atomized population, makes them realize the possibility of further autonomous action (Scott 1990). Acting in common makes community.

Folklorists looking at the persistence of ethnic identifications and at the creation of new coalitions and interest groups in the Civil Rights movement saw how performance made these groups real to their potential members. At first, the emphasis was on discourse: the collective construction of tradition as a means of naturalizing the group. More recently, we have talked about the cognitive and bodily consequences of collective action and, indeed, the existence of a specific set of techniques for community making.

One must first recognize that the performance of community reinforces its own social base by fostering dense and potentially multiplex interaction. Brazilian samba schools, Philadelphia mummers' clubs, or Swiss amateur theatrical societies need year-round planning, rehearsal, and material preparation to put on their elaborate annual performances. All this labor and the fund-raising that must accompany it remobilize local networks, keeping up many ties that might otherwise slip into desuetude. In making work, the voluntary association also fosters recreation: the choir rehearses, then goes out for a drink. Often a formalization of an existing network, the voluntary association creates a further base for dense multiplex sociability—for what is affectively defined as "community" (see Bendix 1989).

The performance itself adds something important, however, and can extend this feeling of community to a larger social body. Community is made real in performance by means that seem to be cross-cultural. Simplifying, we can specify these means as repetition, formalization, and "consensus."

Repetition works both synchronically in a given performance and diachronically as a performance reenacts a precedent. Richard Schechner's definition of performance as "restored behavior" (1985) conveys the sense of recovery effected especially by calendar customs and historical reenactments such as passion plays or the climb up to Masada, in which "a historical narrative is transformed into a personal narrative" (Bruner and Gorfain 1984). The conservatism of such performances, the insistence on exact reproduction, has the effect of reducing dialogicality between performances and collapsing the distance between past and present (Briggs and Bauman 1992:150). Insofar as the past invoked stands for the community and its origins, repetition also effaces present contentions in the collective restoration of a unity understood as primordial. As long as there is the Patum, there will be Berga; conversely, "the demise of the ballads will coincide with the disappearance of this imagined community," notes McDowell of a Mexican case (1992:415). The community exists in its collective performances: they are the locus of its imagining in their content and of its realization in their performance.

Repetition is made possible by formalization, the controls placed on such features as prosody, register, and lexicon that both limit reference and assist memory.[11] The monologism imposed by formalization on texts is reinforced by the univocality it makes possible in performance. A rhythmic slogan, a song in stanzas, or a soldiers' chant imposes a rhythm on collective motion and enlarges the individual voice by coordinating it with all the others (Ayats 1992). The crowd that becomes one body and one voice becomes more than the sum of its parts. The strength of the individual is identified with the strength of the whole, and ventures impossible or abominable for individuals—public protest or murder—become not only thinkable but achievable.

With the coordination of collective action—be it in chanting slogans, walking in pilgrimage up a hot mountainside, or dancing with the devils of the Patum—participants achieve what James Fernandez calls "consensus," from its etymological root of "feeling together." This confluence of feeling happens both within the individual, as different senses carry in coordinated messages, and in the collectivity, as individuals undergo the same experience in concert (Fernandez 1988).[12] At the most attenuated level, we may see the process in the global televisual community created by "media events," as families in their living rooms consume the same breakfast as Charles and Diana on their wedding day, the menu having been distributed in advance by Buckingham Palace to enable this act of communion (Dayan and Katz 1992:98).

More usually, consensus arises from co-presence. The great emphasis in many religions on communions or sacrificial meals—a collective sharing of substance—points to the bodily basis of community. The mutual incorporations of sexuality and nurturance keep the human community alive, and their invocation in performance recalls this common humanity, the foundation of any more specific solidarity.

Participants do not only take the community in, but receive its outward marks. In many Spanish and Southern Italian festivals, the everyday marks of identification in costume and conduct give way to more spectacular immersions in community. In what is generally said to be a reenactment of a founding battle, citizens pelt each other with rotten blood oranges, tomatoes, or bags of flour. In Berga, the annual blessing of pack animals with holy water from the balcony of the church on the feast of St. Eloi has become a general inundation. The families who live along the parade route spend all night filing pitchers and pails and barrels on the balconies of their flats; some just attach garden hoses to the kitchen faucets. In recent years, the people in the street have taken to throwing water back up through the windows, and there is increasing interchange between balconies. Some people are thrown into the public washhouse along the route for more complete "baptisms." At the end, you can easily tell who's loved, who's central: they're drenched.

Sometimes that cost is higher. Here we may think of the circumcisions, scarifications, and other mutilations of the body described by Pierre Clastres as the inscription of the community's law upon the individual (1989). These too are shibboleths, boundary mechanisms: in Berga you must have scars from burns received in the Patum on your hands and arms to show that you have participated fully in the community's central self-realization.

But a community-making festival is generally a more complexly orchestrated mechanism of consensus (and all Berguedan factions agree that the goal of the Patum is to "make union"). The Patum's techniques of the body, imposed by powerful social controls, effect a gradual transformation from mimesis to vertigo, a development that Caillois suggests is cross-culturally frequent (1979:87–97). The festival's dancing effigies clearly represent and, in their comportment, mimic the various social divisions that have defined the community historically: male and female, upper class and lower class, native and foreigner, human and animal. As the five days of the festival progress, as the dances are repeated over and over, as the great drum keeps beating "Pa-tum" into your head and the band and your neighbors force your feet to dance, as you drink more and more and sleep less and less, as the smoke of the firecrackers blackens your face and the crush of bodies takes from you the control of your own movements, the giants and the dwarves spin into one, the royal eagle becomes as fierce as the flaming mule. You lose your everyday name and position: no longer distinguished by them, you are a part of the sweating dark mass. Under such conditions no signification is possible; there is nothing apart from this sensation. The Patum is pure immanence. In the last grand explosion of the *plens*, the "full ones," devils covered in vines and firecrackers among whom the entire community dances, community is at once generated and reproduced for another year in what Berguedans describe as simultaneous orgasm and rebirth. Then the lights come up—there is a gasp of collective self-recognition—and the moment is over.

Such an experience leaves traces in the body. When the Patum is at last over and you can sit or, better, lie down, your body continues to vibrate as it does after a long plane or boat trip. Uninterrupted sleep will not come for several days: you keep waking up in great jerks, thinking you're dancing. The tunes won't get out of your head: people sing them to themselves for weeks afterward. The burns, of course, itch and scab and scar, often staying with you till the next year. No common experience touches you in this literal and pervasive way, and nothing can really release the tension left in you but a return to performance. For at least a month before Corpus Christi the Berguedans are like horses pawing the ground before a race—their bodies erupt into the dance, their voices into the music, and then they check themselves. The Patum breaks out of Berguedan bodies—as if it were always down there, simmering—on occasions of collective rejoicing or reassembly: an important victory of the Barcelona football team or a gathering of Berguedans abroad.

And the Patum is introduced to Berguedan children as the very foundation of culture. Children learn its tunes and its movements at the same time they are learning to walk and speak. "Show me how the dwarves go, au!" "What does the mule do?" In the same way that even urban Americans teach their children the sounds made by cows and roosters as part of their civilizing process, Berguedans teach their children that culture is about the difference and the relationship between the mule and the giants.[13]

This performance of community has thus very nearly naturalized itself in the body: it can get no deeper. When Berguedans say, "We carry the Patum in our blood," they are not talking about race or birth, but about a rhythm that seems to have mastered their heartbeats.

However, the ineffability of the sensation makes such verbalizations dangerous, a fact the Berguedans understand well and have endeavored to impress upon me. With the language of the body as shifter between experience and essence, it would not be hard for race and birth to enter this discussion. The Patum carried "in the blood," "suckled in with our mother's milk," is genuinely different for someone who has grown up with it. Some Berguedans draw the conclusion that only a native can ever be a member.

Happily, this argument is not hegemonic in Berga, where some of the most fervent local patriots are of immigrant birth. But we need not look far to see the dangers of such powerful bodily performances. The desire for return to that sensation of perfect plenitude, perfect wholeness, total presence can lead to intolerance of less coherent and cohesive everyday conditions. The moment of performance itself, enhanced as it often is by alcohol or other drugs, sometimes finishes in acts of purificatory violence intended to bring the empirical into accordance with the imaginary (e.g., Davis 1974). The reality without is annihilated to make room for the reality within.

Reconciling Network and Community: The Appeal of the Local

Plainly, the community is in no way independent of the network. The performance that constructs the community ideologically and emotionally also strengthens or changes the shape of networks by promoting interaction; it may even have the effect of breaking up a network by redrawing the boundaries within it. The community of the social imaginary coexists in a dialectical tension with the empirical world of day-to-day network contacts. The imagined community offers a focus for comparison and desire, and, at the same time, is itself subject to re-visionings in the light of everyday experience. This productive tension is the complex object we denote with the word *group*.

The community exists as the project of a network or of some of its members. Networks exist insofar as their ties are continually recreated and revitalized in interaction. To my suggestion that central members have the greatest interest in such revitalizations, I would add Benedict Anderson's observation on "limited pilgrimages": he noted that when colonial elites restrict the careers of native officials to their own colonies, the unintended consequence is the creation of solidarities, common resentments, and, crucially, a common horizon among the native administrative class (Anderson 1983). This intelligentsia, because it cannot participate in empire, makes the national revolution. Similarly, the Italian immigrant professionals who could not get to the mayoralty of Philadelphia invented Italian Americans as a constituency from a much more heterogeneous body of people (Noyes 1993); and one might reasonably describe the invention of the working class as a consequence of lack of access to the means of production. When rights in a larger whole are denied, a smaller whole will declare itself against that unity, now understandable as "false" or "imposed."

We might also consider Victor Turner's notion of "star-groupers": "Every objective group has some members who see it as their star group, while others may regard it with indifference, even dislike" (1981:146). Star-groupers are not necessarily in accord with each other, he adds, rather competing both for position and for the definition of the situation. They are, indeed, the makers of social drama (1981:145–46). Social drama is an inherent consequence of their role as the makers of community: the givers of names, definers of boundaries, and sponsors of collective effervescences. The process is, however, circular, for the experience of an efficacious performance of community is probably what makes a star-grouper in the first place. Certainly the Berguedan *integristes* have become such from their experience of the Patum, so intensely felt a reality that nothing else will ever feel as real. Their cultivation of the local is an attempt to enlarge and make permanent this reality.

Which brings us to the habit of thinking of local community as primary and natural, a habit common also to folklorists, as our recent self-criticisms have remarked (Kirshenblatt-Gimblett 1992b; Shuman 1993). In fact, I thought of beginning this article not with the greased pole, but with another picture that has stayed in my mind. Henry Glassie opened his "Introduction to Folklore" course at the University of Pennsylvania with an image that must now sum up the discipline for hundreds of Penn graduates: a breathtaking aerial slide of the open-field village of Braunton, Devonshire, surrounded by its countryside, centered by its church with the bell tower. The lecture went on to demonstrate the overwhelmingly centripetal social life and expressive culture of Braunton, supported by images of concentric spatial form and culminating at the heart of the matter, with twelve villagers in the church belfry ringing the changes in a pattern of perfect reciprocity and equality.

The village community gives us the idea made visible, the performance made permanent, in architecture. Here group is territory and performance, social ideal and lived reality. Here is the community as "bounded individual" (Handler 1988), like a body writ large. Here is the emblem. Here are the city walls as the limits of interaction, the reach of the sound of the bells as the limits of meaning.

As soberer Berguedans will tell you, this is a fantasy.[14] But it is significant that it is their favorite fantasy. It may well be that the Internet is a more important realm of interaction than the neighborhood for many in at least the Western world.[15] However, even for those of us who will never live in one, the face-to-face village community is a salutary reminder that life is still material, that really important things like eating and reproduction still take place in common space, and that violence, however remote and rational its sources, is felt close up and in person.

I fear mediation: I fear the interactant I cannot see, whom I cannot oblige to see me. Recent history surely justifies my fears. All of us at the mercy of abstract "global forces" that assume the responsibility for what must, somewhere, be the acts of men—is it any wonder that both left and right are fighting for more local control? No, the local is not natural, the local community is not a given, but it deserves special status in the discipline all the same. For we too have our empirical reality and our disciplinary imaginary, and as an emblem of the latter I prefer the village to its recent rival, the marketplace.

I just can't get enthusiastic about the marketplace. No doubt it looked appealing to Bakhtin from the Soviet Union, but those of us who live in its midst can better see its shortcomings. Certainly it offers liberty in relative abundance—if you can afford it—but equality and fraternity are goods in much shorter supply.

I admit that we have to live with commodification: our disciplinary practice has from the beginning been complicitous with the process (Cantwell 1993; Kirshenblatt-Gimblett 1992a; Stewart 1991). And as contemporary scholars, we have no choice but to participate in the system. Have we not reached the end of history?

One last gasp of the old Marxist history came in 1968 when French students tried to uncover reality beneath the society of the spectacle by picking up the paving stones of Paris. "Sous les pavés, la plage," they said, and then cast the stones through shop windows. They were utopians, to be sure, and their failure was recently confirmed by the suicide of Guy Debord, their key ideologue. There is no beach beneath the paving stones. There is no village community, Salvadoran collectivists learned, when their government, supported by ours, came to bomb it into deniability.

But I see no honor in celebrating the conditions of our imprisonment. I grant that the marketplace is the vitiated air we breathe and consequently deserves all the scholarly attention we have begun to give it. But let us not allow the empirical to kill off the imaginary entirely. Folklorists have already provided the nation-state with a human face: I fear that, with our tendency to celebrate what we describe, we may unwittingly do the same for the multinational.

I will conclude, however, on a more hopeful and more American note, turning descent into consent, circumstance into choice, and novelty into romance (Cantwell 1993; Sollors 1986). I returned to Italian Market Days in the fall of 1994 and found an Italian man in his twenties showing a group of small children—female, black, Vietnamese, and all—how to climb the greased pole. Perhaps that Asian man is adding his own discreet recommendations to a child in some house on Eighth Street. Network keeps trying to reach community. We know it to be a slippery ascent, but that knowledge has not yet deterred us, and it should not.

Notes

My thinking on these matters has benefited from conversations with Roger D. Abrahams, Michael Krippendorf, and William Westerman, and from time spent with the Bar La Barana, Berga, and the Philadelphia Folklore Project; my thanks to the latter for permission to cite material derived from fieldwork I undertook for them. None of these persons or entities should be held responsible for the results.

1. See Philadelphia Folklore Project 1993 for an account of Odunde.
2. I do not mean to disparage the endeavor by calling it a "would-be scientific revolution," only to point out that this was indeed its goal: the creation of a new paradigm, and one rather social-scientific than humanistic. See also Shuman and Briggs 1993.
3. I owe this point to Michael Krippendorf.
4. Bauman described von Sydow as emphasizing the local and the obstacles of political boundaries. I think we must see this in Harold Bloom's terms as a "Young Turk's" willful misreading, productive in its moment.
5. I take my account of sociological network theory primarily from Boissevain 1989 and from the excellent summary in Milroy 1987. Milroy and Milroy 1992 and Hannerz 1992 offer helpful updates.
6. See Meltzer 1994:47 on the apparent impossibility of women alone ever constituting a public.
7. For an exemplary case, see Evans-Pritchard 1987 on the complex dynamics of ownership in Southwest Indian jewelry.
8. We might translate this as "fundamentalist": the analogy is to a militantly conservative Catholic tendency in nineteenth- and twentieth-century Spain. But the emphasis on integrity is appropriate: their concern is with the wholeness and completeness of Berga.
9. "Sixteen judges from a courthouse eat the liver of a hanged man." The founders of the Catalan New Song movement of the late Franco period called themselves the Sixteen Judges.
10. I will not sport with the reader's impatience by summarizing this familiar discussion, but refer him or her to some basic sources: Bendix 1997, Dorst 1989, Handler 1988, and Handler and Linnekin 1984.

11. The classic but controversial reference is Bloch 1989 [1974]; for versions that do not see formalization as exclusively a tool of domination, see Ayats 1992; Briggs 1988:289–339; and McDowell 1992.

12. And see Sklar 1994 on "kinesthetic empathy."

13. It is worthwhile remembering that such festivals often have children's versions: this is true of the Giglio in Brooklyn and of the Palio in Siena as well as of the Patum, and I would expect to find it more generally.

14. See Albera 1988 for an Italian anthropologist's refutation of the assumptions of isolation and boundedness in European community studies. But see also Caro Baroja 1957 for the Mediterranean village ideology of concentricity or "sociocentrism"; the Italian notion of *campanilismo* is substantially the same.

15. But we should beware of assuming that our latest thing is the only thing, particularly when we are trying to think globally; cf. Glassie 1991 and Klein 1995.

References Cited

Abrahams, Roger D. 1981. "Shouting Match at the Border: The Folklore of Display Events." In *"And Other Neighborly Names": Social Process and Cultural Image in Texas Folklore.* Ed. Richard Bauman and Roger D. Abrahams. 303–22. Austin: University of Texas Press.

———. 1983. *The Man-of-Words in the West Indies.* Baltimore: Johns Hopkins University Press.

———. 1993. "Phantoms of Romantic Nationalism in Folkloristics." *Journal of American Folklore* 106:3–37.

———. n.d. "The Winking Gods of the Marketplace." Ms.

Abrahams, Roger D., ed. 1970. *A Singer and Her Songs: Almeda Riddle's Book of Ballads.* Baton Rouge: Louisiana State University Press.

Albera, Dionigi. 1988. "Open Systems and Closed Minds: The Limitations of Naivety in Social Anthropology." *Man* (n.s.) 23:435–52.

Anderson, Benedict. 1983. *Imagined Communities: Reflections on the Origin and Spread of Nationalism.* London: Verso.

Appadurai, Arjun. 1986. "Introduction: Commodities and the Politics of Value." In *The Social Life of Things.* Ed. Arjun Appadurai. 3–63. Cambridge: Cambridge University Press.

Ayats, Jaume. 1992. "'Troupes françaises hors du Golfe': Proférer dans la rue—les slogans de manifestation." *Ethnologie française* 22:348–67.

———. n.d. "Emblematic Songs: Marks of Identity and of Distance." Ms.

Bahloul, Joelle. 1983. *Le culte de la table dressée: Rites et traditions de la table juave algérienne.* Paris: Eds. A.-M. Métailié.

Barrera González, Andrés. 1990. *Casa, herencia y família en la Cataluña rural.* Madrid: Alianza.

Bauman, Richard. 1972. "Differential Identity and the Social Base of Folklore." In *Towards New Perspectives in Folklore.* Ed. Américo Paredes and Richard Bauman. 31–41. Austin: University of Texas Press.

Bauman, Richard, and Charles L. Briggs. 1990. "Poetics and Performance as Critical Perspectives on Language and Social Life." *Annual Review of Anthropology* 19:59–88.

Bell, Michael. 1983. *The World from Brown's Lounge: An Ethnography of Black Middle-Class Play.* Urbana: University of Illinois Press.

Ben-Amos, Dan. 1972. "Toward a Definition of Folklore in Context." In *Towards New Perspectives in Folklore.* Ed. Américo Paredes and Richard Bauman. 3–15. Austin: University of Texas Press.

Bendix, Regina. 1989. *Backstage Domains: Playing "William Tell" in Two Swiss Communities.* Bern: Peter Lang.

———. 1997. *In Search of Authenticity: The Formation of Folklore Studies.* Madison: University of Wisconsin Press.

Benjamin, Walter. 1969. "The Storyteller: Reflections on the Work of Nikolai Leskov." *Illuminations.* Trans. Harry Zohn. 83–110. New York: Schocken.

Bloch, Maurice. 1989 [1974]. "Symbols, Songs, Dance, and Features of Articulation." *Ritual, History, and Power.* 19–45. London: Athlone.

Boissevain, Jeremy. 1989. "Networks." In *The Social Science Encyclopedia.* Ed. Adam Kuper and Jessica Kuper. 557–58. London: Routledge.

Bott, E. 1971. *Family and Social Network.* 2d ed. London: Tavistock.

Briggs, Charles L. 1988. *Competence in Performance: The Creativity of Tradition in Mexicano Folk Art.* Philadelphia: University of Pennsylvania Press.

Briggs, Charles L., and Richard Bauman. 1992. "Genre, Intertextuality, and Social Power." *Journal of Linguistic Anthropology* 2 (2): 131–72.

Bruner, Edward M., and Phyllis Gorfain. 1984. "Dialogic Narrations and the Paradoxes of Masada." In *Text, Play, and Story.* Ed. Edward M. Bruner. 56–79. Prospect Heights, Ill.: Waveland Press.

Burke, Kenneth. 1957. "Literature as Equipment for Living." *The Philosophy of Literary Form.* 253–62. New York: Random House.

Butler, Judith. 1988. "Performative Acts and Gender Constitution: An Essay in Phenomenology and Feminist Theory." *Theatre Journal* 40:519–31.

Caillois, Roger. 1979. *Man, Play, and Games.* Trans. Meyer Barash. New York: Schocken.

Cantwell, Robert. 1993. *Ethnomimesis.* Chapel Hill: University of North Carolina Press.

Caro Baroja, Julio. 1957. "El sociocentrismo en los pueblos españoles." *Razas, gentes y linajes.* 263–92. Madrid: Revista de Occidente.

Clastres, Pierre. 1989. "Of Torture in Primitive Societies." *Society against the State.* Trans. Robert Hurley. 177–88. New York: Zone Books.

Davis, Natalie. 1974. "The Rites of Violence." *Society and Culture in Early Modern France.* 152–88. Stanford: Stanford University Press.

Dayan, Daniel, and Elihu Katz. 1992. *Media Events: The Live Broadcasting of History.* Cambridge, Mass.: Harvard University Press.

Dégh, Linda. 1994. *American Folklore and the Mass Media.* Bloomington: Indiana University Press.

Dégh, Linda, and Andrew Vászonyi. 1975. "The Hypothesis of Multi-Conduit Transmission in Folklore." In *Folklore: Performance and Communication*. Ed. Dan Ben-Amos and Kenneth S. Goldstein. 207–52. The Hague: Mouton.

Dorst, John. 1989. *The Written Suburb: An American Site, an Ethnographic Dilemma*. Philadelphia: University of Pennsylvania Press.

Downes, William. 1984. *Language and Society*. London: Fontana.

Dundes, Alan. 1965. "What Is Folklore?" In *The Study of Folklore*. Ed. Alan Dundes. 1–3. Englewood Cliffs, N.J.: Prentice-Hall.

Evans-Pritchard, Deirdre. 1987. "The Portal Case: Authenticity, Tourism, Traditions, and the Law." *Journal of American Folklore* 100:287–96.

Falassi, Alessandro. 1980. *Folklore by the Fireside: Text and Context of the Tuscan Veglia*. Austin: University of Texas Press.

Fernandez, James. 1988. "Isn't There Anything Out There That We Can All Believe In?: The Quest for Cultural Consensus in Anthropology and History." Paper read at the Institute for Advanced Study School of Social Science, Princeton, N.J.

Fine, Gary Alan. 1979. "Folklore Diffusion through Interactive Social Networks: Conduits in a Preadolescent Community." *New York Folklore* 5:87–126.

———. 1980. "Multiconduit Transmission and Social Structure: Expanding a Folklore Classic." In *Folklore on Two Continents: Essays in Honor of Linda Dégh*. Ed. Nikolai Burlakoff and Carl Lindahl. 300–309. Bloomington, Ind.: Trickster Press.

Garfinkel, Harold. 1967. "Passing and the Managed Achievement of Sexual Status in an Intersexed Person." *Studies in Ethnomethodology*. 116–85. Englewood Cliffs, N.J.: Prentice-Hall.

Geary, Patrick. 1986. "Sacred Commodities: The Circulation of Medieval Relics." In *The Social Life of Things*. Ed. Arjun Appadurai. 169–93. Cambridge: Cambridge University Press.

Geertz, Clifford. 1980. *Negara: The Theatre State in Nineteenth-Century Bali*. Princeton: Princeton University Press.

Glassie, Henry. 1991. "Studying Material Culture Today." In *Living in a Material World*. Ed. Gerald R. Pocius. 253–66. St. John's: Institute of Social and Economic Research, Memorial University of Newfoundland.

Goffman, Erving. 1959. *The Presentation of Self in Everyday Life*. New York: Doubleday.

Goldstein, Kenneth S. 1963. "Riddling Traditions in Northeastern Scotland." *Journal of American Folklore* 76:330–36.

———. 1972. "On the Application of the Concepts of Active and Inactive Traditions to the Study of Repertory." In *Toward New Perspectives in Folklore*. Ed. Américo Paredes and Richard Bauman. 62–67. Austin: University of Texas Press.

Granovetter, M. 1982. "The Strength of Weak Ties: A Network Theory Revisited." In *Social Structure and Network Analysis*. Ed. P. V. Marsden and N. Lin. 105–30. London: Sage.

Handler, Richard. 1988. *Nationalism and the Politics of Culture in Quebec.* Madison: University of Wisconsin Press.

Handler, Richard, and Jocelyn Linnekin. 1984. "Tradition, Genuine or Spurious." *Journal of American Folklore* 97:273–90.

Hannerz, Ulf. 1992. "The Global Ecumene as a Network of Networks." In *Conceptualizing Society.* Ed. Adam Kuper. 34–56. London: Routledge.

Hobsbawm, Eric, and Terence Ranger, eds. 1983. *The Invention of Tradition.* Cambridge: Cambridge University Press.

Ives, Edward D. 1964. *Larry Gorman: The Man Who Made the Songs.* Bloomington: Indiana University Press.

Jordan, Rosan A., and Susan J. Kalcik, eds. 1985. *Women's Folklore, Women's Culture.* Philadelphia: University of Pennsylvania Press.

Kapchan, Deborah. 1993. "Hybridization and the Marketplace: Emerging Paradigms in Folkloristics." *Western Folklore* 52:303–26.

Keeler, Ward. 1987. *Javanese Shadow Plays, Javanese Selves.* Princeton: Princeton University Press.

Kirshenblatt-Gimblett, Barbara. 1992a. "Mistaken Dichotomies." In *Public Folklore.* Ed. Robert Baron and Nicholas Spitzer. 29–48. Washington, D.C.: Smithsonian Institution Press.

———. 1992b. Presidential address. American Folklore Society Annual Meeting, Jacksonville, Fla.

Klein, Barbro. 1995. "Folklorists in the United States and the World Beyond." *AFS Newsletter* 24 (1): 12–15.

Klusen, Ernst. 1986 [1967]. "The Group Song as Group Object." In *German Volkskunde: A Decade of Theoretical Confrontation, Debate, and Reorientation, 1967–1977.* Ed. James R. Dow and Hannjost Lixfeld. 184–202. Bloomington: Indiana University Press.

Kodish, Debora. 1993. "On Coming of Age in the Sixties." *Western Folklore* 52:193–207.

Le Goff, Jacques. 1988. *The Medieval Imagination.* Trans. Arthur Goldhammer. Chicago: University of Chicago Press.

Le Page, R. B., and Andrée Tabouret-Keller. 1985. *Acts of Identity: Creole-Based Approaches to Language and Ethnicity.* Cambridge: Cambridge University Press.

Mathias, Elizabeth, and Richard Raspa. 1985. *Italian Folktales in America.* Detroit: Wayne State University Press.

McDowell, John. 1992. "Folklore as Commemorative Discourse." *Journal of American Folklore* 105:403–23.

Meltzer, Françoise. 1994. "Ghost Citing." In *Questions of Evidence.* Ed. James Chandler, Arnold I. Davidson, and Harry Harootunian. 43–49. Chicago: University of Chicago Press.

Miami Theory Collective. 1991. *Community at Loose Ends.* Minneapolis: University of Minnesota Press.

Mills, Margaret. 1993. "Feminist Theory and the Study of Folklore: A Twenty-Year Trajectory toward Theory." *Western Folklore* 52:173–92.

Milroy, Lesley. 1987. *Language and Social Networks.* Oxford: Basil Blackwell.

Milroy, Lesley, and James Milroy. 1992. "Social Network and Social Class: Toward an Integrated Sociolinguistic Model." *Language in Society* 21:1–26.

Nora, Pierre, ed. 1984. *Les lieux de mémoire.* Paris: Gallimard.

Noyes, Dorothy. 1989. *Uses of Tradition: Arts of Italian Americans in Philadelphia.* Philadelphia: Samuel S. Fleisher Art Memorial and the Philadelphia Folklore Project.

———. 1992. "The Mule and the Giants: Struggling for the Body Social in a Catalan Corpus Christi Festival." Ph.D. diss., University of Pennsylvania.

———. 1993. "From the *Paese* to the *Patria:* An Italian American Pilgrimage to Rome in 1929." In *Studies in Italian American Folklore.* Ed. Luisa Del Giudice. 127–52. Logan: Utah State University Press.

Philadelphia Folklore Project. 1993. *Works in Progress.* Special issue of ODUNDE 6:2.

———. n.d. *The Palm Weavers* (videotape). Philadelphia: Philadelphia Folklore Project.

Schechner, Richard. 1985. *Between Theater and Anthropology.* Philadelphia: University of Pennsylvania Press.

Scott, James C. 1990. *Domination and the Arts of Resistance: Hidden Transcripts.* New Haven: Yale University Press.

Shuman, Amy. 1993. "Dismantling Local Culture." *Western Folklore* 52:345–64.

Shuman, Amy, and Charles L. Briggs. 1993. "Introduction." *Western Folklore* 52:109–34.

Sklar, Deidre. 1994. "Can Bodylore Be Brought to Its Senses?" *Journal of American Folklore* 107:9–22.

Sollors, Werner. 1986. *Beyond Ethnicity: Consent and Descent in American Culture.* Oxford: Oxford University Press.

Stewart, Susan. 1991. "Notes on Distressed Genres." *Journal of American Folklore* 104:5–31.

Streicker, Joel. 1995. "Policing Boundaries: Race, Class, and Gender in Cartagena, Colombia." *American Ethnologist* 22:54–74.

Thomas, Gerald. 1983. *Les deux traditions.* Montreal: Bellarmin.

Thompson, E. P. 1993. "Custom, Law, and Common Right." *Customs in Common.* 97–184. New York: New Press.

Turner, Victor. 1981. "Social Dramas and Stories about Them." In *On Narrative.* Ed. W. J. T. Mitchell. 137–64. Chicago: University of Chicago Press.

Velasco, Honorio. 1986. "Sobre los procesos de la tradición oral: Las adivinanzas, mediaciones de poder y de saber." In *Culturas populares: Diferencias, divergencias, conflictos—Actas del Coloquio celebrado en la Casa de Velázquez, los días 30 de noviembre y 1–2 diciembre de 1983.* 171–84. Madrid: Universidad Complutense.

von Sydow, Carl W. 1948. *Selected Papers in Folklore.* Copenhagen: Rosenkilde and Bagger.

Wallerstein, Immanuel. 1983. *Historical Capitalism.* London: Verso.

2 Art

Perhaps of all the words that surround us in our daily life, *art* is one of the most contentious, most controversial. In part, this is because *art*—like the term *folklore*—has a popular as well as academic parlance. While abstract concepts such as "text" or "identity" rarely enter common discourse, our daily lives frequently encounter popular notions of "art": our cities are filled with establishments that sell "art," we take "art appreciation" courses, we buy the products of "recording artists." We become disparaging when our governments fund certain varieties of "art" over others, and we lump different artworks together under categories such as "highbrow" or "kitsch." We can even turn to our phone books to see entries in the yellow pages under "art": galleries, supply shops, and much more (Maquet 1986:14). The term *art* often is subtly associated with class, or money, or a particular historical period, and perhaps with categories of writing, performances, or objects. Such popular stereotypes mean that the concept of art for the general public is frequently influenced by deep-seated cultural attitudes.

For folklorists, however, art has always been a fundamental concept, a term repeatedly used in discussions of issues that are central to the discipline. Folklore scholarship is filled with words such as *art, artist, creativity,* or *aesthetics,* yet little of a systematic reflexive nature has been written about such key concepts and what they cover. In approaching the issue within folklore studies, we come up against many diverse and often implicit assumptions of what the word *art* means. Part of the difficulty in defining art is that the concept of art might well be thought to cover most of the materials of expressive culture studies, while much research within the discipline of folklore often focuses on only one art form (such as song, or narrative, or painting). Art, as that which represents a specific culture's notion of excellence, becomes central to the folklorist's understanding of a particular group. We folklorists, therefore, have come to believe that art is central to our discipline, so much so, in fact, that the term *folklore*, according to one writer, is actually another way of saying *art* (Glassie 1989:36). We have concentrated on artistic products and activities of cultures. But in spite of this emphasis, we have often spent our time agonizing over the term *folklore* and what it covers, while assuming that the concept of art is a platonic given that needs no obvious explication.

Several fundamental assumptions shape our understanding of what art is. First and foremost, art is a universal phenomenon, yet at the same time it is culturally specific. We think of something designated as art as a distinct product of skill that fulfills certain culturally derived aesthetic criteria at the same time that it answers basic human needs. While this seems almost contradictory, it leads us to explore a number of issues and methodologies. When we theorize about folklore, we are often theorizing about art; thus, when we search out the universals of folklore, we are searching for the universal laws that govern art. But while folklore searches for the universal, it also grounds its studies in the culturally specific, guided by cultural relativism. The products of each culture—what might be considered as art and what might not—can be properly explained only with the help of participants from the culture itself. While the concept of art is universal, it cannot be defined except as it is perceived by those who create and experience it.

This leads us to the series of dichotomies within the framework of cultural relativism: those of insiders and outsiders, emic and etic, academics and art producers or audience. Trying to understand the art of others is often difficult. Our goal as scholars and analysts is to clarify the characteristics of art, but not every culture has a traditional vocabulary of criticism that can elucidate what its art is, how it is created, or how it is judged (Dark 1978:36). The elaborate discourses of evaluation that each of us uses in the study of *our* own art often have no analogous vocabulary in other cultural groups; societies with extensive divisions of labor are more likely to have designated critics who articulate artistic norms (Bell 1984:221; Anderson 1990:226). Indeed, even the word *art* itself does not exist in many cultures (Anderson 1992:927).

Our goal is to construct as accurately as possible the categories of art of those people we study and to determine how art is assessed by that culture. Lack of articulation by others does not mean that we somehow cannot study art, that these issues cannot be confronted, but it does bring us to the fundamental problem: does an actual category of art exist in every culture? Is the concept of art alien to many people of the world (Firth 1992:26)? What exactly is art? Folklorists believe that all peoples have the ability to produce exceptional things that analysts label as art. Our dilemma is often how to recognize the things that others consider as art. Much of what folklorists study is not considered to be art, in this sense, by the people who produce it (Griffith 1988:5). We believe that while the category of art may not be a specific category, all people engage in a wide range of creative acts that are judged by standards of excellence (Carpenter 1969:203). Our difficulty in recognizing these may be related to our own ethnocentric notions of art as something created by, and for, a limited few. What we realize in our struggle against this elitist view is the potential that what many Westerners consider quite ordinary things might well fall under the rubric of art. Our own assumptions about art—is it a product exceptional or is it ordinary?—have been shaped by how the concept developed within the Western intellectual tradition.

The Emergence of Art

Art, as Westerners envision it, is a conceptual category only recently introduced to the analysis of everyday life. In Greek and Roman antiquity, those who specialized in painting and sculpture were sometimes singled out for what were considered special innovations, but it is clear that not until Renaissance times did such creators—certainly in secular circles—have special status (Brendel 1963:248–49). In the medieval European world, there was certainly no concept of art as we use it in the modern sense (Eco 1986:97). People did not consider things that were created as means of individual expression; creators simply worked with words or physical materials to construct products that reflected the divine order inherent in all worldly things. Individual styles followed shared aesthetics.

The medieval mind knew the rules governing the proper way to produce a certain product; notions of what was practical and what was aesthetically pleasing were inseparable. Medieval European objects possessed many of the characteristics that later would be attributed to "folk" art. All objects had practical aims. All that was fabricated moved humans toward their quest for salvation. Artisans, by definition, were those who skillfully produced cultural products. The original meaning of the word *art* was quite clear: it derived from a Greek term meaning "useful skill," and it applied to *any* kind of skill (Anderson 1990:278; Williams 1983:41).

With the Renaissance came the division between utility and aesthetics that would eventually produce the modern Western concept of art. As a humanistic worldview began to fragment the universe, it eventually led to the belief that there were special products—individual items, created by exceptional persons—whose inspiration was of a higher order than the accumulated wisdom of the culture. During the Renaissance, certain objects were set apart as exceptional.

At this time, people came to believe that inspiration for creation came not from knowledge learned from previous practitioners but from the wellspring of creativity within the individual. Michelangelo, for instance, "broke the bonds and chains" that had previously confined all painters to replicate ideas from previous epochs. More and more, for those who created, "nature was their authority, not an inherited tradition" (Lucie-Smith 1981:156). Inspiration became personal, not collective; the "imaginative truth" of the individual rather than the maturation of human skill produced the well-made item. Emphasis on skill was replaced by emphasis on sensibility (Williams 1963:53, 60).

This Renaissance ideal brought with it an increasing dichotomizing of the world: in the realm of art versus craft, what was deemed to be aesthetically inspired was separated from the purely functional (what in later years we would contrast as expressive versus instrumental culture). Much of what we would now consider under our Western rubric of art went this route: certain authorities (designers, composers, writers) created conventional cultural forms considered as art, while practitioners—craftspeople, performers—executed the ideas. In furniture, in music, in architecture—in so much of what we consider as art—the split between designer and maker occurred because of these historical shifts (e.g., Mercer 1969:116–18, 130–31). Art changed from that medieval unity, where artisans brought widely known forms into existence, to a hierarchy of practitioners—some considered by patrons to be more highly skilled than others. The assumption would eventually be that art came from the genius of a limited number of individuals, not from ordinary people drawing on the consensual wisdom of both past and present.

The concepts that govern so much of our research on art are therefore relatively recent in the history of Western ideas. Whereas in medieval times any activity requiring skill was considered as art, during the Renaissance art became the product of the special skills of privileged individuals. Secularization meant that, instead of serving both aesthetic and utilitarian functions, artifacts increasingly became symbols of newly acquired wealth. When objects needed to be bought, statements about status could now be made through an acquisition.

Members of the middle class looked for ways to display their new economic power, and objects often fulfilled that need, through both the collecting of antiquities and the commissioning of new artifact forms (Hooper-Greenhill 1992:23–132). The epitome of art as status was the rise of first the illustrator and then the portrait painter, whose products became demonstrations of wealth (Mukerji 1983; Vlach 1988). It is not surprising, then, that this illustrative work soon became synonymous with Western art. In popular parlance an artist was a painter, yet, with the rise of materialism, Western art gradually became associated with other media: sculpture, music, and literature. At the same time, other products, usually objects with utilitarian functions, came to be considered as more mundane and were categorized as craft. Eventually the arts were divided into greater or lesser, major or minor, basically along the art and craft dichotomy that exists today. Applied or utilitarian arts are still considered by many to be diminished forms of art; an instrumental use somehow negates them being pure art (Dormer 1994:27–28; Morris 1962:89). Whether labeled "craft" or "decorative art," these "lesser arts" were often stereotyped, as Morris argued, as "trivial, mechanical, unintelligent, incapable of resisting the changes pressed upon them by fashion or dishonesty," while elitist art was "nothing but dull adjuncts to unmeaning pomp, or ingenious toys for a few rich and idle men" (Morris 1996:157).

In the medieval world, artisans created works that were part of a divine plan, and each product drew from God's designs, contributing to God's plan for humankind. With the Renaissance, individuals came to draw upon personal inspiration rather than on the collective wisdom of a religious society. With organized religion no longer providing answers to basic questions about existence, intellectuals turned to this new basis of inspiration: art. Questions about life's meaning would now be answered, in part, not by ordinary objects informed by a medieval worldview but by the inspired and exceptional objects of the Renaissance artist.

At the same time that inspired creators were beginning to give modern intellectuals secular and individualistic visions of the world in new works now categorized as art, Westerners began to discover peoples they perceived as mentally different from them. Western intellectuals discovered "art" at the same time that they discovered "the Other," what by the nineteenth century had been labeled "folk" or "primitive" (Graburn 1976:3; G. Shapiro 1989:73). While for some Europeans secular art provided keys to life's meaning, for others, the lifestyles of folk or primitives held the key to the emergent secular worldview.

Voyages of European discovery and subsequent colonialization of "primitive" lands often were spurred on by a quest for the Other and the subsequent appropriation of cultures uncorrupted by Western values

(Cocchiara 1981 [1952]:13–43). Like the uses for the new category of art, this creation of certain people as Other was in part an appropriation of cultural traits that might provide answers to questions once answered by religion (Coutts-Smith 1991:18).

Westerners assumed that other people perceived life—including art—differently from the way they did, and that these different people might provide insight into the process by which Western "civilization" had emerged from its "primitive" state. These Others were somehow more cohesive, more integrated, closer to humans' primitive state; their lives exhibited the meaningfulness that Western peoples no longer had after the radical break brought on by Renaissance humanism (Miller 1991:51, 55, 62).

There is an inherent irony here, however: Post-Renaissance intellectuals sought what they perceived to be the "folk" or "primitive" equivalents of art products. In this case, they coveted material artifacts that approximated painting and sculpture, the Western norms that they believed embodied true artistic excellence (Price 1989:68–81). But the art created by these Others, while providing researchers with alternative sources of insight into Western values, was also implicitly thought of as somehow of secondary quality (that it, for example, fell first under the rubric of craft). Westerners came to believe that their elite culture had produced the only truly inspirational art, an art that gave them insightful visions of humanity (be it the communal vision of medievalism or the fragmented individualism of modernism). Objects of other peoples, however, were functional artifacts that were thought of as utilitarian by their makers and consumers; it was only *we*, in the West, who recognized their aesthetic qualities. In spite of this increasing appreciation of the art of the Others, Westerners implicitly devalued these products by labeling them—"folk" art or "primitive" art—setting them up as different from the elite creations that they regarded as sophisticated or cultured or "art" (Glassie 1986:271). For many, Western elite products remained the epitome of culture, the art by which the works of all others were judged (Clifford 1988:235). The art of the Other needed to be prefixed, qualified.

Certainly, as the discipline of folklore developed, researchers came to regard the exceptional product of the Other as a form of art (sometimes written about as "peasant"), although its nature was never fully discussed (e.g., Granlund). Folklorists in late-nineteenth-century Europe and North America sought to study vernacular European versions of those products already singled out in the postmedieval West as exceptional: painting, sculpture, music, and literature (including narrative and poetry). There were folk parallels for high art: märchen for novels, wall paintings for gallery portraits, painted furniture and ironwork for sculpture, ballads for poetry. While folklorists recognized the theoretical possibility that many different activities might be labeled as artistic, it was usually these specific vernacular analogues—indigenous versions of elite art—that they researched as art (Boas 1955 [1927]:9–10; Bronner 1988:79).

Art has been the underlying organizing criterion of what it is that folklorists have studied. But unlike in art history or aesthetics, research in folklore has basically been on the art of the Other—first the primitive, later the peasant or folk. Under the guise of cultural relativism, we folklorists ironically remained ethnocentric, for we continued to look for stories and poems and paintings: *their* versions of *our* art forms. And by creating an Other, we implied that people were indeed different, that other cultures produced art different from ours. With art prefixed with qualifiers such as "verbal," "folk," or "primitive," the unintended implication is that the art of the Other was not as sophisticated as ours.

The concept of art remains implicit rather than explicit in what folklorists decide to study. Yet no matter what type of questions we raise, we might think about our concern with art under three different emphases: art as product, art as process, and art as behavior. Emerging from these concerns, we can consider artistic items, artistic performances, and artistic everyday activities. Each has brought specific questions to the forefront.

Art as Product

Much of our thinking about art carries with it the assumption that something designated as "art" is clearly a discrete product. In many cases, this has meant that we think of art as both tangible and intangible products (generally objects, but also oral forms such as narratives, poetry, song, and rhymes). We think about art, then, as discrete quantifiable items covering certain limited categories. This is clear when we look at how, historically, we folklorists have thought about the term in our research.

We regard cultural products as art because of their particular form. In recent years some folklorists have argued that form is an arbitrary construct, that items are artificially abstracted from their emergent context; there are not stories, for example, but storytelling events (Georges 1969). But in many instances, it is a specific form that is associated with particular pleasurable experiences, and a culture links form and experience together into what can be considered as art. For many people, as Boas and others have pointed out, art becomes involved with formal perfection, repeating forms that have specific aesthetic impacts (Boas 1955 [1927]:10). The most basic notion of art is that it is the technical production of particular forms, the replication of the form judged to have been well done (Jones 1989:255, 257).

If art is form replicated well, two issues arise: the demarcation of those forms, particularly the stylistic elements that call attention to a form, and how form links to emotion. Which forms please? What other issues in culture do they speak to (Layton 1991:22)? Who is able to read the forms and discern "good" performance?

Much concern in recent years has focused on how to recognize cultural forms; researchers have often explored this issue by looking at the concept of genre. Folklorists have been interested in how each culture constructs repetitive behaviors following particular forms, each form marked by specific features. The textual focus of much genre theory is but one indication of folklorists' concern with pattern and form; and genre issues are one of folklorists' important contributions to cultural studies (Ben-Amos 1976; Glassie 1968; Hymes 1975b:351–52). Some forms are open to more individual variation than others, and some can be altered more easily by audience response at the time of creation, but the presence of form means that certain behaviors are recognized as art by a particular culture—regardless of how variable or rigid the forms are (Abrahams 1976).

Certainly one concern is whether a particular form is one recognized by the cultural group that produces it or one constructed by the researcher (Ben-Amos 1976). Once forms are isolated, their stylistic features—tones, gestures, inflections, designs, and so on—reveal more fundamental values. What seems to determine a focus on particular items is this issue of style, the surface attributes of the cultural product that call attention to its form rather than to referential or functional domains (Hymes 1974:133). Stylistic features are obviously a part of all cultural products (see M. Shapiro 1953:287; Silver 1979:270 ff.), but it is often the ability to vary those features more easily in certain media that causes such forms to be more readily considered as art in the group that produces them. Art forms often rely on stylistic foregrounding, what folklorists have written about in other instances as "texture." With verbally performed materials, stylistic elements are brought to the forefront of each event, reinforcing to an audience the prominence of such style features over any referential issues. Henry Glassie has written extensively on how style and form reflect shifts in basic cultural values: changes in Western cultures from a medieval to a modern worldview and the importance of repetition in many Anglo-American artistic forms (Glassie 1970; 1975).[1] Form and style remain fundamental indicators of pervasive cultural values (e.g., Lomax 1968; Pocius 1979).

With its development as a concept in the West, art was generally considered a discrete item, a product that could be collected, quantified, and displayed. What folklorists considered art depended upon the individual researcher's orientation. For some folklorists art was textual: "artistically creative" elements found in indigenous versions of the literary text (Krohn 1971 [1926]:22). Early in the history of the discipline, literary folklorists often searched texts for such artistic elements reflecting cultural universals, believing that any literature as art would provide insights into the human condition (Lüthi 1984 [1975]; Olrik 1965 [1909]).

Those more influenced by the forces of field research–based cultural relativism, however, were less willing to make sweeping judgments about universals in art, and ironically—in spite of their relativistic stance—they limited their idea of what constituted art to the forms closest to Western patterns: painting and sculpture. For some, in the early years of the discipline, art remained largely tied to material things. Folklorists studied the cultural activities of other groups under categories such as narrative or song or belief, but when they used the term *art*, it was almost always reserved for decorative objects, and it was usually qualified with the addition of the word *folk*. Folklorists began to codify what they considered to be art by qualifying certain behaviors by group (e.g., "folk craft") while others remained unqualified (e.g., "tale") (Oring 1986:4). Verbal traditions had always been a primary focus of study; but if art were considered, it would be a concern with decorative artifacts labeled as "folk art" (e.g., Barbeau 1948).[2] And up until the 1940s, North American folklorists primarily studied "tales and songs," not "art," that is, not material things (Bronner 1984:xxi–xxii).

Shifts gradually began to occur, however, which we can explain in part by the need to recognize what had always been implied: that our studies concentrated on the creative dimensions of ordinary human activity. We still focused on products, but now we claimed openly what the occasional literary folklorist had argued before: that texts were art, just as were artifacts. If, in our Western culture, literature was art, then the literatures of the Other—oral literature—could be considered art as well. Next to the earlier rubric of folk art (as artifact) appeared the new term *verbal art* (Bascom 1955). Verbal art now would subsume the spoken equivalent of the written literatures of dominant cultures.

This definition also brought attention to the fact that widely diverse literary creations exhibited highly stylized forms. Attention to stylized forms meant that such products were not simply utilitarian, thus maintaining the Renaissance notion that art had to go beyond utility. And it was not long before anthropologists would consider not just texts or artifacts as art but a wide range of behaviors as well. Art was no longer primarily found in material expression but manifested itself in a number of media. William Bascom argued that indigenous arts encompassed creations graphic, plastic, literary, and verbal, although he maintained that many items considered as folklore were not art (Bascom 1973:374). For anthropological folklorists, the "arts" now covered all the vernacular analogues of Western art: music, drama, dance, and literature, as well as material creations (Merriam 1977).

Historically, the issue of whether items were useful or artistic was central to the concept of what constituted art. What was considered art was limited to those things "with elaboration beyond the point of utility" (Bascom 1955:247). However, this distinction has caused problems in some media more than others. In terms of objects, the issue of art versus craft clearly has plagued much interpretation, a false dichotomy that assumes art must be something other than useful (Glassie 1997:83, 351, 463). Research has often focused on the most decorative, the most elaborate creations—the vernacular versions of Western art. Objects perceived to be purely practical rarely are considered to have an aesthetic dimension (for an exception that examines tools, see Pope 1985). Yet other cultural items have been accorded de facto status as art; it has been assumed that purely because of their form—literature, poetry, dance, music—the aesthetic dimension is dominant in their creation.

But if art as product succeeds in a culture because of both a replication of certain forms and the predominance of style features that call attention to these forms, then it is often the importance of association that makes a work of art successful. Boas, and Michael Owen Jones after him, have pointed to how artistic impact is often dependent not just on producing a pleasing form but on the ideas that are culturally associated with that form (Boas 1955 [1927]:13; Jones 1971:82). Forms have to relate to some aspect of personal experience; they have to elucidate that experience, often bringing pleasure in this elucidation (Anderson 1990:275; Jones 1971:80).

A work of art, then, through form and through association of that form to particular aspects of daily life, succeeds by eliciting some type of emotional response in the observer. Again, folklorists have long recognized this emotional impact but have only begun to attempt to venture into the field of psychology to understand its mechanisms. This emotional impact of a work of art has been written about under a number of guises; it has been thought of as an "affecting presence" (Armstrong 1971) or as a type of "magic" (Zeitlin et al. 1979:8). Because of its cultural association, the work of art produces an intense emotional reaction in those exposed to the work. One writer considered this component as an "emotional core" that, like

T. S. Eliot's objective correlative, triggers by its content a series of intense basic emotions to which humans react (Coffin 1961).

Up until the 1960s, "art" as studied by folklorists covered stylized products created by cultural Others, products that somehow approximated versions of what Western intellectuals had always considered as art. Narrative approximated literature, ballad approximated poetry, song approximated symphonies, and decorative objects approximated painting and sculpture. Theorists working under the umbrella of cultural relativism simply accepted what had been sundered by the Renaissance—art versus craft—so that certain products (art) were excellent and others (craft) ordinary. "Folk art" might include products such as oral literature relabeled as verbal art. Or it might be more limited, covering only material artifacts. Yet in many of their studies, folklorists investigated the issue of cultural form and its replication in particular contexts, research that would eventually lead to a broader notion of art. The study of art would shift from things to the entire creative act.

Art as Performance

Early folklorists considered art as discrete items, such as poetry, drama, or sculpture, but in the past twenty years we have broadened the concept beyond items to include the situations in which these items are found. This is the shift from "text" to "context." In this reformulation of folklore studies, art has remained one of the defining criteria, as in Ben-Amos's now classic definitional statement of folklore as "artistic communication in small groups" (1972:13). This reorientation led scholars to question the methods that were, in the past, often inattentive to the societal details of the creative act and the multiplicity of uses of particular forms. Particular events came to be characterized as artistic events, with their own overall messages communicated through many channels and codes. Emphasis changed from the item (text or object) to the producers of art and to the contexts of production and use (Babcock 1992:206).

Research shifted from the historical to the ethnographic. Believing that the study of the past somehow condemned folklore studies to a devolutionary dead end where all genuine art was slowly disappearing, a new focus on the contemporary meant that new forms were emerging. And even more important, this reorientation meant that new questions might be asked, questions about creativity, innovation, and aesthetics. Yet in many instances, art merely became a substitute for the old items of folklore, with the added gloss that it was now a dynamic rather than a static concept. "Folklore was art born in the aesthetic 'event'" (Oring 1994:221). It is important to realize that a number of key studies of folklore as art guided by this performance orientation have produced insights not about art per se but about other issues such as identity (Oring 1994:222).

In this shift from product to performance, there still remained in many cases an implicit reliance on the standard categories of art that had been settled upon by earlier researchers. While much new rhetoric expounded on how various forms of behavior considered artistic could now be understood by focusing on art as process—the process of performance or communication—what was regarded as art was still largely restricted to items that were vernacular versions of elite art. Although in many cases we might think of this reorientation as an attempt to consider art as a unique form of communication, the media for that communication remained the same. Instead of reexamining our fundamental assumptions about what art was, we implicitly continued to believe we knew what art products were, and we merely searched for the events, the performances, that contained them. We studied the "artist-performer," who fabricated an "artistic object, an *item* of performance" that was involved with the "dialectic between art and life" through "the artist and his genres" (Abrahams 1977:83). In many cases those genres were already defined as art before research started.

The study of much art was thus linked to the notion of performance, but artistic performances were recognized often by how closely they resembled forms canonized as folklore. The cues of what was verbal art, for example, remained textual rather than in the nature of the performance itself (Bauman 1975:295; Briggs 1988:8–10, 14). We took canonic items of art—our long-standing genres—and reexamined them within this new framework of performance: how, for example, did audience participation alter specific texts? (Murphy 1978:125–26). This is why—in spite of the new performance paradigm—folklorists did not study the opera or the ballet or the artist's studio. What was gained was not a new appreciation for what the notion of art might really be all about but rather a shift to understanding the dynamics of the creation of long-recognized forms and their variations, all of which were dependant on particular contextual scenes. The new concerns for performance, communication, and event removed the limitations of the concept of tradition from definitions of what might be studied as folklore, and therefore art (Ben-Amos 1972:13). But, ironically, the disciplinary tradition of folklore studies itself meant that in many cases what were always considered as art forms continued to be studied. We asked new questions of the same old items.

Art as Behavior

The concept of art as a category created by the split of skillful activities (the work of artisans) into art and craft, instrumental and expressive, fell increasingly under scrutiny in the 1960s. Folklorists came to realize that the concept of art often did not exist for the person or group that was being studied. Instead, in many cultures a wide range of activities could be judged to be pleasing as well as useful, and behaviors with aesthetic dimensions could encompass a wide spectrum of everyday life. Clearly, for some, a notion of artistic behavior would cover not just certain items, the items focused on under earlier rubrics of "art," but would also cover many activities that required skill. Instead of "art" as item, "art" could include the aesthetic dimension of everyday life, in whatever form that might take, forms as diverse as belt buckles made from trunk ornaments on a Detroit assembly line, vanity car-license plates, gardens decorated with rubber tires and beer cans, clothing ensembles such as the "preppy" look of L. L. Bean moccasins without socks, or monograms and signet rings (Kirshenblatt-Gimblett 1983:221). As Boas recognized in his early findings, all human activities could contain an aesthetic (and therefore artistic) dimension (Boas 1955 [1927]:9). Hymes echoes this position, noting the stylized content and conduct of most communication (Hymes 1975a:11).

With this perspective, folklorists began to associate art not with a limited number of cultural items but rather with any type of everyday activity that required a certain amount of skill to execute. For the farmer, for example, art was everywhere: "beauty could be seen in newly plowed fertile soil, a verdant meadow, or a pregnant cow—a magnificent sight!" (Löfgren 1994:239). But art was also found in modern urban contexts, among all groups. Art was assumed to cover behaviors as wide-ranging as occupations (Jones 1984) such as tending bar (Bell 1976), smuggling (Langlois 1991), or professional wrestling (Gutowski 1972), and activities such as cooking (Austin 1992; Weaver 1989), the creation of privacy (Pocius 1986), or the making of festivals (Prosterman 1995; Smith 1975). One folklorist summarized the pervasiveness of art, pointing out: "people who might never have dreamed of visiting an art gallery or drawing a picture do not hesitate . . . about taking charge of the artistic adornment of their own living room: selecting colors and patterns, arranging furniture, draperies, ornaments, and paintings to achieve a whole. Some of them could even consider spending hours in front of the mirror, so that they themselves can be transformed into works of art on a Friday evening" (Löfgren 1994:236). While some studies may well have ignored "tradition" in its "traditional sense" as a factor in determining what is art (Bendix 1988:12), they moved the term closer to the medieval notion of art as skill that William Morris and others wrote about so eloquently. In a curious way, such a stance is perhaps a reinvention of a new brand of romanticism, a romanticism linked not necessarily to a medieval world but to a modern or postmodern version of it, where the skillful, aesthetic, group-enforced and appreciated activities of all humans can be considered as potential art.

Returning to Skill

One of the central defining characteristics, then, of the concept of art must be the criterion of skill (Glassie 1997:82). Morris recognized that every act (and here we can use *act* to cover all items, no matter what the medium or product) required skill to accomplish (1962:85); certainly this stance is not necessarily Eurocentric (e.g., Coomaraswamy 1924:18). What skill comprises, however, is obviously culturally determined, often gauged by how much talent is required to produce a particular cultural form. Skills are developed gradually by individuals; they are not acquired automatically, and they are often a matter of degree (Anderson 1979:9–10). Audiences recognize that what is considered as art requires special skill above the level of the ordinary, a "wish for perfection, displayed in technical mastery" (Anderson 1990:278; Glassie 1999:186). We all decorate, we all dress up; those who do it best are considered to have aesthetic skills as artists.

Folklorists have often considered art as skill in producing particular cultural forms, and we have classified art by degrees of skill. On our classificatory continuum, we have given preeminence to art as painting—a form uncommon in a global artistic context (Glassie 1999:144)—followed by the visual arts generally, and then all visual and performance arts. But finally, art in its earliest and broadest sense, in its medieval guise, covers the skills of all everyday activities (Munro 1969:49–62). Skill, however, must not simply become a substitute for the category of art itself. Skill manifests itself in a series of operations that produce the cultural behaviors we consider as art. In succinct terms, then, we can define art as the manifestation of a skill that involves the creation of a qualitative experience (often categorized as aesthetic) through the manipulation of whatever forms that are public categories recognized by a particular group.[3] These bring us to the key components of skillful behavior: tradition, group, and emotion.

Although the importance of tradition in defining art has been downplayed in recent years, in doing so folklorists have attempted to move beyond the limited number of forms included in Western notions of appropriate art. Yet the idea of tradition guides the creation of all art forms at the basic level of choice. The concept of tradition does not limit but expands, and the folklorist's long-standing interest in tradition (and therefore choice) is finally a strength to draw upon in order more fully to understand art (Jones 1996:9). Art manipulates traditions while at the same time being shaped by them (Ives 1978:407; Glassie 1999:120).

Art involves creation. And all creation is in part culturally based. Artists live in a particular time and in a particular place. Creation never occurs in a vacuum; it must involve choices of techniques, as well as content, that are all culturally influenced and learned. The creator is never totally isolated, nor does he or she merely repeat what is known. Creation of art, on the one hand, is never truly collective, although folklorists have pointed out the importance of shared aesthetics as a defining feature of what is considered as art (Glassie 1989:26; Hauser 1959:286; Vlach 1985). We create a false dichotomy when we believe that elite art speaks only for the inspired artist and folk art speaks only for the community (Rosenberg 1993:174). Artists of all groups obviously can strive to produce excellent versions of conventional types (Glassie 1993:668). The skill in creation may come in the form of the perfect copy; creation may involve the thrill of exact re-creation (Ben-Amos 1972:7).

Materials from the surrounding culture, whether they are relatively new materials or relatively long-standing, are the basis for much creation (Eliot 1928). The stereotype of art is often a bohemianism, free from any formal restraint, but art is rarely innovation (Firth 1992:17; Ives 1978:408). Recent studies of individual creators demonstrate again and again the scholarly trend toward regarding each act of creation as involving a balance between the individual and the collective, often covered by rubrics such as "tradition and creativity," or "tradition, creativity and the individual" (e.g., Abrahams 1970; Biebuyck 1969). For any art to be relevant, it must have components that explore common human conditions, whether those humans are considered "folk" or "modern." And these conditions are usually a mixture of long-standing standards and new opportunities. The creation of art involves a recognition of a particular formal pattern and how much the individual decides to vary that pattern to address both personal needs and the needs of an audience (Glassie 1972:266; 1993:616, 689). Art involves the relation between "individual creativity and the collective order," the relation of "individual will to collective process" (Glassie 1994b:241). One of the fundamental questions in the study of art remains: "How free can the artist ever be, as a creator and at the same time, a member of the social and cultural community?" (Brendel 1963:263).

Skill in producing art means a recognition that there are group crite-ria for what is produced. Many of the visual arts subsumed under the ru-bric of folk art have quite rightly been recognized as esoteric creations for limited audiences (e.g., Vlach 1986, 1988). Indeed, one of the most recent debates among those researching artifacts stereotypically labeled "folk art" has been critical of how representative such objects really are of a culture—whether a painter such as Grandma Moses, for example, is really a folk artist. One school believes that folklorists focus on shared group values and, therefore, any creative act that does not rely on consensus cannot be considered as "folk." The object may still be art, but it receives other la-bels, such as "naïve," "visionary," or—the most widely used—"outsider" (Cardinal 1972; *Naives* 1974; Metcalf 1986:18). These contrasting inter-pretations have been categorized as "cultural" versus "behavioral" views: cultural theories posit a shared group consensus; behavioral approaches argue that creativity might well be idiosyncratic while still drawing on basic human feelings and emotions. One can gauge the differences here, with folklorists sometimes arguing that group art is "folk," while idiosyn-cratic creations—those that are "too personal, too eclectic"—are "outsid-er" (Zug 1994:145; Burrison 2000:19–20, 29–30). When creators transcend community forms or rules and draw on personal inspirations, their art "is simply not folk, no matter what community its maker was otherwise a member of" (Bergengren 1991:128). The opposite view argues that no art whether labeled "outsider" or otherwise is truly unlearned, self-taught, and without community (Jones 1994:317). Yet, someone like Grandma Moses is drawing more from an elite or idiosyncratic tradition than a "folk" or community tradition. The trend has been that if it is poorly ex-ecuted (by elite art standards), then the elite art world labels it "folk."

Yet, the issue here is, again, not what "folk" might subsume but rath-er that art is situated among a particular group—and that art can be eso-teric, limited, or collective. Historically, groups researched by folklorists have been those considered untouched by Western industrial society; of-ten they have been the colonized. But in recent years, the basis of art has shifted to other groups: ethnic, religious, occupational, recreational, gen-dered, or regional (Teske 1987:4), or quite simply the "small group." What becomes important is not some kind of pristine mind-set that the group holds, but that the art has a public basis. Each group arrives at a consen-sus of what it considers to be appropriate art forms, and individual cre-ators draw on this group consensus (Becker 1982), deciding when "cre-ative deviations" are important to keep traditions dynamic (Beck 1988:41). All art has a social basis, and each artist is part of some kind of collec-tive, whatever it might be. Art is often unique, "intensely personal," yet it still can relate to group concerns; "total conformity is as impossible as total nonconformity" (Beck 1982:25; Anderson 1990:267). When art speaks to the needs of a particular group, we need not worry about taking a cultural referendum to gauge how truly collective an art form is.

Folklorists have always found it difficult to deal with individuality and at the same time champion individual creative acts. With the shift from the study of objects to the study of performers and creators, research has now produced writings about artists as much as about arts.[4] In the study of individual artists, researchers ask questions that could be asked about art in any time or place. One discussion, for example, recently surveyed the reasons why a series of artists made folk art, concluding "they include preoccupation with the sensory, ideational, and instrumental; associations with place, people, and a particular period of time; identity formation, clarification, and reconstruction; and therapeutic benefits that sometimes attend the processes of individuals' grieving over a loss, coping with emotional trauma, or attempting to adjust to changes in their lives" (Jones 1995:271). Such ethnographic findings could illuminate art of any kind, no matter if it be prefixed with "folk" or "fine."

But again, we often attempt to limit our questions. As in the medieval world, the term *artist* may be a misnomer, for skillful acts emerge in many social roles (Torgovnick 1990:133). But our notion of the nature of the artist links the ability to be creative (and often innovative) to attention to group aesthetics. Nonetheless, if something is new, it somehow cannot be totally a collective art. Folklorists' enduring concern with the anonymity of cultural products still dissuades researchers from considering those who excel in new forms, as if somehow these did not draw on an individual's manipulation of past ideas. Folklorists who have studied art have generally attributed it to the "collective genius of the artist's culture," rather than to an insightful individual, yet this betrays the fact that researchers have often worked with things rather than persons (Glassie 1994a:248). In attempts to define our discipline as different, we insist, for example, that the artists we study share an aesthetic, are informally trained, and produce utilitarian products. Somehow, it seems, we can easily draw the line between individual and community aesthetic as if all art is somehow either one or the other (Teske 1988:113, 116) but not both. Art cannot be understood if it is constrained by disciplinary inferiorities that demand that creativity be delimited by prefixes such as *folk-*.

Uniqueness in creation comes, as well, from the fact that skills are sometimes innate. Not everyone can excel equally at all forms of art, even if they have the same background and training. Artists are not simply manufactured by being exposed to equivalent cultural contexts (Ruskin n.d.:23). Just as the culture cannot guarantee uniformity, it cannot mechanically produce the exceptional.

Finally, then, skill in producing art causes desired positive aesthetic reactions among members of a group (Greenfield 1986:6). These emotional responses draw on the aesthetics of the group: what moves some humans to joy, anger, grief, laughter—the wide range of emotions of the human condition that all artists strive to explore. Aesthetic responses seem to be a universal phenomenon (Anderson 1992:927; Wingert 1962:31), and our cultural relativism often makes us shy away from dealing with the universal—unlike our early folklorist ancestors. Yet, as Morris realized, we all delight in beauty (1962:8). Although that beauty might be culturally specific, all peoples recognize beauty as an element of the human condition. Art becomes what is best, deepest, and richest in every culture (Glassie 1989:36).

The impact of the art item or artistic act sometimes forces the folklorist to stretch the boundaries of cultural relativism and return to the early subjective concerns of the universality of human experience. Some have argued, for example, that all art produces "sympathetic vibrations" that are experienced by any person, no matter what their cultural background (Welsch 1980:231). Art and aesthetics, problematically for those laboring under the rubric of science, often become an intuitive pursuit (Merriam 1964:260). And while the mandate of cultural relativism makes folklorists nervous about anything that is not based on an insider's view of art and its characteristics, the ability of the artistic experience to transcend cultural backgrounds is evident. Edward Ives, for instance, links the experience of a Segovia performance at Town Hall to the performances of ballad singers in a kitchen or a field "as moments of great integrity, moments when I have been transformed" (1978:436). For Ives, art is not sundered into categories of "us" and "them" but is an aesthetic activity that links Yeats and popular ballad poetry as one. Art moves us beyond simple skill to emotion: "while good art requires skills . . . art at its best connects words, sounds, movement or color to emotions crystallized within us. It allows us to glimpse something within human reach, to fulfill the unuttered promise of experience, to find poetry in our loneliness" (Schemo 1995:1).

Each group has certain canons of taste that govern which art forms are produced (Dark 1978:35). But these are no different from the canons of taste produced by our own Western elite art worlds (Becker 1982). For the issue of aesthetics has finally to do with judgment, with something done well, with the attainment of excellence (Jones 1980:357, 1987:86). Every act of artistic creation, every performance, carries with it a responsibility to produce a product that will be judged aesthetically appropriate to the particular situation (Hymes 1975b:352). When something is created the creator of this new version of a widely known cultural form (be it verbal, visual, or otherwise) leaves open the question of judgment and critique from both group and individual taste. The skill of anticipating how a creation can or will be judged (be that creation a fleeting performance or a lasting object) is perhaps the most central component of the entire artistic process.

In studying art, we folklorists have devoted most of our energies to the understanding of how some cultural products become involved in the exploration of the human soul. Often we have lost sight of the idealism of our founders, who realized that medieval skills had been broken apart into rationalist categories according to which many labored and only a few were believed to create. Our predecessors knew better, but we feel embarrassed by these early thinkers who looked to other places and people for answers not about who those Others were but about who they themselves were.

In our own scholarship we have come full circle. In our anxieties and insecurities we have slowly shifted art from product to performance to, finally, skillful behavior. And so, in a way, we have returned to William Morris, who lamented the demise of a world in which the ability of all human beings to excel in certain skills was recognized, a world in which skill gradually became restricted to specialized activities referred to as "art." It is unclear what new questions folklorists will ask if art is broadly reconsidered, especially because there is still so much attention on "Others" as our primary focus, where their "art" remains prefixed by qualifiers such as *folk*.[5] And as we recognize the limitations of such qualifiers, we continue to categorize art by other categories such as "vernacular" or "working-class" (Jones 1951:9–10; Cooper 1994:9–13); yet we must be certain that such distinctions do not simply perpetuate the minor status of these creations. We must not believe that skillful acts of the Other are different forms of art, because then we will merely study objects as a dislocation of our own postmodern malaise (Torgovnick 1990:245). We must have the courage and insight to realize that we are dealing with peoples— those similar as well as different—who all create art. And in this creation, we all strive for the skill to create forms that illuminate the human complexities of daily living. All of us share in this. All of us are creating particular forms that move us, and we take pains to excel in that creation.

Notes

This essay has benefited from conversations with Gloria Hickey and Neil Rosenberg, who, along with Shane O'Dea, offered specific comments on the written version. I discussed some of my initial thoughts with students in my advanced folkloristics seminar, winter 1994, at Memorial University: Ellen Damsky, Zainab Haruna, and Seana Kozar; their comments also proved most helpful.

1. Glassie labels this new modern material style as Georgian; his findings have had a pervasive impact on material culture studies, especially historical archaeology. See Deetz 1977; Leone and Shackel 1987; Wenger 1989; Johnson 1996.

2. *Funk and Wagnalls Standard Dictionary of Folklore, Mythology, and Legend,* published in 1949–50, contained no general entry for "art," but one on "primitive and folk art" that covered only artifacts; see Harmon 1950. The recent index of the *Journal of American Folklore* considers the category of art to also cover only artifacts, those objects regarded as "folk art"; see Jackson et al. 1988:325. Working as one of the senior bibliographers for the folklore section of the *Modern Language Association Annual Bibliography* since 1978, we have used "folk art" to cover only material items.

3. This definition of art is based on Firth 1992:18; Glassie 1986:274; Jones 1984:176; Mills 1971 [1957]:95; and Toelken 1979:181, 1980:9. Much that is written about non-Western elite creativity still uses the term *art* primarily for artifacts; such definitions, however, can be broadened to include the full range of aesthetic creativity. The definition of one anthropologist, writing largely about objects, is similar to mine: "art is culturally significant meaning skillfully encoded in an affecting, sensuous medium" (Anderson 1990:238). A recent definition by Henry Glassie is quite succinct: that art is "the conspicuous exhibit of the individual urge to creation coupled with the social need for order" (Glassie 1994a:255).

4. Michael Owen Jones is general editor of the Folk Art and Artists Series, begun by the University Press of Mississippi in 1994. Most of these monographs focus on a folk artist whose works are, in many cases, quite idiosyncratic and are art forms that are not widely made by any particular group. This obviously reflects Jones's behavioral (individual) rather than group approach to creative studies (Jones 1993).

5. The rise of public folklore in the United States has often meant that the idea of art continues to be linked to the canons of "folk art": archaic objects and performance activities that follow stereotypes of vernacular versions of Western elite artworks. Much public folklore work is founded on the fundamental assumption that folk art is somehow different from other kinds of art, that our responsibility is not to understand the fundamentals of art but merely to rescue archaic activities. See Bulger 1980; Dewhurst and MacDowell 1978; and Siporin 1984, 1992.

References Cited

Abrahams, Roger D. 1970. "Creativity, Individuality, and the Traditional Singer." *Studies in the Literary Imagination* 3:5–36.

———. 1976. "The Complex Relations of Simple Forms." In *Folklore Genres.* Ed. Dan Ben-Amos. 193–214. Austin: University of Texas Press.

———. 1977. "Toward an Enactment-Centered Theory of Folklore." In *Frontiers of Folklore.* Ed. William R. Bascom. 79–120. Boulder, Colo.: Westview Press.

Anderson, Richard L. 1979. *Art in Primitive Societies.* Englewood Cliffs, N.J.: Prentice-Hall.

———. 1990. *Calliope's Sisters: A Comparative Study of Philosophies of Art.* Englewood Cliffs, N.J.: Prentice-Hall.

———. 1992. "Do Other Cultures Have 'Art'?" *American Anthropologist* 94:926–29.

Armstrong, Robert Plant. 1971. *The Affecting Presence: An Essay in Humanistic Anthropology.* Urbana: University of Illinois Press.

Austin, Ben S. 1992. "The Vanishing Art of Cooking Table-Grade Molasses." *Tennessee Folklore Society Bulletin* 55:101–7.

Babcock, Barbara A. 1992. "Artifact." In *Folklore, Cultural Performances, and Popular Entertainments: A Communications-Centered Handbook.* Ed. Richard Bauman. 204–16. New York: Oxford University Press.

Barbeau, Marius. 1948. "Folk Arts as Part of Folklore." *Journal of American Folklore* 61:210.

Bascom, William R. 1955. "Verbal Art." *Journal of American Folklore* 68:245–52.

———. 1973. "Folklore, Verbal Art, and Culture." *Journal of American Folklore* 86:374–81.

Bauman, Richard. 1975. "Verbal Art as Performance." *American Anthropologist* 77:290–311.

Beck, Jane C. 1982. "Folk Art and Traditional Culture in Vermont." In *Always in Season: Folk Art and Traditional Culture in Vermont.* Ed. Jane C. Beck. 17–51. Montpelier: Vermont Council on the Arts.

———. 1988. "Stories to Tell: The Narrative Impulse in Contemporary New England Folk Art." In *Stories to Tell: The Narrative Impulse in Contemporary New England Folk Art.* Ed. Janet G. Silver. 38–54. Lincoln, Mass.: DeCordova and Dana Museum and Park.

Becker, Howard S. 1982. *Art Worlds.* Berkeley: University of California Press.

Bell, Michael J. 1976. "Tending Bar at Brown's: Occupational Role as Artistic Performance." *Western Folklore* 35:93–107.

———. 1984. "Making Art Work." *Western Folklore* 43:211–21.

Ben-Amos, Dan. 1972. "Toward a Definition of Folklore in Context." In *Toward New Perspectives in Folklore.* Ed. Américo Paredes and Richard Bauman. 3–15. Austin: University of Texas Press.

———. 1976. "Analytical Categories and Ethnic Genres." In *Folklore Genres.* Ed. Dan Ben-Amos. 215–42. Austin: University of Texas Press.

Bendix, Regina. 1988. "Folklorism: The Challenge of a Concept." *International Folklore Review* 6:5–15.

Bergengren, Charles. 1991. "A Scuffle in the Folk Arts Turf Wars." *New York Folklore* 17:127–33.

Biebuyck, Daniel, ed. 1969. *Tradition and Creativity in Tribal Art*. Berkeley: University of California Press.

Boas, Franz. 1955 [1927]. *Primitive Art*. New York: Dover.

Brendel, Otto J. 1963. "Art and Freedom in Evolutionary Perspective." In *The Concept of Freedom in Anthropology*. Ed. David Bidney. 245–71. The Hague: Mouton.

Briggs, Charles L. 1988. *Competence in Performance: The Creativity of Tradition in Mexicano Verbal Art*. Philadelphia: University of Pennsylvania Press.

Bronner, Simon J. 1984. *American Folk Art: A Guide to Sources*. New York: Garland.

———. 1988. "Art, Performance, and Praxis." *Western Folklore* 47:75–101.

Bulger, Peggy A. 1980. "Defining Folk Arts for the Working Folklorist." *Kentucky Folklore Record* 26:62–66.

Burrison, John A. 2000. *Shaping Traditions: Folk Arts in a Changing South—A Catalog of the Goizueta Folklife Gallery at the Atlanta History Center*. Athens: University of Georgia Press.

Cardinal, Roger. 1972. *Outsider Art*. New York: Praeger.

Carpenter, Edmund. 1969. "Comments." In *Tradition and Creativity in Tribal Art*. Ed. Daniel Biebuyck. 203–13. Berkeley: University of California Press.

Clifford, James. 1988. *The Predicament of Culture: Twentieth-Century Ethnography, Literature, and Art*. Cambridge, Mass.: Harvard University Press.

Cocchiara, Giuseppe. 1981 [1952]. *The History of Folklore in Europe*. Trans. John N. McDaniel. Philadelphia: Institute for the Study of Human Issues.

Coffin, Tristram P. 1961. "Mary Hamilton and the Anglo-American Ballad as an Art Form." In *The Critics and the Ballad*. Ed. MacEdward Leach and Tristram P. Coffin. 245–56. Carbondale: Southern Illinois University Press.

Coomaraswamy, Ananda. 1924. *The Dance of Siva: Fourteen Indian Essays*. New York: Sunwise Turn.

Cooper, Emmanuel. 1994. *People's Art: Working-Class Art from 1750 to the Present Day*. Edinburgh: Mainstream.

Coutts-Smith, Kenneth. 1991. "Some General Observations on the Problem of Cultural Colonialism." In *The Myth of Primitivism: Perspectives on Art*. Ed. Susan Hiller. 14–31. London: Routledge.

Dark, P. J. C. 1978. "What Is Art for Anthropologists?" In *Art in Society: Studies in Style, Culture, and Aesthetics*. Ed. Michael Greenhalgh and Vincent Megaw. 31–50. New York: St. Martin's Press.

Deetz, James. 1977. *In Small Things Forgotten: The Archaeology of Early American Life*. Garden City, N.Y.: Natural History Press.

Dewhurst, C. Kurt, and Marsha MacDowell. 1978. *Rainbows in the Sky: The*

Folk Art of Michigan in the Twentieth Century. East Lansing: Kresge Art Gallery, Michigan State University.

Dormer, Peter. 1994. *The Art of the Maker: Skill and Its Meaning in Art, Craft, and Design.* London: Thames and Hudson.

Eco, Umberto. 1986. *Art and Beauty in the Middle Ages.* New Haven: Yale University Press.

Eliot, T. S. 1928. "Tradition and the Individual Talent." *The Sacred Wood: Essays on Poetry and Criticism.* 47–59. London: Methuen.

Firth, Raymond. 1992. "Art and Anthropology." In *Anthropology, Art, and Aesthetics.* Ed. Jeremy Coote and Anthony Shelton. 15–39. Oxford: Clarendon Press.

Georges, Robert. 1969. "Toward an Understanding of Storytelling Events." *Journal of American Folklore* 82:313–28.

Glassie, Henry. 1968. *Pattern in the Material Folk Culture of the Eastern United States.* Philadelphia: University of Pennsylvania Press.

———. 1970. "'Take That Night Train to Selma': An Excursion to the Outskirts of Scholarship." In *Folksongs and Their Makers.* Ed. Henry Glassie, Edward D. Ives, and John F. Szwed. 1–68. Bowling Green, Ohio: Bowling Green University Popular Press.

———. 1972. "Folk Art." In *Folklore and Folklife: An Introduction.* Ed. Richard M. Dorson. 253–80. Chicago: University of Chicago Press.

———. 1975. *Folk Housing in Middle Virginia: A Structural Analysis of Historic Artifacts.* Knoxville: University of Tennessee Press.

———. 1986. "The Idea of Folk Art." In *Folk Art and Art Worlds.* Ed. John Michael Vlach and Simon J. Bronner. 269–74. Ann Arbor, Mich.: UMI.

———. 1989. *The Spirit of Folk Art: The Girard Collection at the Museum of International Folk Art.* New York: Abrams and Mum of New Mexico.

———. 1993. *Turkish Traditional Art Today.* Bloomington: Indiana University Press.

———. 1994a. "Epilogue: The Spirit of Swedish Folk Art." In *Swedish Folk Art: All Tradition Is Change.* Ed. Barbro Klein and Beate Sydhoff. 247–55. New York: Abrams.

———. 1994b. "On Identity." *Journal of American Folklore* 107:238–41.

———. 1997. *Art and Life in Bangladesh.* Bloomington: Indiana University Press.

———. 1999. *Material Culture.* Bloomington: Indiana University Press.

Graburn, Nelson H. H. 1976. "Introduction: Arts of the Fourth World." In *Ethnic and Tourist Arts: Cultural Expressions from the Fourth World.* Ed. Nelson H. H. Graburn. 1–32. Berkeley: University of California Press.

Granlund, Sten. 1910. "Sweden." In *Peasant Art in Sweden, Lapland, and Iceland.* Ed. Charles Holme. 3–30. London: Studio.

Greenfield, Verni. 1986. *Making Do or Making Art: A Study of American Recycling.* Ann Arbor, Mich.: UMI.

Griffith, James S. 1988. *Southern Arizona Folk Arts.* Tucson: University of Arizona Press.

Gutowski, John A. 1972. "The Art of Professional Wrestling: Folk Expression in Mass Culture." *Keystone Folklore Quarterly* 17:41–50.

Harmon, Mamie. 1950. "Primitive and Folk Art." In *Funk and Wagnalls Standard Dictionary of Folklore, Mythology, and Legend.* 2:886–901. New York: Funk and Wagnalls.

Hauser, Arnold. 1959. *The Philosophy of Art History.* New York: Knopf.

Hooper-Greenhill, Eilean. 1992. *Museums and the Shaping of Knowledge.* London: Routledge.

Hymes, Dell. 1974. *Foundations in Sociolinguistics: An Ethnographic Approach.* Philadelphia: University of Pennsylvania Press.

———. 1975a. "Breakthrough into Performance." In *Folklore: Performance and Communication.* Ed. Dan Ben-Amos and Kenneth S. Goldstein. 11–75. The Hague: Mouton.

———. 1975b. "Folklore's Nature and the Sun's Myth." *Journal of American Folklore* 88:345–69.

Ives, Edward D. 1978. *Joe Scott, the Woodsman-Songmaker.* Urbana: University of Illinois Press.

Jackson, Bruce, Michael Taft, and Harvey S. Axlerod, eds. and comps. 1988. *The Centennial Index: One Hundred Years of the Journal of American Folklore.* Special issue of *Journal of American Folklore* 101.

Johnson, Matthew. 1996. *An Archaeology of Capitalism.* Oxford: Blackwell.

Jones, Barbara. 1951. *The Unsophisticated Arts.* London: Architectural Press.

Jones, Michael Owen. 1971. "The Concept of 'Aesthetic' in the Traditional Arts. *Western Folklore* 30:77–104.

———. 1980. "L.A. Add-ons and Re-dos: Renovation in Folk Art and Architectural Design." In *Perspectives on American Folk Art.* Ed. Ian M. G. Quimby and Scott T. Swank. 325–63. New York: Norton.

———. 1984. "Introduction: Works of Art, Art as Work, and the Arts of Working." *Western Folklore* 43:172–78.

———. 1987. *Exploring Folk Art: Twenty Years of Thought on Craft, Work, and Aesthetics.* Ann Arbor, Mich.: UMI.

———. 1989. *Craftsman of the Cumberlands: Tradition and Creativity.* Lexington: University Press of Kentucky.

———. 1993. "Why Take a Behavioral Approach to Folk Objects?" In *History from Things: Essays on Material Culture.* Ed. Steven Lubar and W. David Kingery. 182–96. Washington, D.C.: Smithsonian Institution Press.

———. 1994. "How Do You Get Inside the Art of Outsiders?" In *The Artist Outsider: Creativity and the Boundaries of Culture.* Ed. Michael D. Hall and Eugene W. Metcalf Jr. 312–30. Washington, D.C.: Smithsonian Institution Press.

———. 1995. "The 1995 Archer Taylor Lecture: Why Make (Folk) Art?" *Western Folklore* 54:253–76.

———. 1996. "Icon Painters in Western Canada and the Conundrums of Classification: Who Creates Folk Art, When, and Why?" In *The Icon in Canada: Recent Findings from the Canadian Museum of Civilization.* Ed. Robert B. Klymasz. 7–34. Ottawa: Canadian Museum of Civilization.

Kirshenblatt-Gimblett, Barbara. 1983. "The Future of Folklore Studies in America: The Urban Frontier." *Folklore Forum* 16:175–234.

Krohn, Kaarle. 1971 [1926]. *Folklore Methodology: Formulated by Julius Krohn and Expanded by Nordic Researchers.* Trans. Roger L. Welsch. Austin: University of Texas Press.

Langlois, Janet. 1991. "Smuggling across the Windsor-Detroit Border: Folk Art, Sexual Difference, and Cultural Identity." *Canadian Folklore Canadien* 13:23–33.

Layton, Robert. 1991. *The Anthropology of Art.* Cambridge: Cambridge University Press.

Leone, Mark P., and Paul A. Shackel. 1987. "Forks, Clocks, and Power." In *Mirror and Metaphor: Material and Social Constructions of Reality.* Ed. Daniel W. Ingersoll Jr. and Gordon Bronitsky. 45–61. Lanham, Md.: University Press of America.

Löfgren, Orvar. 1994. "The Empire of Good Taste: Everyday Aesthetics and Domestic Creativity." In *Swedish Folk Art: All Tradition Is Change.* Ed. Barbro Klein and Mats Widbom. 235–45. New York: Abrams.

Lomax, Alan. 1968. *Folk Song Style and Culture.* Washington, D.C.: American Association for the Advancement of Science.

Lucie-Smith, Edward. 1981. *The Story of Craft: The Craftsman's Role in Society.* Oxford: Phaidon.

Lüthi, Max. 1984 [1975]. *The Fairytale as Art Form and Portrait of Man.* Trans. Jon Erickson. Bloomington: Indiana University Press.

Maquet, Jacques. 1986. *The Aesthetic Experience: An Anthropologist Looks at the Visual Arts.* New Haven: Yale University Press.

Mercer, Eric. 1969. *Furniture, 700–1700.* New York: Meredith.

Merriam, Alan P. 1964. *The Anthropology of Music.* Evanston, Ill.: Northwestern University Press.

———. 1977. "Anthropology and the Arts." In *Horizons of Anthropology.* Ed. Sol Tax and Leslie G. Freeman. 334–43. Chicago: Aldine.

Metcalf, Eugene W., Jr. 1986. "Confronting Contemporary Folk Art." In *The Ties That Bind: Folk Art in Contemporary Culture.* Ed. Eugene W. Metcalf Jr. and Michael Hall. 10–28. Cincinnati: Contemporary Arts Center.

Miller, Daniel. 1991. "Primitive Art and the Necessity of Primitivism to Art." In *The Myth of Primitivism: Perspectives on Art.* Ed. Susan Hiller. 50–71. London: Routledge.

Mills, George. 1971 [1957]. "Art: An Introduction to Qualitative Anthropology." In *Art and Aesthetics in Primitive Societies: A Critical Anthology.* Ed. Carol F. Jopling. 73–98. New York: Dutton.

Morris, William. 1962. *William Morris: Selected Writings and Designs.* Ed. Asa Briggs. Harmondsworth, U.K.: Penguin.

———. 1996. *William Morris on Art and Design.* Ed. Christine Poulson. Sheffield: Sheffield Academic Press.

Mukerji, Chandra. 1983. *From Graven Images: Patterns of Modern Materialism.* New York: Columbia University Press.

Munro, Thomas. 1969. *The Arts and Their Interrelations.* Cleveland: Case Western Reserve University Press.

Murphy, William P. 1978. "Oral Literature." *Annual Review of Anthropology* 7:113–36.

Naives and Visionaries. 1974. New York: Dutton.

Olrik, Axel. 1965 [1909]. "Epic Laws of Folk Narrative." In *The Study of Folklore.* Ed. Alan Dundes. 129–41. Englewood Cliffs, N.J.: Prentice-Hall.

Oring, Elliott. 1986. "On the Concepts of Folklore." In *Folk Groups and Folklore Genres: An Introduction.* Ed. Elliott Oring. 1–22. Logan: Utah State University Press.

———. 1994. "The Arts, Artifacts, and Artifices of Identity." *Journal of American Folklore* 107:211–33.

Pocius, Gerald L. 1979. "Hooked Rugs in Newfoundland: The Representation of Social Structure in Design." *Journal of American Folklore* 92:273 84.

———. 1986. "Parlors, Pump Houses, and Pickups: The Art of Privacy in a Newfoundland Community." Paper delivered at the annual meeting of the American Folklore Society, Baltimore, Md.

Pope, Peter. 1985. "Hand-working Tools: Formal Analysis of a Core Tool Kit." *Culture and Tradition* 9:90–101.

Price, Sally. 1989. *Primitive Art in Civilized Places.* Chicago: University of Chicago Press.

Prosterman, Leslie. 1995. *Ordinary Life: Festival Days—Aesthetics in the Midwestern County Fair.* Washington, D.C.: Smithsonian Institution Press.

Rosenberg, Neil V. 1993. "'An Icy Mountain Brook': Revival, Aesthetics, and the 'Coal Creek March.'" In *Songs about Work: Essays in Occupational Culture for Richard Reuss.* Ed. Archie Green. 163–83. Bloomington: Folklore Institute, Indiana University.

Ruskin, John. n.d. *The Political Economy of Art.* London: Waverley.

Schemo, Diana Jean. 1995. "Between the Art and the Artist Lies the Shadow." *New York Times* January 1, sec. 4.

Shapiro, Gary. 1989. "High Art, Folk Art, and Other Social Distinctions: Canons, Genealogy, and the Construction of Aesthetics." In *The Folk: Identity, Landscapes, and Lores.* Ed. Robert J. Smith and Jerry Stannard. 73–90. Lawrence: Department of Anthropology, University of Kansas.

Shapiro, Meyer. 1953. "Style." In *Anthropology Today: An Encyclopedic Inventory.* Ed. A. L. Kroeber. 287–312. Chicago: University of Chicago Press.

Silver, Harry R. 1979. "Ethnoart." *Annual Review of Anthropology* 8:267–307.

Siporin, Steve, ed. 1984. *"We Came to Where We Were Supposed to Be": Folk Art of Idaho.* Boise: Idaho Commission on the Arts.

———. 1992. *American Folk Masters: The National Heritage Fellows.* New York: Abrams and the Museum of International Folk Art.

Smith, Robert J. 1975. *The Art of the Festival.* Lawrence: Department of Anthropology, University of Kansas.

Teske, Robert T. 1987. "Wisconsin Folk Art: Continuing a Cultural Heritage." In *From Hardanger to Harleys: A Survey of Wisconsin Folk Art.* 1–11. Sheboygan, Wisc.: Kohler Arts Center.

———. 1988. "State Folk Art Exhibitions." In *The Conservation of Culture: Folklorists and the Public Sector.* Ed. Burt Feintuch. 109–17. Lexington: University Press of Kentucky.

Toelken, Barre. 1979. *The Dynamics of Folklore.* Boston: Houghton-Mifflin.

———. 1980. "In the Stream of Life: An Essay on Oregon Folk Art." In *Webfoots and Bunchgrassers: Folk Art of the Oregon Country.* Ed. Suzi Jones. 7–38. Salem: Oregon Arts Commission.

Torgovnick, Marianna. 1990. *Gone Primitive: Savage Intellects, Modern Lives.* Chicago: University of Chicago Press.

Vlach, John Michael. 1985. "The Concept of Community and Folklife Study." In *American Material Culture and Folklife: A Prologue and Dialogue.* Ed. Simon J. Bronner. 63–75. Ann Arbor, Mich.: UMI.

———. 1986. "'Properly Speaking': The Need for Plain Talk about Folk Art." In *Folk Art and Art Worlds.* Ed. John Michael Vlach and Simon J. Bronner. 13–26. Ann Arbor, Mich.: UMI.

———. 1988. *Plain Painters: Making Sense of American Folk Art.* Washington, D.C.: Smithsonian Institution Press.

Weaver, William Woys. 1989. *America Eats: Forms of Edible Folk Art.* New York: Harper and Row.

Welsch, Roger L. 1980. "Beating a Live Horse: Yet Another Note on Definitions and Defining." In *Perspectives on American Folk Art.* Ed. Ian M. G. Quimby and Scott T. Swank. 218–33. New York: Norton.

Wenger, Mark R. 1989. "The Dining Room in Virginia." In *Perspectives in Vernacular Architecture 3.* Ed. Thomas Carter and Bernard Herman. 149–59. Columbia: University of Missouri Press.

Williams, Raymond. 1963. *Culture and Society, 1780–1950.* New York: Penguin.

———. 1983. *Keywords: A Vocabulary of Culture and Society.* London: Fontana.

Wingert, Paul S. 1962. *Primitive Art: Its Traditions and Styles.* New York: New American Library.

Zeitlin, Steven J., Amy J. Kotkin, and Holly Cutting Baker. 1979. *A Celebration of American Family Folklore.* New York: Pantheon.

Zug, Charles G., III. 1994. "Folk Art and Outsider Art: A Folklorist's Perspective." In *The Artist Outsider: Creativity and the Boundaries of Culture.* Ed. Michael D. Hall and Eugene W. Metcalf Jr. 144–60. Washington, D.C.: Smithsonian Institution Press.

JEFF TODD TITON

3   *Text*

Like the word *folklore,* the word *text* is something folklorists can control only partially. I prefer to think of any object of interpretation as a text. But just as the general public has its own understanding of folklore, no matter how academic folklorists may define it, many constituencies are involved in constructing definitions of *text.* In this essay I review what I consider to be the more important meanings of text, and then I consider the special contributions that folklorists can make to an understanding of text. Although text is an exceedingly important concept for folklorists, the folklore text by nature appears as a secondary document, a transformation or transcription of something more original—a performance. First, I explore the uses of transcribed texts, the folklorist's stock-in-trade. Second, I discuss the reconfigurations of the folklore text that emerged in the past three decades from the paradigm shift in folklore studies toward performance theory. Third, looking to the future, I propose what I call "knowing texts," fieldwork-based ethnographic writings that attend to critical issues of representation and authority through writing strategies involving point of view. Fourth, I discuss the use of texts in the age of computers and multimedia representations, particularly in terms of the theory and practice of *hypertext.* (In the context of hypertext, a text is any information that can be digitized, whether words, sounds, or pictures; hypertext may be regarded as linked, nonlinear text: postmodern text.)

In its oldest, narrowest, and still most common usage, *text* means written words, usually words given some kind of authority. Editors preparing literary editions or historical documents seek a text "most nearly representing the author's original work" (Oxford English Dictionary). For literary scholars a text is a work of literature; for historians, a text is a historical document; for musicologists, a text is the words to a piece of music; for folklorists a text is a transcription of a folklore performance: the words of a song or a tale, for example. But as we shall see, in recent years some folklorists have diminished the importance of text while concentrating more upon performance and context. Other folklorists have taken an opposite path, expanding the meaning and significance of *text* so that now it also stands for any interpreted object, verbal or otherwise.

In the narrow sense, as a transcription, the folklore text is peculiar because it is a written representation of an original that is spoken, sung, gestured, or crafted from a larger oral and customary exchange among people. Whereas the original of a literary, historical, or legal text is writing (even if this writing is conventionally understood to represent speech), the original of a folklore text is not writing at all. An individual can produce writing alone, and it takes on a life of its own: newspapers, self-help books, novels, textbooks. These are not meant to be read aloud to others but to be absorbed alone, in a transaction between text and reader; the author is absent. Verbal folklore, on the other hand, lives in the intersubjective process that takes place when two or more people communicate face-to-face. The relationship between folklore and its written representation as text is not the simple equivalence of transcription. Nor is a folklore text a script or score meant for performance. Any written text arising from a communicative event that we recognize as folklore is clearly a transformation and a reduction.

Scholars usually make sense of literary texts using a combination of hermeneutic, phenomenological, and structuralist approaches. Hermeneutics, a method of interpreting meaning in written texts, arose as a means of explicating the Bible. While we still speak of a biblical text and a commentary attached to it, today hermeneutics covers the interpretation of any text, biblical or otherwise. The meaning of a literary text is usually a kind of paraphrase, using other words to express what is said and what is implied in the reader's confrontation with an author's text: what the text is "about." Most of what goes on in undergraduate literature classes, for example, is practical criticism of individual poems, short stories, and novels—what they mean, what they are about—and professors always are returning to the texts, the words on the page, for evidence. These days, individual texts are almost always considered in their historical contexts. The idea that literature inhabits an eternal realm of its own is no longer given credence when interpretive practice is brought to bear on texts. Phenomenological approaches emphasize the experience of the reader: what it feels like to read a particular text. Structuralist approaches, on the other hand, are not concerned with unique meanings in individual texts. Instead, structuralist strategies probe relations and patterns among a group of texts and particularly in "the conditions [of writing and reading] which make literature possible" (Culler 1975:viii). Structuralists not only discuss literary conventions, such as plot, but also theorize about communicative acts in general.

In his well-known essay "Is There a Text in this Class?" Stanley Fish reports the following conversation: A student asked a colleague that very question, and he replied with the name of the textbook anthology that he had ordered at the bookstore. "'No, no,' she said, 'I mean in this class do we believe in poems and things, or is it just us?'" (1980:305). If it is "just us," then meaning is a matter ultimately to be determined by the reader, not by appeals to authorial intention or to evidence in "the text itself." Fish has defended this "just us" theory of reception. A number of literary critics have misread Fish, thinking that he has let loose an anarchy of interpretations, a world in which any interpretation of a given text carries as much weight as any other. Fish's answer is that interpretations carry more or less weight depending on the ideologies of the interpretive communities in which they reside. So, for example, a literal interpretation of the creation as recorded in Genesis carries weight within a fundamental Christian interpretive community but not outside it. Fish's point is that "right" interpretations of texts are right only within particular contexts; there is no universal or foundational or eternally correct interpretation of a text. Among folklorists today, one interpretive community is at home with texts and another is uneasy with them.

As a model of text, literature inhabits a visual realm—writing and reading, the words on the page—and that is text's narrowest construction. Broader constructions of text, as is true of any object of interpretation, include the tactile, the oral, the gestural, and so forth. Folklorists can contribute to the dialogue on text, in part, because so many of our objects of study are not written but oral (as a song or a story) or material (as a craft) or gestural (as a dance). For many years folklorists transcribed and transformed them into written texts, and we inclined toward hermeneutic, structural, and analytical interpretation without examining alternatives. Until the 1960s folklorists treated oral folklore as items of literature with a few peculiar features due to their orality. Analysis concentrated on various aspects of the texts, but most importantly on the conditions of their existence, their evolution and the relations among similar texts, their social functions, and what they presumably indicated about the history and culture of the folk or peasant classes of society.

The Transcribed Text, Intertextuality, and Ideology

The narrow meaning of *text* as an inscription of an oral performance remains the most common usage of the term among folklorists today. It has a long and honorable history in folklore studies—some two hundred years. Texts in this sense are most often understood to be the written versions of orally delivered folklore, whether myth, legend, folktale, riddle, proverb, sermon, or something else spoken, chanted, or sung. The conventions of writing for a popular audience moved many folklorists to edit, or improve, the texts they collected; but beginning in the nineteenth century scientific standards required accurate transcription for scholarly purposes, whether deposit in archives or scholarly publication. Faithfully transcribed texts remain so authoritative nowadays that they are expected of students in folklore classes, can be found in many interpretive articles published in the leading folklore journals, and appear in most scholarly books written by folklorists.

Largely absent from those scholarly folklore journals, however, is the former practice of reporting undocumented texts, versions, or variants, without much accompanying theory or interpretation. Concomitant is a decline in the publication of anthologies of folklore texts. In the first half of the twentieth century, for example, anthologies containing regional ballad collections abounded, but few of these are published today (see, e.g., Brewster 1940; Gardner 1939; Henry 1938; Cox 1925; Hudson 1936; Barry 1939; Davis 1929). Folklorists collected and pored over texts, specializing in particular genres, seeking motifs and types, scrutinizing guides, indices, and bibliographies. These amateurs and professionals felt themselves engaged in a collective enterprise, tracking the movements of verbal folklore in textual variation through time and space. Today that activity has declined, while the ratio of interpretation to text in folklore publications has increased. This increase in interpretation is partly the result of a movement toward material culture and the ethnographic methods of cultural anthropology, and it reflects the professionalization of folklore and the increasing number of young folklorists trained in the academy, where for the past twenty-five years or so, in the face of a difficult job market, theorizing has been thought a better bet for an academic career.

Amidst all the theorizing, academics risk forgetting that experiencing a representation of folklore affords pleasure. "Text of pleasure: the text that contents, fills, grants euphoria; the text that comes from culture and does not break with it, is linked to a *comfortable* practice of reading" (Barthes 1975:14; italics in original). Many folklorists began their work with texts before they even thought of themselves as folklorists, simply by collecting and transcribing texts for their own contemplation or perhaps for performance: photographs of barns, for example, or transcriptions of song texts or tunes. Texts have a certain permanency. Transcription has the advantage of taking a performance out of the past and permitting the folklorist to experience it as an aesthetic object, bringing pleasure and knowledge more or less at will.

We like to think of transcribed texts as finite, bounded, and stable, as a novel is compassed between two covers. But a kind of indeterminacy principle is at work in any orally performed text, whether we think of text as words, event, or artifact, because its "motion"—that is, its unfolding process, considered in terms of its production and its reception—is anything but stable and replicable. Instability in the folkloric text derives from intertextuality, or the way texts exist in relation to other texts: there is no single authoritative text, but rather a folkloric text exists in multiple versions and variants, similar to one another and thereby referencing one another, generally exhibiting "major variation over space and minor variation through time" (Glassie 1968:33).[1] And the instability of a folkloric text is the result of its emergent, processual character, stressing the dialectic of innovation and tradition within community-based expressive culture and the relations between the performer and audience.

The life of a particular verbal text clarifies what I mean by intertextuality and emergence in this context. More than twenty years ago, in an article entitled "The Life Story," I used for illustration a story that blues singer Son House told me (Titon 1980). It was his conversion narrative, a story of how he experienced the presence of God and felt redeemed. Although the story was deeply personal, it shares the same pattern and indeed some of the very same words and phrases as countless other Christian conversion narratives, whether written, as that of Saul/Paul on the road to Damascus, Augustine's *Confessions*, or Jonathan Edwards's *Personal Narrative*, to name a few, or oral, as one can see expressed every Sunday in religious broadcasts on television and in thousands of churches. Interpreting Son House's life story, I stressed the emergent qualities of its enactment, or its reenactment, as for the moment he and I were bound up imaginatively in re-creating this event.

Instability in texts presents difficult problems for representation and interpretation. "What is the text?" seems to be a wrongly formulated question, in which the word *is* receives more pressure than it can bear. In "The Life Story," I represented Son House's story as an oral prose narrative on the printed page. Yet, four years earlier I had inscribed this same conversion narrative as a poem, in an ethnopoetic transcription—a different representation meant to show aspects of oral delivery, such as pauses and shifts in volume and tone of voice, that contributed to the meaning of the performance but would not normally have been notated (Titon 1976). The original tape recording is yet another, and an experientially more satisfying, representation. A reproduction of this representation on a plastic disc recording was bound into the journal that published the ethnopoetic transcription, so that the reader could also hear the inflections of Son House's voice. Under other circumstances, House's conversion narrative would have been different. A former preacher, he surely varied the details of his narrative depending on his audience. Thus far, we have stability of neither text nor representation, and when we consider House's narratives as versions of countless other conversion narratives, we experience what might be called intertextual overload.

Today it is commonplace to speak of intertextuality as a quality of referencing among texts. Literary theorists Robert Scholes, Nancy R. Compley, and Gregory L. Ulmer write, "Once you realize that all texts are reworkings of other texts, that writing comes out of reading, that writing is always rewriting, you can see that the desirable quality we call 'originality' does not mean creating something out of nothing but simply making an interesting change in what has been done before you" (1988:129). Folklorists understood intertextuality through versions and variants and genres of the folklore text long before literary critics began to see it as a feature of all texts. Oral tradition seems to "explain" intertextuality in folklore texts, but if intertextuality is also present in written texts, then orality cannot suffice as an explanation. Instead, intertextuality would appear to be a quality inherent in thought or consciousness.

And if intertextuality inhabits the way we think, it is not much of a leap to consider our minds not so much as socially constructed as textually constructed (see Culler 1982:29). This "textualization" of the self has led to a new way of approaching people as loci of what Roland Barthes and Claude Lévi-Strauss called "mythology" and Michel Foucault termed "discourse." People are viewed as sites of ideological discourse—in other words, as bundles of text. These texts are equivalent to those beliefs and desires that lead to action in the world; indeed, they embody them. "Think of human minds as webs of beliefs and desires, of sentential attitudes—webs that continually reweave themselves so as to accommodate new sentential attitudes" (Rorty 1991:93).

The relation of text to ideology has concerned Marxist critics. "The largely concealed structure of values which underlies our factual statements is part of what is meant by 'ideology'" writes Terry Eagleton. "By 'ideology' I mean, roughly, the ways in which what we say and believe connects with the power-structure and power-relations of the society we live in." Not all beliefs are ideology, but rather "those modes of feeling, valuing, perceiving and believing which have some kind of relation to the maintenance and reproduction of social power" (Eagleton 1983:14–15). Texts are aesthetic cultural productions that provide "experiential access to ideology. . . . It is in [literary texts], above all, that we observe in a peculiarly complex, coherent, intensive and immediate fashion the workings of ideology in the textures of lived experience of class-societies" (Eagleton 1978:101). Among folklorists, Jack Zipes's studies of fairy tales exemplify this approach (1983). Antonio Gramsci's idea of hegemony was enlisted by Tony Bennett in a powerful formulation for cultural studies: that "hegemony specifies that relations between ruling and subordinate blocs are negotiated and that therefore the concept encompasses a theoretical reconciliation between the imposed structures of the dominant ideology and an active cultural expression by the dominated class" (as quoted in Easthope 1994:178). This conception of hegemony provides both rationale and focus for studies of texts from "marginalized" peoples viewed as resistant to the ideology of the central or dominant class as promulgated by the state; an example is early African American hip-hop music and culture.

Text and Performance

A difficulty with texted representations of folklore, then, is that because folklorists do so much trafficking in texts—we transcribe and interpret them, we publish them—texts have a nasty habit of reasserting equivalence; the text comes to stand for the folklore. Some folklorists have responded to the force of textual reification by accepting it, treating texts as the more or less unproblematic stuff of folklore, grist for the mill of analysis and interpretation. Others have diminished the importance of text while seeking other means to represent and interpret folklore. Diminishing means narrowing the definition of *text* as far as possible to written words, while saying that this written text represents but a small portion of the larger process called folklore and searching for alternative means of understanding folklore as human communication. This has led folklorists to ideas of folklore as process, as expressive culture, and most influentially, folklore as performance. Performing (acting and observing, gesturing, speaking, singing) thus replaces literature (reading and writing) as the key metaphor.

Still other folklorists have pursued a third strategy, the opposite of diminishing text—that is, expanding the definition of *text* to include not only words but also things. Expanding the definition, philosopher Richard Rorty makes a useful distinction between texts and "lumps, a division which corresponds roughly to things made and things found" (1991:84). A lump is "something which you would bring for analysis to a natural scientist rather than to somebody in the humanities or social sciences—something which might turn out to be, say, a piece of gold or the fossilized stomach of a stegosaurus" (1991:84–85). In this enlarged sense, a text is any humanly constructed object. It need not be words: it may be an artifact such as a painting or a building or a pot, or it may be an action or event such as a ritual, or it may even be a person or a group of people. Text in this view becomes a key metaphor for any humanly constructed sign system, and we inhabit a semiotic world of signifiers that are not limited to words but include the entire human universe.

While some folklorists have taken up this reconfigured and expanded notion of text, other schools of ethnographic and folkloristic thought emphasize the body, process, feeling, and persons and they reject the idea that understanding expressive culture is like reading a text. Much in the recent history of folklore studies can be seen as an attempt to come to an understanding of folklore either as text or as something else. To paraphrase a philosopher friend of mine, folklorists have sought the varieties of text worth wanting. Is this literary metaphor, folklore as text, reading and writing as our means of representing and understanding the world, still appropriate to folklore? Today the functions of literature for most people in North America are filled by television, movies, and video and computer games, not to mention life stories in ordinary conversation. The school world is probably the last place that still acts as if literature exists mostly in print.

In the 1960s folklorists began to problematize text. A few younger scholars proposed that folklore be conceived of and studied as an unfolding, living process, as performance, not as a product or literary text. Dan Ben-Amos's influential and radical formulation of folklore as "artistic communication in small groups" sounded the battle-cry (1972:13), and Richard Bauman's "Verbal Art as Performance" (1977) solidified the gains against the older generation. Barre Toelken summarized: "If the active part of folklore can be called *performance,* then the actual total occurrence of that performance, including performer, audience, and context in a time-frame, can be called the *event*" (1979:147; emphasis in original). Yet some folklorists resisted. Lamenting that "'Text' is rapidly becoming a dirty word," in his 1972 presidential address before the American Folklore Society, D. K. Wilgus defended the older, item-centered, structural approach: "Text . . . is the item, the artifact, or the record of a mentifact of folklore. . . . it is the manifestation of a folk idea, whether it be a song, a story, a dance, or a cooking pot. . . . There is certainly no reason that the making of a pot cannot be considered a 'performance,' even a kind of rhetoric in clay, but the concreteness of the pot calls attention to the artifact as survival, and 'survival' is another bad word these days" (1973:244).

For Wilgus, a text was a "thing," and as a thing it had its advantages: already objectified, it could be studied as a historical object, its path traced over time and space. He illustrated this in the balance of his address by performing a historical analysis of related song texts. Wilgus's defense of text was a defense of a structuralist method exemplified both in classic historical approaches (what Richard Dorson [1972:7–15] has called historical-geographic and historical-reconstructional) and also, by implication, in the pattern analyses of folklorists such as Vladimir Propp (1968 [1928]) and Albert Lord (1960).

Some "new folklorists" of the 1970s and 1980s continued to seek patterns and employ structuralist methods, now applying them to performances and to the "conditions which make [folklore] possible." Influenced by an interdisciplinary confluence of work in sociology (particularly that of Erving Goffman), ethnography of speaking (in sociolinguistics), and ethnoscience in cultural anthropology, Richard Bauman, Roger Abrahams, and several others took care to point out that performance events were signaled or marked as separate from ordinary goings-on and that they proceeded by rules understood, but largely unarticulated, by the participants. Deriving these rules from performance was one of the chief preoccupations of performance analysis (e.g., Glassie 1975b, a structural analysis of vernacular house types). But the new folklorists also applied hermeneutic approaches to performance; Henry Glassie's *All Silver and No Brass* is an attempt at a cultural hermeneutics of Irish mumming (1975a) and prefigures his holistic approach to Irish folklife in his widely admired *Passing the Time in Ballymenone* (1982).

The paradigm shift to performance created a movement away from the objectified text-as-folklore-item. Because text *was* a dirty word to some folklorists, they took care to avoid using it. Some writers took up the ritual metaphor implied by performance and found, in the anthropological work of Victor Turner and in the sociological analyses of Erving Goffman, frameworks that enabled them to interpret repetitive, ritual events. Others took very seriously the theatrical aspects of performance, thinking of a text as no more important to an event than a script is to a play or a film. The formal rigidity of a written text as a reader experienced it, its fixed nature on the page (despite variants and versions) seemed to ossify the living process of performance. And since the usual medium in which academic folklorists communicated was the world of the written scholarly text, many felt stymied. Some explored other media, such as film, but found that costs of production were substantial and academic rewards minimal. Others threw their energy into public sector (applied) folklore, working as cultural advocates and bringing about events such as festivals that featured performances directly. In one sense the slow institutional decline of academic folklore since the 1970s reflects not only the diminished academic job market but also a declining interest in text-based research.

For those who gave up on text-in-itself and embraced performance, what was gained and what was lost? Gained was a more holistic enterprise and the possibility of doing justice to an intuitive sense of folklore as living process. Gained was an emphasis on persons as well as things, an emphasis on attitudes as well as acts. Gained, I think, was a sensitivity to the human exchanges involved in fieldwork, as folklorists did away with the notion that they were merely collecting data. Folklorists instead embraced reflexivity and intersubjectivity, becoming more aware of authority, power, reciprocity, and representation. Exchanged were one set of metaphors belonging to writing and reading for another belonging to the theater. To some, one of the more troubling implications of the theatrical metaphor, in a discipline that historically has placed such weight on sincerity and authenticity, is that performances imply inauthenticity—that is, staging, acting, and people playing roles different from their presumed real selves. Yet these implications do not trouble those postmodern folklorists who believe that there are no autonomous selves anyway, only a variety of roles available to a self that is constituted by ideology from without. A deeper dilemma turns on the practice of performance analysis, for insofar as analysis constitutes its object, it is forced to remove performance from living process and treat it as if it were a text. This dilemma appears to be inherent in our scholarly procedures, not only because we write our scholarship as text but because analysis and interpretation are directed at objects; and if a text is anything that can be interpreted, then there is no interpretation without text. And so even when performance theory has driven folkloristic analysis, transcribed texts remain in our work, embedded now in new interpretive contexts.

Powerhouse for God, a folklife ethnography about language in religious practice among a community of worshippers in Virginia's Blue Ridge Mountains, is filled with textual transcriptions of songs, sermons, prayers, testimonies, and conversion narratives (Titon 1988). When I began this project in 1976 I deliberately turned to long-term fieldwork and contrived a text-heavy hermeneutic model involving affect, performance, community, and memory, as I recorded, transcribed, and interpreted texts from these performances of religious folklife. At the same time that I was recording and transcribing the texts for *Powerhouse for God*, I understood them within a performance framework. That is, I took texts like testimonies, sermons, and prayers to be products that people generated in performances. Conversations became occasions for generating metatexts—texts about texts—as we spoke about the meaning of the morning's sermon or a song that had a visibly powerful effect on someone in the congregation. From a theoretical point of view I was interested in how language in religious performance brought about certain ideas, feelings, and actions and how it helped give meaning to the lives of people who had become my acquaintances and friends. But in order to gain any insight into their lives—how their lives worked—I had to try to understand who they were, as persons.

Over and over I learned that performances are intersubjective, emerging from personal relationships and to some extent shaped by them. Even though the texts were objects, I could not consider them objectively. My friends did not think of themselves as generating texts; they were talking to each other and to me. Always there were persons behind texts. I became aware that my presence must have affected certain performances. For example, a number of people gently "witnessed" their experiences of God to me hoping that by example I might see how I could become born again. In so doing, they were not behaving unusually; they believe God requires them to witness and evangelize. Had I become born again, I would have been the recipient of performances that, as an outsider, they did not disclose to me.

We folklorists do not only study texts; we do not only study performances. We try to understand persons in performance generating texts and giving and finding meaning in their lives. That is what the film *Powerhouse for God* is meant to portray (Dornfeld, Rankin, and Titon 1989). In a different field project, the Reverend C. L. Franklin's life history emerged from our conversations, but it emphasized the kinds of things I asked to hear and the kinds of things he was interested in revealing to me. The text would have been significantly different had he been speaking with a person from a different background with different interests (see Franklin 1989). If we overlook the relations between individual people and the texts that they (we) generate, we never will understand texts—or people.

Recognizing these relations, many folklorists have embraced a newer sense of text as process. Rather than trade text for performance, we treat texts as performances and performances as texts, blurring the distinctions between them and extending the meaning of *text* to cover any object of interpretation. Metaphorically, then, artifacts, performances, events, and so forth are regarded as textual inscriptions to be read and interpreted: the performance, in this view, does not merely *have* a text (script) as a part of its totality. Rather, its totality *is* a text. Performances cannot be reduced to texts; rather, performances are texts. The movement away from the older concept of text-as-item can thus be understood as a broadening and reconfiguration of text. Evidence of scholarly movement in this direction has also appeared in American cultural anthropology where, at about the same time, there was an "interpretive turn," usually traced to Clifford Geertz, who wrote that just as words can be read so events can be "read" as texts. Textual analysis of events attends to "how the inscription of action is brought about, what its vehicles are and how they work, and on what the fixation of meaning from the flow of events—history from what happened, thought from thinking, culture from behavior—implies for sociological interpretation. To see social institutions, social customs, and social changes as in some sense 'readable' is to alter our whole sense of what such interpretation is toward modes of thought rather more familiar to the translator" (1980:175–76). Geertz demonstrated just such a "reading" in his famous article on the meaning of the Balinese cockfight, where he likened culture to "an assemblage of texts" (1973:448).

Although Geertz's formulation of a cultural hermeneutics greatly influenced the ethnographic enterprise in North America, he was operating within a European tradition of inquiry into the human sciences, emphasizing a humanistic approach to what Americans call social sciences. In a 1971 essay, "The Model of the Text: Meaningful Action Considered as Text," Paul Ricoeur wrote, "the human sciences may be said to be hermeneutical (1) inasmuch as their *object* displays some of the features constitutive of a text as text, and (2) inasmuch as their *methodology* develops the same kind of procedures as those of Auslegung or text-interpretation" (1981:197; italics in original). William Dilthey's insistence on the "humanness" of the nonnatural sciences and on the differences between explanation (the result of scientific method) and understanding (the result of interpretation in the human sciences) inaugurated this tradition. Dilthey stressed "the lived experience in cultural expressions rather than reducing experience to a system of semiotic exchange" (as quoted in Rajan 1994:378). For Dilthey the human sciences were hermeneutic, their constituents the objects of interpretive acts. Geertz had identified three competing social science paradigms in his "Blurred Genres" article: life is a game, life is a drama, life is a text (1980). While happiest with the text metaphor, Geertz looked forward to the possibility of a reconciliation among them. Turner, arguing against Geertz, wrote that texts "are like the shucked-off husks of the living process" (Schechner and Appel 1990:16). Turner's argument gave weight to those scholars in performance who felt that the word *text*, like the word *folklore*, was hopelessly outdated. Indeed, a new graduate field, performance studies, was established at N.Y.U. and Northwestern; it drew upon folklore, theater, and cultural anthropology.

Ethnography and the "Knowing Text"

Within the discipline of folklore, text remains a problematized concept showing, among other things, that despite attempts to defeat it, the concept retains force. Among American academic folklorists, the performance-oriented theorists have succeeded in diminishing the older idea of text-as-item and the historical-geographical methods that accompanied it. But the attack on text resulted in a reconceptualization of text as any object of interpretation. This defense of text, if it is to be effective, does not merely return us to the older procedures of textual analysis; rather, the new text is open to the kinds of interpretations folklorists are interested in making, yielding to the new questions folklorists are interested in asking. Such questions, nowadays, involve postmodern critiques of scholarship; and they focus on ideas such as experience and belief and categories such as class, gender, ethnicity, region, and sexual orientation.

To make text responsive to current ideas in the discipline, folklorists will continue to make use of transcribed performances as objects of interpretation. But representations of these performances today enlarge to include far more than just objectified verbal discourse or artifact; wherever possible, they now include gestures, feelings, intentions, reception and resulting behaviors, and so forth: not so much text-and-context, but text-in-process, text as experienced. This reflects a general shift of interest in experiential social science. The old questions involving origins, pattern, diffusion, and transmission of folklore never were answered satisfactorily and possibly never will be; whereas questions having to do with the uses of tradition, with tradition-bearers' own ideas about folklore, with folklore as it is experienced in human consciousness are the more interesting questions today.

Those of us who broaden the meaning of text so that we may in effect read performance events also consider the interpretive books (and articles and films) we produce to be texts. We view ourselves as authors engaged in the cultural production of texts. Not only do we "collect" and transcribe texts in the field, not only do we interpret verbal and other texts, but we understand our scholarly productions themselves as texts because they too are objects of interpretation: we and our readers interpret them. I propose here that we write "knowing texts." By a knowing text I mean a text that a reader will find to be self-knowing (reflexive), aware of the basis for and limits of its knowledge-claims (authority). I mean a text skillfully crafted, particularly in terms of point of view, to establish an intersubjective relation among author, text, the "characters" (persons represented in the text), and reader. I mean a text written to take full advantage of the techniques available to authors. What follows is meant to be a preliminary discussion of the knowing text, not a definitive exposition.

In the 1970s as performance theory was turning folklorists towards context, European folklife studies attracted folklorists toward ethnographies focused on expressive culture and the lived experiences of tradition-bearers. Folklorists, after all, did fieldwork; and in an academic world grown sensitive to power relationships and exploitation of the marginalized groups folklorists traditionally studied, the image of the folklorist as collector, strip-mining folklore while traveling and surveying the field, was not a pleasant prospect. Some adopted Malinowski's fieldwork model, in which rather than traveling, surveying, and collecting, the fieldworker takes up residence in the native village and tries to understand, through close observation over a relatively long period, the way of life of the natives—which, for folklorists, meant understanding the performance of expressive culture in its context. Just as cultural anthropologists in this tradition produced ethnographies—descriptions of aspects of native life that included texts, contexts, native points of view, and interpretations by the anthropologist—so did these folklorists produce studies of aspects of folklife among individuals in particular folk groups. With hindsight it is now possible to see that, ironically, just when American literary critics were abandoning certain tenets of the New Criticism in favor of a structuralist poetics (Culler 1975), folklorists gave up the text-centered structuralism that had constituted the issues (design, structure, and transmission over time and space) that they had sought to explore. While performance took center stage, some folklorists came to prefer the term *folklife* to describe their interests in a more holistic and affective approach to expressive culture. Insofar as a life-centered, rather than lore-centered, approach is an interpretive move in the direction of affect, it is also, ironically, a move toward the New Critics' emphasis on understanding not just how and what a literary work means, but how it feels to experience that work.

As American folklorists moved more toward anthropological research, some became involved in the anthropological reaction against older models of objectively reported text. Beginning with the essays collected in *Reinventing Anthropology,* a radical critique of the field based on the radical politics of the sixties generation, and later in *Anthropology as Cultural Critique* and *Writing Culture,* the two most widely read works of anthropological theory in the 1980s, a new kind of ethnographic text was called for, one appropriate to the "experimental moment" of cultural relativism when scientific objectivity no longer seemed adequate, epistemologically or ethically, in a postcolonial world (Hymes 1972; Marcus and Clifford 1986; Fischer and Marcus 1986). This new text would be experiential, self-reflexive, and it would recognize, as Geertz did, that ethnographies were made, not found, that they were rhetorical, not scientific. In a word, the new ethnographic text would be literary.

But would it succeed? Why produce a literary text when powerful currents pulled many toward feminist, Marxist, and other ideologically driven texts whose mark is an apparent outward sincerity, the writer speaking without artifice in his or her real voice? Why produce a literary text when contemporary reactions against political correctness pulled others back toward a purportedly objective stance? Isn't a literary text ambiguous when an ethnographer should be striving for clarity? How can we write fiction when our aim is truth? In answer I claim that all interpretive texts are literary. All writing is artifice. The ethnographic text is a fiction in the root sense (*facio*) that it is a making, not in the sense that it is false. There is a difference between imaginative fiction and ethnographic fiction, of course. The novelist or short story writer is free to invent in ways that the ethnographer is not. The fieldwork-based claim of the ethnographer is "I was there," whereas the novelist's witness is chiefly in his or her imagination. Novels and short stories are made up, invented, whereas ethnographic fiction is made after experience is found out. But if we who author fieldwork-based ethnographic texts conceive of our work as rhetorical, literary, and self-reflexive, and so long as we continue to be concerned with issues of representation and authority, then we will write "knowing texts" whose epistemological ground is realized through self-conscious management of point of view to establish the nature of the author's authority and the relation between author, text, character, and reader.

My advocacy of knowing texts requires some background, particularly in an intellectual atmosphere in which the concepts of culture and fieldwork have been problematized to the point where, like text, there are those who would discard them entirely. It was with a shock of recognition that I read Clifford, Tyler, Marcus, and others in the 1980s, for I had come to the same conclusions about the literariness of ethnographic texts independently and earlier. When I came to read popular ethnographies in the

1960s and 1970s I responded to them as if they were literature. I am thinking especially of Colin Turnbull's *The Forest People* (1961), but also of Michael J. Harner's *The Jivaro* (1972), Carlos Castaneda's *The Teachings of Don Juan* (1968) and, most influentially, *Tristes tropiques* (1974), Levi-Strauss's brilliant travelogue of ethnography and memoir.

While teaching at Tufts in the 1970s I devised a freshman English course and called it "Inventing Anthropology." In this course, typical of its time in that instructors taught writing by choosing subjects and readings centered on a particular theme, we read popular ethnographies and works of fiction, considering how each conformed to similar and different rhetorical and literary conventions. In addition to the above-mentioned anthropological works we read Ursula Le Guin's *The Left Hand of Darkness* (1969) and discussed to what extent science fiction and ethnography employed similar devices, what they had in common, and how we understood their truth-claims and authority-claims. We read Thomas Pynchon's *The Crying of Lot 49* (1966) as (among other things) a work of detective fiction and asked how it differed from ethnography.

Thinking about ethnography, autobiography, and fiction led me to reconsider the assumptions connected with the autobiographical texts that fieldworkers obtain from the people they speak with. In "The Life Story" I claimed such talk was better understood as fiction, a making, rather than as something factual that the fieldworker discovered or found out (Titon 1980). I responded, also, by writing stories about the practice of public folklore, stories in which I established a fiction writer's point of view. To the amusement of a few, I delivered some of these as papers at folklore and ethnomusicology conferences. But the aim was more than to amuse myself; story and irony presented themselves as time-honored means toward truths. Besides, narrative, if done gracefully, can embed interpretation into the flow of ongoing events. One story, "Murder at the Folk Festival," permitted me, in the narrative voice of a detective who knew nothing about folk festivals and was impatient with their rhetoric, to explore some of the festivals' assumptions of representation (Titon 1979) which Robert Cantwell later questioned in *Ethnomimesis* (1993). Another was cast in epistolary form, a series of letters from a putative fieldworker traveling through Maine in search of performers for a national folk festival (Titon 1983). This epistolary point of view encouraged me to pursue discrepancies between festival views of authenticity and those of tradition-bearers and revivalist performers. I think of these as imaginative fiction, not as knowing texts. I knew something about folk festivals because I had participated in them, but I invented these stories. On the other hand, the prologue, first chapter, and epilogue in *Powerhouse for God* are my renderings of events that did happen, "knowing texts" where I maintain narrative points of view (Titon 1988; see below) different from the general exposition in a book that has become known for careful textual procedures.

By point of view I do not mean the author's personal opinions. Instead I use the term in its conventional literary sense, to mean the author's relation to the text and reader. What options are open to authors of ethnographic texts? Typically, an ethnographer begins by writing narrative in the first person, in his or her own voice, not only to introduce the subject but also to establish authority. This authority is based on witness: the author did fieldwork, was there, was engaged long enough to understand something of what was going on. But once these credentials have been established, the "I" seems to be in the way; and so the author shifts to third-person exposition to describe those aspects of the culture that appear to be there for anyone to see. Those aspects often include verbal texts, artifacts, customary behavior, and so forth, along with native interpretations of them. From a literary standpoint, our ethnographer has moved from a position of limited, first-person authority to the position of omniscient author. Reading a work of fiction, one might find this shift in point of view puzzling. Reading ethnographic writing, one ought to be similarly skeptical. Claims to authority are undermined when authors move from their initial, limited, first-person points of view to omniscience because nowadays most are uncomfortable with the pretense of omniscience. In fiction these claims can succeed only under a special set of circumstances: if the initial "I" is understood as a creation of the author, at best an alter ego, but not the author directly. Yet this strategy is unavailable to the ethnographic author who wishes to write directly of him or herself in the first person. What other possibilities might there be? The knowing text offers one such.

A widely used book that teaches writing discusses point of view in terms of the following questions: Who speaks? To whom? In what form? At what distance? With what limitations (Burroway 1987)? (In what follows we may take the "characters" in the story to be the fieldworker's consultants, informants, or colleagues who are written into the ethnographic text, sometimes given their own voice, edited or not.) Whatever the point of view, an author is admonished to stick to it throughout the text. The author may speak in the third person, omnisciently, or with partial omniscience (favoring the point of view of a single character, going into his or her mind and telling the reader what is passing there). The author conventionally speaks to the reader, but in a folklife ethnography the author is understood, also, to be speaking to the characters in his text,

some of whom will read it. The author gives the story a form: it may be
represented as something written or spoken; it may take the form of a
report, a monologue, a dialogue, a diary, and so forth. The authorial point
of view may be based on a close identification with the action of the story, as a central participant in it; or it may be the point of view of a peripheral participant or witness; or it may be removed in space or time.
Finally, the narrator may be limited by who he or she is or by what he or
she knows about the story, and those limitations may produce degrees
of unreliability, as for instance when the narrator is ill, clearly biased,
ignorant, unsympathetic, and so forth; and in those circumstances the
reader is meant to know more than the narrator.

In short, point of view permits the writer of an ethnographic text to
begin experimenting with more solutions to the problems of representation and authority than omniscience, first-person confessional, or the
conventional but awkward shift from the latter to the former. If in the
course of our fieldwork we have recorded dialogue, we can present it
verbatim or edited, from different points of view. An interview conversation need not be excerpted in the course of an expository argument (the
conventional representation); it may be presented and interpreted as it
goes along. Folklife performances may be represented evocatively, narrated as a story, with interpretation coming from the narrator's point of
view. The narrator might be the folklorist but need not be. Or, as in the
well-known 1950 film *Rashomon*, there might be multiple narrative
voices, each with a different understanding of what was taking place
(Kurosawa 1969).

Powerhouse for God is presented for the most part in the third person as text and interpretation, with the occasional presence of an "I"
meant to represent me, the scholar in the process of thinking and writing
it; but in three places I experimented with point of view. The prologue is
the story of an encounter and conversation between the book's chief tra-
dition-bearer (character) and a folklorist from Washington, Carl Fleisch-
hauer. The conversation took place in a fast-food restaurant in Luray,
Virginia, and I sat in the booth and witnessed it. Better, I made a tape recording of it, and when it came time to represent it, I could transcribe it
and present the conversation verbatim. The words, at any rate, could be
presented thus; but I told the story of the encounter, recalled and represented the setting, and gently put a few perceptions into the characters'
minds based on my understanding of what transpired. I wrote the prologue
entirely in the voice of a first-person narrator, an "I" who represented the
author taking part in the action at a particular time and place when he
did not know what he knew later on. This "I" was the "I" at the start of

the project and at the start of the book. The first chapter of *Powerhouse*, on the other hand, is an evocative representation of a homecoming service—again, one that was tape-recorded and videotaped—but from the point of view of an omniscient author at the end of the project, ten years after he first witnessed it. That point of view was informed by years of observations and by hours and hours of conversations with the book's characters about the meaning of the events. At the same time, I kept in mind as audience for this chapter a thoughtful and well-educated adult who, nevertheless, had no experience with this kind of worship or language in religious practice. The epilogue, also a narration, revisited the town homecoming, a secular version of the most important annual occurrence in the church's calendar. The town homecoming was one of the very first events I had observed while doing fieldwork in that community, but it seemed appropriate to end the book with a story that took the reader out of the close confines of the church, congregation, and pastor's family who are its center, and into the larger world. Embedded in that story is the pastor's own story, a reminiscence how one year he appeared in the town homecoming on a float, preaching to the crowd, caught up in it so completely that he did not know when he passed by the judges' stand.

Clifford Geertz has defended a hermeneutics of observation, one in which the interpreter deliberately stands outside of and apart from the cultural production that is the object of interpretation. In this formulation experience is the experience of others, conveyed in part insofar as these others are able to articulate it and in part as it is "caught" through cultural metaphor by an observer who occupies a privileged position to understand it. "Understanding the form and pressure of . . . natives' inner lives is more like grasping a proverb, catching an allusion, seeing a joke—or, as I have suggested, reading a poem—than it is like achieving communion" (Geertz 1977:49). In so saying, Geertz put himself in opposition to Dilthey and others who espoused a hermeneutics of empathy, in which the interpreter claims to understand "Others" through friendship and by imaginatively changing places with them.

Geertz's objectivity is not a necessary component of hermeneutic approaches to text, however. Dennis Tedlock and Barbara Tedlock, for example, have both undertaken a hermeneutics of empathetic participation in which the hermeneutic circle extends to include the relationship between the interpreter and those people who are the subjects of an intersubjective interpretation. In the classic Malinowskian formulation of participant-observation, "participation" meant living among one's informants but refraining from fully participating in that life. Yet for the Tedlocks, as for others, participation meant apprenticeship and adoption into the culture (B. Tedlock 1992). The resulting representations have included, for example, Dennis Tedlock's attempts to convey experience by writing poems (1990). Ethnomusicologists nowadays participate in the musical life of the people they observe (see Titon 1995). Of course, in some circumstances, full participation is impossible because one lacks ability or time to learn, or feels that to participate will be to change one's being and identity in an unwanted way. And in some situations people being "studied" are suspicious, hostile, not very forthcoming, dissembling, or bored—reactions that occur more frequently in the postcolonial world.

Many fieldworkers understand that they have been, to some degree, transformed by their experiences. Until recently most did not make personal transformation a part of their ethnographic text. It was not appropriate. Now that ethnographic writing has become more reflexive, and some ethnographers now choose to write in the first person, in their own voice, representing themselves, the urge to confess sometimes results in texts that foreground the author. Unfortunately, no matter how sincere the attempt, the products can be, and have been, dismissed as self-indulgent, displacing the reader's attention from the subject of the ethnography to the fieldworker, whose personal epiphanies are not rendered sufficiently compelling. The reader, who expected to learn of a particular people's way of life, feels short-changed, perhaps even a victim of bait-and-switch. And the ethnographic subject, in the words of a joke that has become commonplace among ethnographers, says to the author, "That's enough about you; now what about me?"

How, then, to handle the problem of the author in the text? Some readers simply will not accept ethnography as memoir or autobiography in any form. For the rest, if compelled to write about one's personal transformation, one may write a story that implicates the reader directly. One chooses a different point of view, one that best permits the reader to experience, through identification, the author's transformation. Let the reader experience the transformation as the author does, but vicariously. The move toward this point of view and the reasons for it were discussed by the literary critic Percy Lubbock seventy-five years ago. Lubbock's subject was imaginative fiction writing, but what he wrote seems equally relevant in the case of transformational ethnography:

> If [the narrator] has nothing to do but relate what he has seen, what anyone might have seen in his position, his account will serve very well; there is no need for more. . . . But if he is himself the subject of his story, if the story involves a searching exploration of his own consciousness, [then] an account in his own words, after the fact, is not by any means

the best imaginable. Far better it would be to see him while his mind is actually at work in the agitation. . . . The matter would then be objective and visible to the reader, instead of reaching him in the form of a report at second hand. (1957 [1921]:252)

Lubbock next asks how this can be managed through point of view. Rejecting the "account in his own words, after the fact," in the first person, he suggests that the author bypass the idea of the report and let the reader into the writer's consciousness as the action occurs, not in retrospect:

> But how to manage this without falling back upon the author and his report, which has already been tried and for good reasons, as it seemed, abandoned? It is managed by . . . a further shift of the point of view. The spectator, the listener, the reader, is now himself to be placed at the angle of vision; not an account or a report, more or less convincing, is to be offered him, but a direct sight of the matter itself, while it is passing. Nobody expounds or explains; the story is enacted by its look and behaviour at particular moments. . . . Now . . . the narrator is forestalled; he is watched while the story is in the making. (253)

This strategy suggests that authors of knowing texts deliberately create a character, a fieldworker-ethnographer who is meant to resemble the author during the stage of fieldwork. This character may write in the first person, as an unreliable narrator who becomes more reliable as the story moves along, understanding occurs, and the transformation is effected. Or the fieldworker character may be observed by yet another character, who writes in the first person—a narrator who observes the fieldworker-ethnographer's experiences. Or there may be no narrator but just an omniscient voice, writing in the third person, who chooses to limit the point of view to the consciousness of the fieldworker-ethnographer, and allows the reader to witness the transformation by seeing the ethnographer's mind "at work in the agitation," as Lubbock writes above.

Knowing texts are addressed to readers for whom the older ethnographic models no longer suffice. Readers today are skeptical; they are bored. "How can we take pleasure in a reported pleasure (boredom of all narratives of dreams, of parties)?" writes Barthes. "How can we read criticism? Only one way: since I am here a second-degree reader, I must shift my position: instead of agreeing to be the confidant of this critical pleasure—a sure way to miss it—I can make myself its voyeur" (1975:17). Because the reader already has shifted "position" and turned the ethnographic work into "a text, a fiction, a fissured envelope" (ibid.), the author responds by shifting point of view and making a knowing text.

Postmodern Representations in Hypertext and Multimedia

Ideology figures importantly in the theory of the "virtual class," technocrats (including professors and students) who spend many hours each day in front of a computer, viewing text on a screen. Arthur Kroker and Michael A. Weinstein suggest that in their eagerness to embrace virtual reality as a substitute for full sensory, face-to-face participation, the virtual class has found a way to interact in the world without bodies and without risk (1994). Kroker is thinking primarily of those who search the Internet for pleasurable interactions in cyberspace: examples are multiplayer game sites in which World Wide Web surfers take on the attributes of various characters and interact through role-playing. Channeling their energies into virtual reality, where cyberpunk ideology reigns, this virtual class challenges the hegemonic discourse without risk (unless behaving as a criminal, for example, hacking one's way into a corporation's presumably secure computer system).

But there are less dramatic and more powerful forces at work in the virtual world, forces that are reconfiguring our notions of text yet again. Variously described as hypertext, multimedia, and hypermedia, a new kind of computer representation models the world, one which combines words, sounds, and images (can touch and smell be far behind?). What is hypertext? The word suggests hyperactivity, and that is not a bad way to begin thinking about it. "Hypertexts are electronic documents, read on the screen of the computer rather than printed on paper" (Bolter et al. 1993:21). So states the instruction manual for Storyspace, one of the better computer programs that enable one to write hypertexts. "In a conventional book, one page follows another in a single, fixed sequence. In a hypertext, writing spaces are linked together. Frequently a writing space may offer several different links, each leading to different information" (Bolter et al. 1993:25). Hypertexts are nonlinear. Several writing spaces can appear on the screen simultaneously. The reader of a hypertext often feels hyperactive, jumping around by means of links from one space to another in a sequence of his or her own choosing. In a hypertext, the reader is always offered multiple pathways through the information, and the reading will be different depending on which pathways are chosen and what is read and not read.

Hypertext offers, first of all, a superior environment for modeling intertextual relationships among texts traditionally considered as "things." Suppose one chose several performances of a native American ballad such as "Poor Omie" (Laws F31, F4) as the subject of a hypertext. An imaginary hypertextual construction for folklorists might consist of the following writing spaces. Ten writing spaces could be given over to ten versions and variants of the words to the ballad, one space to each version. Each version could be linked to any number of the other versions, perhaps on the basis of similarities. Readers could activate the links by pressing on-screen virtual buttons with a mouse or set of keyboard commands: press the button and another writing space appears. Other linked writing spaces could contain contextual information. For example, one or more could contain newspaper reports and other chronicles of the murder of Naomi Wise by John Lewis (the event on which the ballad was based). One or more could contain musical transcriptions of performances of versions of the ballad, and these could be compared by means of links and on-screen juxtapositions. Singers' ideas about the ballad could occupy other spaces. An essay on balladry could occupy others. Performance analysis still others. Links to other American murder ballads, still others. This hypertext is an open text with many possibilities.

Hypertexts may also contain multimedia presentations such as sounds. In our imaginary construction, there is no reason why one or more writing spaces could not contain buttons that, when activated, could "play" a digitized field recording containing one or more of the versions of "Poor Omie" under discussion. These sounds could be stored on the hard drive, CD-ROM, or DVD for that purpose. In fact, one could "play" a video clip in the same way. And these days computers have the capability of recognizing sounds. So, for example, one could "practice" singing any of these versions of "Poor Omie" and the computer would not only tell how accurate the melody was but suggest where and how one could improve it.[2] Finally, one can, in some hypertexts, add material and modify the whole. Reader additions may take the form of comments that can be seen by the next reader, new links to already-established writing spaces, and new writing spaces with reader-generated material (one's own version of the ballad, perhaps) linked to other writing spaces.

The possibilities of hypertext have not yet been fully realized. Many of the early hypertexts were little more than books on the computer screen, or versions of booklike activities made more convenient through the computer. *The In Memoriam Web* (Landow 1992) centers upon the text of Alfred Lord Tennyson's long poem. Links are provided not only to explain words in the poem but to contextual essays having to do with aspects of Victorianism. Such a construction may be considered to have a central hub (the poem text) and several interlinked spokes (the contextual essays). The experience of reading this hypertext is meant to suggest the experience of a scholar in a library doing research. *The Clyde Davenport Web* (Titon 1991) is an early model of hypertext that takes the reader to visit with Kentucky old-time fiddler Clyde Davenport. Links are provided to members of his family, to various incidents in his life, to some of his fiddle tunes (which are given as sounds and as musical transcriptions), to his aesthetic preferences, and to brief essays on old-time fiddling and on bluegrass. One writing space discusses the relationship between Clyde and the author of the hypertext. In the original HyperCard version, every writing space offers readers an opportunity to comment and thereby alter the text for the next reader. An unusual feature of this hypertext is that it offers the reader opposite conclusions without resolving the difference, thereby modeling some of the ambiguity a researcher faces. For example, the reader hears Clyde play two tunes and is told that musical analysis suggests that they are quite similar. Transcriptions illustrate the similarities. But another path leads to Clyde saying that these same two tunes are different, then demonstrating the difference.

The centralized hypertext invokes a hierarchical structure, in which there is always a core text and varying degrees of peripheral information and interpretation. This text evokes an impression of an omniscient point of view. In a second type of hypertext, a central text is absent or undermined in some way, and the experience of reading the hypertext is more like playing a game than doing a research assignment. Without a single central text the branching structure is nonhierarchical; instead it is like a web or mosaic, with some nodes more central and important than others. *Afternoon* (Joyce 1990) is a work of hypertext fiction in which the narrative depends on the reader's choices. The narrator is unreliable. Readers learn more or less about the characters and events depending on the paths that they choose and the order in which they choose them. The reading is complicated in that certain links become available only after the reader has activated other links. *Uncle Buddy's Phantom Funhouse* (McDaid 1993) is also a work of fiction, but it has no narrative structure. In this hypertext, the reader enters the virtual house of "Uncle Buddy," a writer, who has disappeared, leaving only his artifacts: desk, file cabinets, screenplays, music, and so forth. The hypertext reader rummages around Uncle Buddy's effects and tries to understand who he was on the basis of various clues, some contradictory, others secret. In some ways the reader is placed in the position of a detective; in other ways, a fieldworker.

Hypertexts are unlike conventional books in important ways. They do not have the same kind of closure; they do not end, but readers stop. J. Yellowlees Douglas likens them to

> the elaborate memory palaces constructed by Greek and Roman speakers which once enabled them to memorize vast chunks of perfectly finished oratory. . . . Where ancient rhetoricians strolled through every

room . . . you'll be wandering through this narrative edifice more or less as you would through a museum. You don't need to peer intently at every exhibit in every room of a museum to feel that you've "done" the museum. What prompts us to leave the museum is not the sense of having digested its every aspect, but the sense of having satisfied—or exhausted—something in ourselves. (1991:n.p.)

People will increasingly experience text as hypertext in the twenty-first century. Text will be digitized, stored, and available on-line as information. Scholars will continue to write books, but more and more will work in hypertexts. It would seem that hypertext offers many advantages over linear text, and indeed I believe it does. For one thing, it offers grand opportunities for producing knowing texts and virtual realities. At the same time, there are reasons to be cautious and critical. Many hypertexts at present are dull and annoying, and hypertexts are never any better than their contents. Access to hypertexts is limited at present to the segment of the population that can afford it.[3] Issues regarding copyright of intellectual property are extremely difficult to resolve in this new medium because policing is much more problematic. And linear forms of text organization offer a kind of representation that for many is reassuring. Indeed, most of the information available on the World Wide Web today is organized with links designed to mimic the linear world insofar as possible. A case in point: the "back" and "forward" buttons on today's Web browsers encourage movement back and forth in a straight line. Ambiguity, unreliable narrators, and lateral movement to another world are unsuitable and irritating when using the Web to find, for example, the cheapest airfare to a travel destination. But although the Web has now become the way most people experience linked text, for representations of lived experience the information retrieval model on the Web cannot provide the richness of knowing texts. Fortunately, as I mentioned earlier, hypertexts that operate on a virtual reality model are also available in electronic form on the Web and in CD-ROM and DVD format.

Virtual reality does not mirror reality any more than other "realist" representations do. It is a representation of its own: the experience of a person at a computer mentally confronting a text. Is a computer merely a channel through which minds communicate via texts? Can a computer offer a virtual performance? One of the lessons that performance-oriented folklorists learned is what Nathaniel Hawthorne taught over and over: that the life of the intellect, divorced from human contact and pursued single-mindedly, leads to madness. Ethan Brand and Roger Chillingworth would have been cybersurfers today, no doubt about it. The reason why the new folklorists were interested in performance was that they were interested in persons. What kind of experience is the experience of a virtual world of text without risk, without responsibility?[4] How fulfilling are experiences of virtual reality? If our minds are but bundles of texts, sites of competing ideologies, how do we account for our minds becoming critically self-aware? Can a text become aware of itself? It would seem a logical impossibility. Critics of text who view the problem as one of disembodiment will be little comforted by the virtual reality of hypertext.

Despite this critique of text, it is clear that just as we are being led to understand text in new ways, we are being led to understand mind and self in new models. Rorty's notion of minds as self-reweaving webs is very close to the concept of interactivity in hypertext, particularly as readers become authors. Further, Rorty emphasizes that "there is no self distinct from this self-reweaving web. All there is to the human self is just that web" (1991:93). And for Rorty there is no mind-body problem, either: the body is one with the mind and self, the web of desires continually reweaving as it acts and is acted upon in the world. Jacques Derrida's view of the new and "transformed" text sounds very suspiciously like a hypertext version of the world:

> a "text" that is henceforth no longer a finished corpus of writing, some content enclosed in a book or its margins, but a differential network, a fabric of traces referring endlessly to something other than itself, to other differential traces. Thus the text overruns all the limits assigned to it so far (not submerging or drowning them in an undifferentiated homogeneity, but rather making them more complex, dividing and multiplying strokes and lines)—all the limits, everything that was to be set up in opposition to writing (speech, life, the world, the real, history, and what not, every field of reference). (1979:83–84)

The Indo-European root of text, *tek*, means to weave, to fabricate. Texts are not a given in the world; they are made. Even if we are inhabited by language and constructed by texts, if our selves are webs of beliefs and desires, I am not ready to believe our experience always comes to us already textualized, in language, bit by bit. Ecstasy or transcendent experience seems to me to be outside of textualization, at least initially, and language can only point to it, not model it, though occasionally it can induce it. Texts may make us, but we also make texts; we translate, we represent. Texts in this sense are always nostalgic, longing for experience. The pre-texted world is a processual world. It is the flow that, for example, most people recognize when making or listening to music: an unfolding. Texts considered as digitized information are reproducible, exactly replicable; experiences (including experiences of texts) are not. Texted, language seems to be a reasonable translation; the stuff of thought, it represents thought. Notated, music is only a fair translation; its realization requires much more in the way of context. Experience ordinarily is texted as art: we tell stories about ourselves (often to ourselves), we write poems, we make films, we paint, we draw, we make music, we build houses, we cook, we arrange our lives, we express ourselves; this is our expressive culture. Texts about texts, metatexts, are representations of texts that already are representations. This is the textualized world that scholars inhabit. This world of text is an already virtual world. Hypertext representations encourage artful authoring and reading, and good hypertexts turn readers into authors. Like the best texts, the best hypertexts are not ends in themselves but means that return us refreshed and knowing to the world of people, performance, and community.

Notes

For helpful comments on this topic, I am grateful to Steven Taylor, Barbara Kirshenblatt-Gimblett, Marta Daniels, Patrick Mullen, and Burt Feintuch. An earlier version of this essay, but without the section "Ethnography and the 'Knowing Text,'" appeared in the *Journal of American Folklore* 108 (1995): 432–48.

1. A few folklorists have argued that multiple versions and variants are not a necessary condition of folklore and that other conditions, such as expressive quality, the folk community base, aesthetics, and so forth, are more fruitful avenues for interpretation. When text is understood as a representation of a process, rather than as an item, however, this problem disappears.

2. In 1995, when this essay was first published, Claire, the "personal music coach," was commercially available software that taught sight-singing on any Macintosh computer. In this software, musical notation appears in exercises on the screen, the student "sings" into the computer's microphone, and the computer calculates the pitch accuracy. Unfortunately the manufacturer abandoned the software about 1997.

3. Efforts have succeeded to make the Internet free to the general public, however, through public library workstations.

4. *Per,* an Indo-European root of *experience,* means to try, to risk, to lean forward.

References Cited

Barry, Phillips. 1939. *The Maine Woods Songster.* Cambridge, Mass.: Powell Printing Co.

Barthes, Roland. 1975. *The Pleasure of the Text.* Trans. Richard Miller. New York: Hill and Wang.

Bauman, Richard. 1977. *Verbal Art as Performance.* Prospect Heights, Ill.: Waveland Press.

Ben-Amos, Dan. 1972. "Toward a Definition of Folklore in Context." In *Toward New Perspectives in Folklore.* Ed. Américo Paredes and Richard Bauman. 3–15. Austin: University of Texas Press.

Bolter, Jay David, Michael Joyce, and John B. Smith. 1993. *Getting Started with Storyspace.* Cambridge, Mass.: Eastgate Systems.

Brewster, Paul G., ed. 1940. *Ballads and Songs of Indiana.* Bloomington: Indiana University Press.

Burroway, Janet. 1987. *Writing Fiction.* 2d ed. Boston: Little, Brown.

Cantwell, Robert. 1993. *Ethnomimesis: Folklife and the Representation of Culture.* Chapel Hill: University of North Carolina Press.

Castaneda, Carlos. 1968. *The Teachings of Don Juan: A Yaqui Way of Knowledge.* Berkeley: University of California Press.

Cox, John Harrington, ed. 1925. *Folk-songs of the South.* Cambridge, Mass.: Harvard University Press.

Culler, Jonathan. 1975. *Structuralist Poetics.* Ithaca: Cornell University Press.

———. 1982. *On Deconstruction.* Ithaca: Cornell University Press.

Davis, Arthur Kyle. 1929. *Traditional Ballads of Virginia.* Cambridge, Mass.: Harvard University Press.

Derrida, Jacques. 1979. "Living On/Border Lines." In *Deconstruction and Criticism.* Ed. Geoffrey Hartman. 75–176. New York: Continuum.

Dornfeld, Barry, Tom Rankin, and Jeff Todd Titon. *Powerhouse for God.* 1989. Color, VHS and 16mm, 58 min. Watertown, Mass.: Documentary Educational Resources. Also available on <http://www.folkstreams.net>

Dorson, Richard, ed. 1972. *Folklore and Folklife.* Chicago: University of Chicago Press.

Douglas, J. Yellowlees. 1991. "Are We Reading Yet?" In brochure notes to *Victory Garden* by Stewart Moulthrop. Cambridge, Mass.: Eastgate Systems.

Eagleton, Terry. 1978. *Criticism and Ideology.* London: Verso.

———. 1983. *Literary Theory: An Introduction.* Minneapolis: University of Minnesota Press.

Easthope, Anthony. 1994. "Cultural Studies 1." In *The Johns Hopkins Guide to Literary Theory and Criticism.* Ed. Michael Groden and Martin Kreiswirth. 176–79. Baltimore: Johns Hopkins University Press.

Fish, Stanley. 1980. *Is There a Text in This Class?: The Authority of Interpretive Communities.* Cambridge, Mass.: Harvard University Press.

Fischer, Michael M. J., and George Marcus. 1986. *Anthropology as Cultural Critique.* Chicago: University of Chicago.

Franklin, Reverend C. L. 1989. *Give Me This Mountain: Life History and Selected Sermons of the Rev. C. L. Franklin.* Ed. Jeff Todd Titon. Urbana: University of Illinois Press.

Gardner, Emelyn Elizabeth, ed. 1939. *Ballads and Songs of Southern Michigan.* Ann Arbor: University of Michigan Press.

Geertz, Clifford. 1973. *The Interpretation of Cultures.* New York: Basic Books.

———. 1977. "From the Native's Point of View: On the Nature of Anthropological Understanding." In *Symbolic Anthropology*. Ed. Janet Dolgin et al. 480–92. New York: Columbia University Press.

———. 1980. "Blurred Genres." *American Scholar* 49:165–79.

Glassie, Henry. 1968. *Pattern in the Material Folk Culture of the Eastern United States*. Philadelphia: University of Pennsylvania Press.

———. 1975a. *All Silver and No Brass*. Bloomington: Indiana University Press.

———. 1975b. *Folk Housing in Middle Virginia*. Knoxville: University of Tennessee Press.

———. 1982. *Passing the Time in Ballymenone*. Philadelphia: University of Pennsylvania Press.

Harner, Michael J. 1972. *The Jivaro*. Garden City, N.Y.: Doubleday.

Henry, Mellinger Edward, ed. 1938. *Folk-songs from the Southern Highlands*. New York: J. J. Augustin.

Hudson, Arthur Palmer. 1936. *Folksongs of Mississippi and Their Background*. Chapel Hill: University of North Carolina Press.

Hymes, Dell. 1972. *Reinventing Anthropology*. New York: Pantheon.

Joyce, Michael. 1990. *Afternoon*. Cambridge, Mass.: Eastgate Systems.

Kroker, Arthur, and Michael A. Weinstein. 1994. *Data Trash: The Theory of the Virtual Class*. New York: St. Martin's Press.

Kurosawa, Akira. 1969. *Rashomon: A Film by Akira Kurosawa*. New York: Grove Press.

Landow, George. 1992. *The In Memoriam Web*. Cambridge, Mass.: Eastgate Systems.

Le Guin, Ursula K. 1969. *The Left Hand of Darkness*. New York: Ace Books.

Lévi-Strauss, Claude. 1974. *Tristes tropiques*. Trans. John Weightman and Doreen Weightman. New York: Atheneum.

Lord, Albert B. 1960. *The Singer of Tales*. Cambridge: Harvard University Press.

Lubbock, Percy. 1957 [1921]. *The Craft of Fiction*. New York: Viking Press.

Marcus, George, and James Clifford, eds. 1986. *Writing Culture*. Berkeley: University of California Press.

McDaid, John. 1993. *Uncle Buddy's Phantom Funhouse*. Cambridge, Mass.: Eastgate Systems.

Propp, Vladimir. 1968 [1928]. *Morphology of the Folktale*. Trans. Laurence Scott. Bloomington, Ind.: Research Center in the Language Sciences.

Pynchon, Thomas. 1966. *The Crying of Lot 49*. New York: Perennial Library.

Rajan, Tilottama. 1994. "Hermeneutics 1." In *The Johns Hopkins Guide to Literary Theory and Criticism*. Ed. Michael Groden and Martin Kreiswirth. 375–79. Baltimore: Johns Hopkins University Press.

Ricoeur, Paul. 1981. *Hermeneutics and the Human Sciences*. Ed. and trans. John B. Thompson. Cambridge: Cambridge University Press.

Rorty, Richard. 1991. *Objectivity, Relativism, and Truth*. Cambridge: Cambridge University Press.

Scholes, Robert, Nancy R. Compley, and Gregory L. Ulmer. 1988. *Text Book: An Introduction to Literary Language*. New York: St. Martin's Press.

Schechner, Richard, and Willa Appel, eds. 1990. *By Means of Performance.* New York: Cambridge University Press.

Tedlock, Barbara. 1992. *Time and the Highland Maya.* Albuquerque: University of New Mexico Press.

Tedlock, Dennis. 1990. *Days from a Dream Almanac.* Urbana: University of Illinois Press.

Titon, Jeff Todd. 1971. "Ethnomusicology of Downhome Blues Phonograph Records, 1926–1930." Ph.D. diss., University of Minnesota.

———. 1976. "Son House: Two Narratives." *Alcheringa: Ethnopoetics* (n.s.) 2 (1): 2–9.

———. 1979. "Murder at the Folk Festival." Paper read at the conference of the Society for Ethnomusicology, Northeast Chapter, Brown University, April 5.

———. 1980. "The Life Story." *Journal of American Folklore* 93:276–92.

———. 1983. "Captain Tradition and the Folklore Police." Paper read at the conference of the Society for Ethnomusicology, Northeast Chapter, Middlebury College, April 16.

———. 1988. *Powerhouse for God.* Austin: University of Texas Press.

———. 1991. *The Clyde Davenport Web.* HyperCard stack, freeware. Providence, R.I.: Jeff Todd Titon. Available online at <http://www.stg.brown.edu/projects/davenport/CLYDE_DAVENPORT.html>.

———. 1995. "Bi-musicality as Metaphor." *Journal of American Folklore* 108:287–97.

Toelken, Barre. 1979. *The Dynamics of Folklore.* Boston: Houghton-Mifflin.

Turnbull, Colin. 1961. *The Forest People.* New York: Simon and Schuster.

Wilgus, D. K. 1973. "The Text Is the Thing." *Journal of American Folklore* 86:241–52.

Zipes, Jack David. 1983. *Fairy Tales and the Art of Subversion.* New York: Wildman.

4   Genre

The word *genre*, derived from French and Latin, means "kind"
or "genus." *Genus* in turn means "a class," "kind," or "sort," with the
accompanying expansion in logical usage of being a class of like objects
or ideas having several subordinate classes or species. Genre is thus an umbrella concept that allows many disparate, and often related, concepts to
be conveniently divided and subdivided. The word has some specialized
usage, as in "genre painting," which realistically depicts subjects or scenes
from everyday life. In its usual context of classification, however, genre
can be as expansive or confined as disciplinary usages demand. In literature, for example, scholars and teachers usually refer to fiction, poetry, and
drama as the "primary genres," though there are myriad and often rather
technical subdivisions within each. To illustrate the point, consider some
of the subdivisions within the genre of poetry: subgenres include the epic,
heroic, mock-heroic, lyrics, ballads, sonnets, dirges, threnodies, monodies,
epigrams, epitaphs, verse epistles, pastorals (a pastoral poem can also be
referred to as an eclogue, a bucolic, or an idyll), and a host of others (Bain
et al. 1973:708–12). For most general readers and students, such fine distinctions fade in the face of the more popular subgenres.

Genre has been one of several defining concepts folklorists have used
in carrying out their work over the past hundred years. One of folklore's
most necessary concepts, genre has also been one of the most difficult to
contain. While the notion of genre was useful in classification and worked
relatively well to create boundaries, it also inadvertently allowed for cross-
over between boundaries. The history of the use of genre in folklore studies is one in which initial efforts to stabilize the concept in the late-nine-

teenth- and early-twentieth-century beginnings of the discipline gave way in the mid-twentieth century to recognition that any system of classification is ever evolving, ever subject to new subgroups and new categories.

In recent decades, folklorists have come to the conclusion that genre is a continuous site of contestation; with the acceptance of merging, blurring, and overlapping categories of classification, folklore scholars have changed the questions they ask about the urge to classify. They have embraced theoretical rather than empirical approaches to genre and have joined literary scholars, linguists, and anthropologists in the recognition that porous categories lead to more fruitful lines of inquiry about the items treated within a discipline. How these items interact with and upon each other—their intertextuality, their written texts, the speech acts and language used to create them, the people who perpetuate them, and the environments and the performance contexts in which they are perpetuated—provide the base for questions that engage most contemporary folklorists.

In the Interest of Discipline: Establishing Genre

Throughout the history of folklore study, scholars have sought recognition of folklore as a singular *distinct* discipline. Viewed in the eighteenth and nineteenth centuries as integrally tied to anthropology and, in more recent decades of the twentieth century, sometimes blurred with oral history, popular culture, or cultural studies, folklore has been on the defensive since William J. Thoms coined the term in 1846. Critics have maintained that practitioners had no methodology of their own and that they borrowed from more established and perhaps more well-respected disciplines.

One of the first efforts to counter such accusations and to formalize the separateness of the discipline was the establishment of the American Folklore Society in 1888. This organization provided the official sanction for practitioners who looked for a site of their own from which to voice the business of their profession. Officialdom was an important first step to establishing legitimacy and an important forum from which early folklorists could present ideas, confront the challenges to them, and work out the refinements that would further distinguish their work from that of others. One of the primary reasons for establishing the professional organization was to found a publishing outlet from which its members could present their research findings. The *Journal of American Folklore*, as the official publication, served its purpose well in moving the discipline up the notches of scholarly credibility and acceptability.

Nevertheless, the first folklorists entered the American academic community as stepchildren with identity crises or, at best, with burning urges to break the ties with the anthropological father who initially held their hands, if he did not actually sire them. Consequently, early on they worked as hard as they could to define as clearly as possible the kinds of things that they did. Definitions were key to autonomy. Folklorists from William Wells Newell to Stith Thompson to Francis L. Utley to Alan Dundes to Jan Harold Brunvand worked to make sure that folklorists conveyed to each other as well as to the world at large that the ground on which they stood was not just unique but solid (Brunvand 1968; Dundes 1965; Newell 1906; Thompson 1955b; Utley 1965). But folklorists themselves frequently muddied the waters by being inconsistent in their application of terms to phenomena and in their orderings of classifications for various folk forms. Dan Ben-Amos and a host of well-known folklorists continued the efforts at clarification, tackling the issues of definitions and classifications again in 1976 in *Folklore Genres* (Ben-Amos 1976).[1] Ben-Amos found Dundes's assertion that "not so much as one genre has been completely defined" (1964:252) as still an accurate one. This probably rested in part, Ben-Amos concluded, on folklorists' adopting terms from common parlance in English and then trying to imbue them with theoretical and specialized meanings. The quest for solidity in folklore studies seemed to remain as current in the eighth decade of the twentieth century as it had been in the last decade of the nineteenth.

Solidity in turn rested upon authenticity, the foundation on which the discipline would be built. If folklorists could show that there were forms, traditions, events, practices, and narratives that could not fit comfortably into the purview of any other discipline, they would go a long way toward carving out the space they needed to conduct their field research and library work and earn their academic credibility. Isolating distinctive forms and articulating how folklorists' training was essential to understanding them led folklorists to adopt a broad-based concept of genre. A slippery concept, genre was nonetheless a crucial starting point for a discipline that was at times itself rather less than firm.

The concept of genre thus became for folklorists the basis for classifying and authenticating forms they judged to be within their realm of training, expertise, and scholarly supervision. Genre served a dual purpose: it provided a system of classification as well as a conceptual framework for articulating the characteristics of components within a classification. With orality (word-of-mouth transmission), tradition, anonymity, community, formularization, multiple versions, demonstration, and imitation as some of the authenticating features setting the parameters of their claims, folklorists set out to classify everything from myth to personal narratives, shotgun houses to straw baskets, spirituals to folksongs.

Genre has proven to be a stabilizing as well as, when necessary, flexible concept. For example, the genre of folksong[2] shares common ground with the discipline of literature and its genre of poetry. Initially unwieldy, especially in its uncertainty about the placement of ballads, folksongs usually emphasize the feature of orality to distinguish them from, as Brunvand argued in 1968, "art songs" and "popular songs," both of which have written texts. Folksongs immediately subdivide into sacred and secular; these categories have remained fairly stable, although a blues singer may occasionally call upon the Lord in his or her lyrics. Within sacred folksongs, spirituals, hymns, and gospels are the generally recognized American subgenres.[3] Within secular folksongs, the pre-1950 categories that included blues, ballads, corridos, cowboy songs, and a few other types have been expanded to include rockabilly, zydeco, and banjo songs (black and white), and more will probably very quickly be added. The subgenre of blues has been divided into country blues, city or classic blues (dominated primarily by the famous women blues singers of the 1920s), and urban blues, with the accompanying focus on vocalization and instrumentation that follows each; and there followed further regional subdivisions such as Delta blues, Memphis blues, Chicago blues, Durham blues, and so on. More recently, the blues subgenre has evolved to include posturban blues, and considerations have focused on who is singing the blues, who is perpetuating a tradition once identified with a lone musician and his guitar. Genre subdivision in the case of the blues allows for how the music was originally transmitted in the nineteenth and early twentieth centuries, by whom, and where, and it also allows for the transformations affecting the music over the past several decades. It further allows for focus on the traits characteristic of the subgenre: word-of-mouth transmission; the repetitive *a-a-b* stanzaic form; minor "blue" notes; themes of lost love, natural disasters, and racial prejudice, among others; the prevalence of imagery such as mojos and trains; and call and response interactive engagement with audiences.

The genre of folk narratives has proven equally stable and flexible. Indeed, the word *narrative* is primarily a post-1970 usage applied to what most folklorists traditionally identified as folk literature or folktales.[4] One could speculate that the use of the word *literature* was perhaps also tied to the quest for legitimacy. On the one hand, it suggested that stories from the folk could be placed in a comparable position of interpretation to those literatures usually recognized to be worthy of scholarly interpretation, such as Chaucer's *Canterbury Tales* or Hawthorne's *The Scarlet Letter.* On the other hand, it was a salvaging gesture for the folk; while the creators of the stories might have been less educated and less urban, their imaginations were no less fertile, folklorists implicitly argued, and they could create narratives with plots, villains, heroines, and moral values as readily as their upper-class counterparts. The use of *literature* was by no means an innocent or casual choice in this early classification system. Folk literature as a genre was usually subdivided into myths, legends, and something several scholars persisted in calling "ordinary folktales," which meant that they were the ones usually told for purposes of entertainment.

When the genre became known as folktales, it would be subdivided into myths, legends, folktales, and fairy tales. (Some early classifications made an entirely separate genre of myths and legends.) Unfortunately, there was a classification problem in including the subgenre folktales, usually understood to mean the common, nonsacred categories of stories that people circulate mostly for entertainment, within a genre of the same name. Opting for the use of the word *narrative* enabled folklorists to clarify inclusion and to regularize the understood outline of types, allowing them more easily to place not only folktales, myths, legends, and fairy tales but also animal tales, fables, tall tales, jokes, anecdotes, and shaggy dog stories in the genre. Prior to the widespread use of the word *narrative,* scholars and teachers relied heavily upon Stith Thompson's six-volume *Motif-Index of Folk-Literature* (1955a) and *The Folktale* (1946), Aarne and Thompson's *The Types of the Folktale* (1961 [1928]), Vladimir Propp's *Morphology of the Folktale* (1975 [1928]), and Ernest W. Baughman's *A Type and Motif-Index of the Folktales of England and North America* (1966) to draw the fine lines in narrative folkloric constructions.

Adopting folk narrative to replace folk literature and folktales stabilized subgenres that sometimes leaned into one another or could not distinguish between being parents and children. It also paved the way for inclusion of as-yet-undiscovered folk stories that needed a greater number of words than usually allotted to riddles or formula tales and short jokes. That flexibility has been tested in recent years by the inclusion of personal-experience narratives and the increased value given to tales traditionally called memorates, which were historically a subcategory of legends. Individual lived experiences have become as significant in the classifying structure as tales several hundred years in age.[5] In their willingness to incorporate new subgenres, folklorists have institutionalized flexibility within their discipline and have kept folklore alive and healthy long after its official acceptance into the halls of academia.

While genre as folklorists use it shares kinship in other disciplines, it is imbued with distinguishing characteristics that enable it to be recognized as autonomous. When any form claimed for folklore overlapped with other disciplines, folklorists turned to whatever authenticating feature they needed to reassert their hold on the classification. For example, one of the hardest genres for folklorists to hold on to as their own was that of myth. Scholars in literature, comparative religion, and anthropology all have legitimate reasons for focusing investigative and interpretive research on myth. Folklorists highlighted the feature of orality, the community's belief factor in relationship to the myth, and the interpretive qualities that issued from the value the people placed on the myth.[6] Folklorists also exhibited flexibility in not fighting the war of denial, in recognizing that the tools of their discipline could be used to perform unique interpretive functions even as comparatists or literary scholars similarly employed unique methodologies for opening their windows on myth.

Genre allowed for the taming of what was, at times, an unruly monster whose many tentacles reached across disciplines and scholarly endeavors and frequently seemed unwilling to let go of attachments outside folklore. Both religious scholars and folklorists study spirituals; folklorists, feminist scholars, and sociologists study the blues; women's studies scholars, African Americanists, and historians all join with folklorists in studying personal-experience narratives, oral histories, and narratives focusing on race, sex, and culture. Flexibility within stability and uniqueness within commonality have perhaps been the guidelines that have enabled folklorists to claim their own space and affirm their discipline, and yet be viewed as integral contributors to the production of knowledge within university and public societies of scholars.

Resistance to Stabilization: Blurring and Blending of Genre

Even as folklorists initially worked for the purity and uniqueness of their discipline by identifying authentic folk forms as broadly as they could, they were almost immediately faced with challenges to those claims for authenticity. While genres and subgenres could stabilize, they could not prevent encroachment from a variety of directions. Certainly the history of those challenges is illuminating, but it is to the credit of folklorists as a group and to folklore as a discipline that both have withstood, rather genially, the various assaults.

The first major challenges were to the discipline itself. Since folklore has historically been viewed as the "lore" of the "folk," both parts of the term have frequently had to answer to critics, at times including folklorists themselves, seeking clear definitions. If the producers of folk materials (in the broadest sense) were the folk, and the lore was what they produced, then who were they and what did they authentically produce? From the earliest definitions of the folk as rural, isolated, basically uneducated people, folklorists expanded the term to include practically every people that has traditions, which means every human society and group of people. Cotton pickers or railroad workers in Alabama in the late nineteenth century could produce work songs that were considered folk by virtue of being transmitted orally and learned by imitation, and college students and professors at Cornell University in 1970 could circulate absent-minded professor jokes and anecdotes that also reflected their inclusion in authentic folk communities. Urban dwellers could perpetuate stories of rats in Kentucky Fried Chicken in the 1980s and earn their place as an authentic folk group just as assuredly as quilters in Mississippi could sit on their porches in the 1930s sewing and telling tales about superstitions that midwives practiced. By the late 1960s, folklorists seemed to have accepted the fact that flexibility in identifying the folk and folk communities was the only viable path for the future.

The same was true for folk creation. Verbal lore and other folk creation that in the early and middle decades of the twentieth century folklorists worked hard to authenticate has given way, in the past two or three decades, to a sort of "mellowing out" on the part of folklorists. Instead of trying to locate the exact origin of a particular tale or joke in the much-touted historic-geographic method that identified most midcentury graduate study in folklore, folklorists have begun to place less emphasis on the need to validate an item of folklore through hundreds of years of circulation, countless versions, anonymity of creation, or location of circulation and have turned their attention more to the function of lore within communities, to valued forms with much shorter story-lives, and to other considerations that would perhaps make the dust of the late-nineteenth-century folklorists swirl in their graves. The initial thirsty desire for authenticity gave way to a more realistic recognition of the value of forms *in culture*, to the myriad links between producers and their products, and to the immediacy of performance issues over historically static texts. Folklorists have perhaps experienced a more humanizing and people-directed tendency in their discipline beyond the fieldwork stages that has overshadowed the traditional, stodgy, library-oriented focus that previously followed field research.

Challenges to the discipline of folklore and to the genres within it have also come in response to its placement within the academy. Even as folklorists fought for recognition of their area of study as a distinct discipline with distinct methodologies, they had to face the reality that few universities had separate folklore departments. And that is still true today: there are fewer than ten full-fledged departments of folklore in American universities. Practicing folklorists have found themselves keeping company with English or linguistics or anthropology or religious studies professors or serving as adjuncts to departments or centers. Those lucky enough to become state folklorists or to find work in other areas of public-sector folklore have also, in some ways, been betwixt and between, suffering perennial identity crises as they try to pursue the work integral to their chosen profession. Battles for finances and space have occupied almost as much of their time as scholarly endeavors. Isolated folklorists may have been hard put to keep disciplinary identity intact in their university environments, but they have reaffirmed the value of what they do through interactions with scholars outside their universities as well as through attending meetings of the American Folklore Society, state folklore societies, and, in some instances, even local folklore meetings. The challenge has been for folklorists to maintain identities as folklorists even when there are no living mirrors around them.

Folklorists have also been challenged to maintain a high level of scholarly productivity in comparison to the small numbers in the profession. Small numbers overall mean that some ethnic and racial communities have had the majority of their lore studied by folklorists who are not members of their ethnic or racial groups. This has historically been the case with African American folklore, as Zora Neale Hurston, J. Mason Brewer, Julius Lester, and a handful of other African American folklore scholars before the middle of the twentieth century gave way to Roger Abrahams and his contemporaries in the 1960s and 1970s. It is now increasingly the case with Latino and other Spanish-oriented lore, with Native American lore, and with American folklorists generally looking across the ocean to study European communities. The insider/outsider, emic/etic clash continues to be relevant to how scholars define, describe, and interpret genre.

One of the longest debates of definition, origin, and analysis has centered on spirituals. That subgenre of folksongs has been challenged and rechallenged as scholars have tried to make several determinations. First of all, did African Americans create songs independent of the influence of European Americans? If they drew upon European American sources, how extensive was that borrowing, and can we determine where the lines of influence should be sketched? Should we properly recognize two forms of the subgenre, "black spirituals" and "white spirituals"? Were African sources important to the creation of spirituals? If so, can such sources be documented conclusively in the songs as we currently know them? Some scholars have viewed these debates as efforts to detract from African

American creativity, as a racist refusal by scholars of the dominant culture to allow black folks anything, even the songs they made up. Other scholars perhaps wanted to give credit, if it were due, to joint black and white inspiration for what has become one of the distinctively American folklore subgenres. While recent African American folklorists such as John W. Roberts have added their investigative and interpretive skills to the debate, it is still not yet conclusively settled.[7]

Other challenges have come to particular subgenres of folk materials within the discipline of folklore as well. Where was the distinction to be made between ballads as literature and ballads as songs? English and Scottish ballads, long fixed in form and structure through centuries of written texts, were also passed on orally among settlers in the United States, particularly in Appalachia. Were these versions collected by folklorists to be considered as authentic as those in literary anthologies? Were folklorists simply satisfied to confront and accept the intersections of levels of cultures—art and folk culture—or to try to enumerate the separateness of the two? Were folklorists really within the purview of their discipline in embracing variants of the Child ballads that had not been truly oral forms for centuries, variants that Child himself had taught as literature at Harvard University in the 1890s? Perhaps these are the kinds of questions that prompted some folklorists to separate ballads from the category of folksongs, though they still studied them.[8]

Other questions arise about some manifestations of the blues as *folk*songs. With the traditional expectations of orality in folkloristic transmission, many skeptics questioned the actual *writing* of lyrics for blues songs that many of the classic blues singers recorded in the 1920s. And with the initial focus on acoustic guitars as the instruments of choice for early blues singers, the use of electric guitars and the addition of pianos created immediate problems for persons concerned about the authenticity of folk transmission. Retaining purity in folk creation through the process of transmission as well as in the instruments of transmission led to much critical discussion. By the 1990s, however, the music had won, for the ranges of its instrumental accompaniment would have astonished those black musicians singing at house parties in the 1870s or at jook joints in the first two decades of the twentieth century.

Blues music and the changes in its instrumentation and the community surrounding it reveal yet another challenge to folklore genre. What happens when the community that has created a folklore genre *seems* to abandon it? What happens when another community *seems* to show more respect for the genre than the community in which it originated? That has certainly appeared to be the case, with necessary qualifications of

course, with the blues. As more and more church-based African Americans identified the blues as the devil's music, and as more and more col-
lege-educated, upwardly mobile African Americans considered it "country" and "backward" and turned away from it as they reached for their
piece of the American democratic pie, blues suffered a slump in popu-
larity in some African American communities. On the other hand, non-
blacks, particularly Britishers and young white Americans, turned to the
music with unqualified appreciation. A folklorist in the 1980s could have
found a young white man from England much more informed about the
blues than a young black man living in Memphis, Tennessee, one of the
cities where the blues originated. Economics, history, class, and race were
all factors in the blues' becoming a floater of sorts across races and national boundaries. In recent years, however, some blacks who earlier
neglected the form are returning to it and finding singers like Koko Taylor much to their liking.

The issue of instrumentation as the source of attack for determining what is authentically a folklore genre is rooted in a progression that
no scholarly discipline could control: technology. The impact of technology on folklore genre has been wide-ranging. On the lower end of the
scale, the purchase of cloth to use in quilting caused traditional quilters
to raise their eyebrows. Historically, quilting was a recycling art, one in
which quilters took pieces of material from partly frayed clothing of long-
dead relatives or scraps from other salvaged clothing and fashioned them
into new bedclothes. Since quilts were to be functional, "something to
keep you warm," as a quilter told photographer Roland Freeman, the art
was seldom in the matching and use of the same two or three colors
throughout a quilt; instead, the art was in imaginatively using up, through
traditional designs and elaborate stitches, materials that were readily
available. With the advent of quilting catalogs, the increase in economic
opportunities to purchase cloth that would ensure look-alike patches, and
the onslaught of "art" quilts, the practice has changed so dramatically
that the idea of quilts being a record of "worn" and "warm" family history is almost passé. Now, art quilts (made entirely with purchased materials) that focus on family history or abstract designs, which have become the subject of museum-sponsored quilt shows, have significantly
transformed the art. From documenting family and family history, quilts
have progressed to documenting AIDS and rape victims, and to being
communally inspired and executed creations rather than the work of a
single individual. If Harriet Powers were making quilts today, she would
probably have two hundred helpers in fifty different American cities contributing to a quilt that could be draped halfway around the Washington

Mall. Quilts as official documentaries have combined with quilts as documents (artifacts) to change forever the shape of that folklore genre.

The making of cloth, however, is an age-old art on the scale of technological advancement. Other steps along that scale would mean other
changes to folklore genre. Electric guitars may now seem a minimal encroachment upon the blues in comparison to the impact of technology
upon folk narratives. Telephone pranks, a part of the subgenre of jokes
under the genre of folktales, were one of the first categories of folk transmission influenced by technology that folklorists and popular culturists
were willing to accept. Borrowing from the well-recognized formula tales
and the question-and-answer endemic to riddles, telephone pranks are the
particular purview of adolescents. Retaining a transformed anonymity by
the inability of their audiences to see them, they subvert traditional transmission even as they perpetuate a revision of it. Wholly dependent for
its success upon the telephone, the subgenre of telephone pranks represents one of the earliest challenges to authenticity; the genre's survival
reiterates the concept of flexibility inherent in genre classification.

Radio and television have also had their impact upon folklore genre.
Radio announcers such as Wolfman Jack have earned perhaps as many
imitators as they have listeners. The oral poetry and quick verbal retorts
identified with many black radio announcers have also earned their an-
tics a place in American folklore.[9] Scholars identify the poetry of their
creations as readily as they discuss the poetry of contemporary rap lyrics. Television viewers have learned from the miniscreen jokes, gestures
(such as the over-the-head, fist-rolling woofing of Arsenio Hall and the
wave identified with spectators at sports activities), and the styles and
mannerisms (such as "snapping") characteristic of a number of situation
comedies. These influences illustrate how directly and effectively various levels of culture—the folk and the popular—interact with and have
an impact upon each other. While folklorists have not yet defined new
genres for these forms, certainly the old subgenre classification of gestures has been radically expanded with these visual additions.

In recognition of these impinging influences, one of the most prominent folklorists has recently published a study of the ties between mass
media, including television, and folklore genre.[10] Linda Dégh (1994) includes in her discussion "magic for sale," that is, märchen and legend in
television advertising; magic as a mail-order commodity; and the influence
of fairy tales, with their emphases on beauty, wealth, and power, upon career choices women make in the modern media. The undertaking of such
a project is comparable to literary scholar Jane Tompkins's (1992) focus on
Louis L'Amour and the western novel in American culture, a genre pro-

fessors of literature traditionally dismiss. Their works illustrate the extent to which Dégh and Tompkins recognize that the *purity* traditionally harbored toward particular genres in their disciplines has changed substantially over the decades. The western as a well-respected television genre finally became a well-respected literary genre, and the lines between popular and folk culture were blurred even more as fairy tales and legends shook hands with television to form unions for which we do not yet have names.

As technology expands, so does the possibility for broadening categories of folklore genres. With the widespread introduction of photocopying machines into offices around the country in the 1970s and 1980s, narratives that were seldom circulated orally began to be typed and copied for wider circulation. Office workers across the United States formed a new kind of folk community, one that could anonymously produce and rapidly reproduce tales, jokes, or other words of wisdom for mass consumption. Xerox lore, as it came to be known, with its features of mass production and fast access to a large number of willing readers, combined the problematic literacy feature with a hand-delivered rather than an oral transmission and further expanded genre and the idea of authenticity in folk materials. The repetitiveness of transmission and the recognized, though revised, patterns on which Xerox lore rested enabled folklorists to accept its kinship to more traditional forms in the discipline. For example, the following frequently circulated discourse on the parts of the body has documented counterparts in verbal lore. It is called "The Boss":

> When the body was first made, all the parts wanted to be boss.
> The brain said, "Since I control everything, and do all the thinking, I should be boss."
> The feet said, "Since I carry man where he wants to be and get him in position to do what the brain wants, I should be boss."
> The hand said, "Since I do all the work and earn all the money to keep the rest of you going, I should be boss."
> The eyes said, "Since I must look out for all of you and tell you where danger lurks, I should be boss."
> And so it went, the heart, the ears, the lungs, and finally the asshole spoke up and demanded that it be made boss. All the other parts laughed and laughed at the idea of an asshole being boss. The asshole was so angered that he blocked himself off and refused to function. Soon the brain was feverish, the eyes crossed and ached, the feet were too weak to walk, the hands hung limply at the sides, the lungs and heart struggled to keep going. All pleaded with the brain to relent and let the asshole be boss.
> And so it happened. All the other parts did the work and the asshole just bossed and passed out a lot of shit.
> THE MORAL: You don't have to be a brain to be boss—just an asshole.[11]

The subject matter of the item clearly identifies its concerns with those of office workers, many of whom probably circulated "The Boss" behind the backs, so to speak, of difficult bosses. More recently, fax machines have probably taken over this function from photocopying machines.

When personal computers reached near epidemic use in the mid-1980s, folk forms followed rapidly, and they are ever-increasing today. With the institution of the Internet and with more programs available than the originators of the "information superhighway" ever imagined, the impact of this technology on folklore genre will not go unnoticed. For example, computer programmers and interested persons with sufficient programming skills are creating new kinds of games that involve role-playing, myth, and narrative. When scholars seek information from others around the world, competition ensues when a bright young rebel in Tokyo decides that he can get the answer more quickly than a middle-aged scholar somewhere in Brazil. Electronic mail (e-mail) is transforming the tradition of conversation and face-to-face interaction for people within a given community; indeed, the concept of community itself is being expanded so rapidly that the children's song "The World is Getting Littler Every Day" is coming true by the hour. As jokes, stories, and other information fly through telephone cables, the ideas Axel Olrik and Robert A. Georges articulated about the dynamics of a storytelling situation have been transformed forever.[12] The genre of folk narrative will need further refinement as issues of technology, traditionality, and circulation within particular communities lead folklorists to revise and expand definitions in ways that their predecessors could not have anticipated a mere ten years ago.

For every healthy use of technology, there is the corresponding shady side, and that is no less true with computers. As a counterpart to the subgenre of dirty jokes, computer programs, games, Web sites, and chat rooms can cross the border into the pornographic, with so many sex networks currently available that no one nosy scholar can keep track of all of them. With the technological possibilities for color, graphics, sound, and interaction, the intensity of this computer sex lore outstrips the mere telling of tales and jokes. These challenges to the traditional genre of folkloric entertainment will force folklorists to find the terminology and the skills to incorporate this body of lore into their studies.

The greatest challenge to folklore genre remains documentation and reproduction. From the earliest points at which tales, stories, songs, and other folk forms were written down or recorded and transcribed, the issue of authenticity surfaced. How could a folksong, inherently transmitted by word of mouth, still be a folksong once its text had been "fixed" by an article, a book, or a recorder? How could a folksong, traditionally circulated by word of mouth within particular groups in which elders taught the songs to youngsters, still be a folksong in the mouth of Joan Baez, who certainly did not fit the expected criteria for a singer of such songs? How folk were the songs Pete Seeger and Woody Guthrie sang if the lyrics had been composed instead of passed down orally or if they had been taught in formal, nearly schoolroom settings such as the Highlander Folk School instead of learned in the usual manner of sitting at the knee of an ancestor? Was a storytelling session really that if it were reduced to black squiggles on a white page? What did a Native American rain ceremony lose by being caught in static pictures? How, in other words, could the lore, actions, manners, and gestures be separated from the mouths, bodies, and communities of the folk and still be authentic? These issues notwithstanding, folklorists soon accepted the fact that, since they were not all griots and could not possibly remember *everything* from their field research, some technological form of documentation had to be allowed into the profession.

Indeed, folklorists themselves began to increase their use of technology in their own efforts to achieve the dynamism inherent in folk interactions and to counteract the stasis of documentation. Polaroid cameras initially accompanied recorders in a bid to capture some of the liveliness of storytelling sessions or sermons. Then movie cameras and later video cameras were introduced into the discipline in an effort to capture gesture, laughter, and nuances of oral presentation that static cameras could not and to capture the visual images of the people that tape recorders could not. Throughout the history of the discipline, folklorists have been adaptable to whatever technological advances that can reveal the complexity and power of the forms and people they study.

The constant in technological documentation has been the book. Publishing houses have posed as great a challenge to folklore genres as any of the more seemingly insidious technological advances. In the face of the advent of desktop publishing, journals that exist only on computer networks, and the increasing tendency of libraries to rely more upon virtual reality than tangible volumes, the technology of the book may be so dramatically transformed that questions of "fixity" will be moot and will yield to some of the same questions now raised in connection with computer network lore. Technological challenges to folklore genres mean an ongoing dialogue, desired or not, between practicing folklorists and the world in which they carry out their scholarly pursuits. The dialogue has illustrated conclusively that purity and authenticity are negotiable traits and that viable continuation of folklore studies depends upon the competence and willingness with which folklorists effect those negotiations.

Beyond Genre and into Theory

The blurring and blending of folklore genres might be viewed as an analogue of American society itself. As more and more diverse ethnic and racial groups have made their claims upon American democracy, they have inspired folklorists to be responsive to the expansiveness of cultures, to the ever-increasing plurality within the singularity of American society. The need to broaden conceptualizations of folklore in context, of the functions folklore serves, of the kinds of people and groups who perpetuate folk traditions, and of the folklore itself is the corollary to the mixing and matching of genres, to the various encroachments upon once clearly established and clearly understood folk forms. If the discipline of folklore represents America in this analogy, then it is an America far removed from the one in which folklorists initially set out to make their claims for uniqueness within academic and social communities.

Consider the recent developments in performance studies as one kind of blending. Traditionally, folklorists have certainly recognized the interactions of performers and their audiences, but more recently, the value, so to speak, of the audience has been upgraded.[13] Where folklorists once spoke of call and response, they now speak of co-performance. When once there seemed to be tellers of tales and listeners, everyone involved in a folklore event these days seems to have equal value to, and responsibility for, the success of the performance. This is especially apparent in the delivery of sermons, where the minister, the "Amen corner," and the rest of the congregation have all been recognized as constructing an incredible visual, aural, and oral presentation; each is on stage in a particular way. Indeed, performance has been broadened to include what folklorists themselves do in the presentation of their research materials, so that a speaker performs even as he or she is discussing performance; their re-creation of gestures and voice adds to their performance. Folklore thus, in turn, draws more heavily upon linguistics in its discussions of such patterns as well as upon theater and the emerging discipline of oral interpretation. Conception and performance of certain types of shows, such as *The Gospel at Colonus* (Breuer 1989), have transformed the mythical and religious to the realm of the blues and the variety show, if not the musical comedy itself. Previously discrete notions of appropriateness and setting for a particular genre have changed in the presentation of material lifted from literary texts and presented before live audiences, with tones and moods dramatically different from those suggested in the original.

One might anticipate, in the further blurring of genres, that video equipment, formerly used to "authenticate" traditional genre, will become central in the formation of new genres. If it has not already been done, surely some folklorist will shortly isolate an entire category of media lore, of which videos will be central.[14] From the initial documentary function, the use of videos will expand to become key to understanding various peoples and cultures. Consider, for example, the genre of family folklore (which is itself a mere toddler in comparison to myths and legends). Family folklore, already subdivided into many categories, might reasonably see one of its subgenres dominated entirely by videos: family reunion videos, birthday party videos, marriage videos, "baby learning skills" videos, and perhaps even funeral videos (these last three could properly be called "rites of passage" videos as a tie-in to traditional Gennepian documentations of these significant points in an individual's incorporation into and separation from his or her folk or family community). Pregnant women might even decide to make videos for their unborn children, or new mothers might decide to document early life for their rapidly growing children (as in a recent movie focusing on a young mother dying of cancer). With this blending of narratives, visual arts, family traditions and events, celebrations, and ceremonies, folklorists will have to categorize, name, and find ways of interpreting these blurred genres.

Another new development in genre might be named graphics lore, in which practitioners would draw upon the advances in medical and business technology (virtual reality) and interactive computer technology to pass along gestures, dramatize folktales (for themselves or their children), or create the puzzles and riddles that occasionally allowed pencil and paper historically to enter the domain of what was considered folk. Graphics lore will enable participants to see, hear, and feel their interaction with other human beings through machinery and with the machinery itself. This total immersion in a transformed folk experience, this sense of *being there,* will almost enable individuals to become self-contained folk communities, active participants in a variety of newly conceived folklore genres.

These speculative, though still concrete, dimensions of genre retain the urge for classification in their very conceptualization. Another direction for contemporary genre discussions, however, has embraced the theoretical bases that inform several other contemporary disciplines, especially literature. Postmodern literary theorists such as Linda Hutcheon have argued for a reevaluation of such disciplines as literature and history by theorizing the inseparability of the two. As a linguistic construction, history is a narrative that cannot contain objective truth; it can only approximate verisimilitude. Since novels similarly can only approximate verisimilitude instead of containing objective truth, the two disciplines conjoin in striking ways. Hutcheon (1988) coins the phrase "historiographic metafiction" to explore these complexities. Another postmodern theorist, Jonathan Culler, has posited the possibility of "nongenre" literature (1975:255). Such theorists challenge traditional divisions among literary genres and narrative in general; they have thereby significantly broadened what is possible in discussing written texts.

Borrowing from such endeavors, many folklorists, instead of naming and ordering new folkloristic items, are challenging the validity of the naming and ordering process itself. They realize that the impulse to separate inherently violates the richness and texturing of folkloric genres. For example, if a folktale contains an instance in which a query is posed as a riddle, it hardly makes sense, simply for purity of classification, to try to distinguish the riddle from the narrative. Similarly, if a riddle is expanded to take the shape of a folktale before it arrives at its intended destination, it is perhaps not a fruitful line of scholarly endeavor to separate and label it for the sake of labeling. Instead, folklorists such as John Dorst have drawn upon the works of P. N. Medvedev and M. M. Bakhtin to explore ways in which such intertwining might not be violated. Borrowing the concept of the dialogic from Bakhtin, Dorst (1983) and others suggest ways in which folklore genres are in dialogue with, interdependent upon, and ultimately inseparable from each other. This meeting of texts and the formation of various intertextual relationships provides a new site on which to approach questions of genre.

In their discussion "Genre, Intertextuality, and Social Power," Charles L. Briggs and Richard Bauman argue that "genre is quintessentially intertextual," that "all genres leak," and that folklorists need "an alternative view of genre, one that places generic distinctions not within texts but in the practices used in creating intertextual relations with other bodies of discourse" (1992:147, 149, 163). Such an alternative view would allow for engaged consideration of a written text, an oral representation or performance of that text, the intended interpretation at its moment of creation versus its contemporary context, the linguistic codes operative at its inception versus its contemporary meaning, past versus contemporary audiences, linguistic differences in performance, varying sites of performances, and varying performance successes or failures.[15] A single text, therefore, can have a variety of relationships to comparable texts and genres that have preceded it. It can breach genre classification and still retain intrinsic interest for scholars. It can also be affected by the posture that folklorists bring to it. For example, in the case of a song that contains a narrative, a folklorist might consider it as narrative, as song, or as the sum of the contextual meaning; the interpretive posture brought to bear can transform the concept of genre. Most of all, theoretical folkloristic interpretations emphasize that genres are made up of speech and language, with constantly increasing possibilities for examination of interactions, both internally and externally, of the item under consideration. These expanded ways of viewing genre reconnect some of the lines of demarcation between linguistics, literature, and anthropology as scholars share theoretical tools that transcend disciplinary boundaries.

From clarification to complexity to even greater complexity: that has been the path of genre application and discussion in folklore studies. So what, ultimately, is genre? From its humble beginning as a system of classification it has progressed to become the springboard for connecting folklore studies to several disciplines that emphasize the linguistic constructedness of all forms of discourse, from the shortest conversational exchange to the briefest construction of a riddle to the complicated construction of an epic. Language as the base of all genre is thereby independent of its own context and construction—not contained by the forms it takes, even as it is wedded to those origins. Theoretical linguistic focus on genre makes genres even more porous and even more a *site* for discussion than a containment of forms and classes.

Genre has become the matrix through which folklorists explore the complexity of creation and the speech acts human beings use to create—across history, cultures, and numerous tangible and intangible factors. With the theoretical concepts that folklorists have brought to bear upon genre, they have catapulted it to an intricacy of interpretive possibilities that seems almost infinite. Indeed, one might reasonably raise a question that some folklorists have hinted at previously: If genre is such an elusive or uncontainable concept, might folklorists not be well served by abandoning it altogether? Chances are that, in spite of its unwieldiness, they will not. Such an attempt would be comparable to asking people to forget that the sky is blue. They might be willing to accept that notion on particularly dark nights or when the sky is cloudy, but ultimately the sunshine would remind them of what they perceive as the natural state of things. For folklorists, genre provides the realm of familiarity, the base of the pyramid whose additional layers might not be formed according to the original plan but which nonetheless rest on recognizable grounds.[16] Genre remains the generally stable trampoline from which folklorists and budding folklorists can spring into the constantly changing future of folk-lore studies. For all its problematic connotations, genre has at least pro-vided folklorists with a basic common terminology and a basic system of classification.

The future of genre in folklore clearly lies in folklorists' embracing theoretical incursions upon traditional classification. Folklore as a dis-cipline is being redefined as a study of much more than static myths and legends, much more than variants of long-learned tales and jokes, much more than music lyrics and sites of performances, much more than iso-lated people with few commercial or technological resources interacting with each other. In contrast to earlier efforts to think of folklore studies as a science, that progression is certainly no longer realistic and perhaps no longer desirable. While the idea that genre was integral to science may have influenced the initial willingness of folklorists to adopt that system of classification, the ties quickly became less valuable. The study of folk-lore cannot be a science as long as dynamism supersedes stasis, as long as theoretical possibilities expand interpretation, and as long as creativ-ity and technology combine to ensure an ever-evolving subject area and ever-evolving ways of viewing it.

Notes

1. The essays included in this volume were originally published in *Genre* in 1969 and 1971; they were written by such illustrious folklorists as Francis Lee Utley, Harry Oster, Linda Dégh, Barre Toelken, and Roger D. Abrahams, among others.

2. I make absolutely no effort in this essay to refer to *every* folklore genre. I have selectively made choices to illustrate points in the larger issues with which folklorists contend in classifying the forms within a constantly evolv-ing discipline.

3. It will quickly become clear that any attempt to classify forms transmit-ted orally is problematic. While spirituals are perhaps closest to orality, hymns and gospels can be composed and written down, though oral "lining out" of hymns and the word-of-mouth transmission of previously recorded gospel songs complicate the issue.

4. Although Stith Thompson used the phrase "oral narrative" as early as 1955, it has been with the explosion of contemporary literary theory that the word *narrative* has gained wide usage among folklorists. Conferences on "narratology," a plethora of critical discussion of "narrative theory," and a general literary trend toward belief in the death of authors and focus on texts and the roles readers play in their shaping have influenced folklorists signifi-cantly. Contemporary literary theorists have also influenced the thinking of folklorists about genre. See Dorst 1983 and Abrahams 1985.

5. For a discussion of personal-experience narratives as a folklore genre, see Dégh 1985:37–54. Such reclassification means that *single individuals*, in their short-lived temporal experiences, have become as important as tradition in folklore studies.

6. See Ben-Amos 1976 for a review of the nuances of these discussions of genre across disciplinary and categorizing lines. See also the several papers from the Symposium on Myth that were published in the *Journal of American Folklore* 68:379–488. Among the scholars who contributed papers were David Bidney, Richard M. Dorson, Claude Lévi-Strauss, Lord Raglan, Stanley Edgar Hyman, and Stith Thompson (Bidney et al. 1955).

7. Roberts 1989 argues for an African influence on the thematic and heroic construction of the spirituals. See especially chapter 4.

8. In a general climate of challenges, some folklorists have been inspired to return to a reexamination of some of the traditional genres. See Stewart 1991:5–31.

9. For a discussion of the importance of disc jockeys, see Abrahams 1970.

10. See Dégh 1994. Dégh cites other folklorists from as early as 1969 who were also interested in the intersections between television and folklore genres.

11. My brother, Peter Harris, gave me a copy of "The Boss" in the mid-1970s when he was working in Arlington, Virginia, and I was on the faculty of the College of William and Mary in Williamsburg, Virginia. Abrahams 1970 also includes a much shorter version of the narrative, along with a headnote from Legman in which he identifies the Abrahams version as a "relic of an extremely ancient folktale," a version of which is included in *Arabian Nights*. See Abrahams 1970:214–15.

12. See Olrik 1965. See also Georges 1969.

13. For a discussion of how performance was viewed earlier, see Abrahams 1976:193–214. See also Hymes 1971 and Bauman 1975, 1977.

14. As I was searching through back issues of the *Journal of American Folklore* in preparation for writing this essay, I came across a recently published article relevant to my point here. See Koltyk 1993:435–49 on video documentation in Hmong communities. It is doubtful that such an article would have been published ten years ago.

15. For an extended discussion of how such factors can effect a particular genre, see Hanks 1987.

16. This recognition of the old in the new can be seen in several recently discussed genres that differ from traditional understandings of that concept. See Alexander 1992, Jones 1993, Smith 1984, Wachs 1982.

References Cited

Aarne, Antti, and Stith Thompson. 1961 [1928]. *The Types of the Folktale.* Helsinki: Suomalainen Tiedeakatemia.

Abrahams, Roger. 1970. *Deep Down in the Jungle: Negro Narrative Folklore from the Streets of Philadelphia.* Chicago: Aldine.

———. 1976. "The Complex Relations of Simple Forms." In *Folklore Genres.* Ed. Dan Ben-Amos. 193–214. Austin: University of Texas Press.

———. 1985. "A Note on Neck-Riddles in the West Indies as They Comment on Emergent Genre Theory." *Journal of American Folklore* 98:85–94.

Alexander, Tamar. 1992. "Theme and Genre: Relationships between Man and She-Demon in Jewish Folklore." *Jewish Folklore and Ethnology Review* 14:56–61.

Bain, Carl E., Jerome Beaty, and J. Paul Hunter. 1973. "The Elements of Poetry: Genres and Kinds." In *The Norton Introduction to Literature.* Ed. Carl E. Bain, Jerome Beaty, and J. Paul Hunter. 708–12. New York: Norton.

Baughman, Ernest W. 1966. *A Type and Motif-Index of the Folktales of England and North America.* Indiana University Publications Folklore Series no. 20. The Hague: Mouton.

Bauman, Richard. 1975. "Verbal Art as Performance." *American Anthropologist* 77:290–311.

———. 1977. *Verbal Art as Performance.* Prospect Heights, Ill.: Waveland Press.

Ben-Amos, Dan. 1976. *Folklore Genres.* Austin: University of Texas Press.

Bidney, David, et al. 1955. "Papers from Symposium on Myth." *Journal of American Folklore* 68:379–488.

Breuer, Lee. 1989. *The Gospel at Colonus.* New York: Theatre Communications Group.

Briggs, Charles L., and Richard Bauman. 1992. "Genre, Intertextuality, and Social Power." *Journal of Linguistic Anthropology* 2 (2): 131–72.

Brunvand, Jan Harold. 1968. *The Study of American Folklore: An Introduction.* New York: Norton.

Culler, Jonathan. 1975. *Structuralist Poetics: Structuralism, Linguistics, and the Study of Literature.* Ithaca: Cornell University Press.

Dégh, Linda. 1985. "'When I Was Six We Moved West': The Theory of Personal Experience Narrative." *New York Folklore* 11 (1–4): 37–54.

———. 1994. *American Folklore and the Mass Media.* Bloomington: Indiana University Press.

Dorst, John D. 1983. "Neck-Riddle as a Dialogue of Genres: Applying Bakhtin's Genre Theory." *Journal of American Folklore* 96:413–33.

Dundes, Alan. 1964. "Texture, Text, and Context." *Southern Folklore Quarterly* 28:252.

———. 1965. *The Study of Folklore.* Englewood Cliffs, N.J.: Prentice-Hall.

Georges, Robert A. 1969. "Toward an Understanding of Storytelling Events." *Journal of American Folklore* 82:313–28.

Hanks, William F. 1987. "Discourse Genres in a Theory of Practice." *American Ethnologist* 14:668–92.

Hutcheon, Linda. 1988. "'The Pastime of Past Time': Fiction, History, Historiographic Metafiction." In *Postmodern Genres.* Ed. Marjorie Perloff. 54–74. Norman: University of Oklahoma Press.

Hymes, Dell H. 1971. "The Contribution of Folklore to Sociolinguistic Research." *Journal of American Folklore* 84:42–50.

Jones, Steven Swann. 1993. "The Innocent Persecuted Heroine Genre: An Analysis of Its Structure and Themes." *Western Folklore* 52:13–41.

Koltyk, Jo Ann. 1993. "Telling Narratives though Home Videos: Hmong Refugees and Self-Documentation of Life in the Old and New Country." *Journal of American Folklore* 106:435–49.

Newell, William Wells. 1906. "Individual and Collective Characteristics of Folk-lore." *Journal of American Folklore* 19:1–15.

Olrik, Axel. 1965. "Epic Laws of Folk Narrative." In *The Study of Folklore.* Ed. Alan Dundes. 129–41. Englewood Cliffs, N.J.: Prentice-Hall.

Propp, Vladimir. 1975 [1928]. *Morphology of the Folktale.* Austin: University of Texas Press.

Roberts, John W. 1989. *From Trickster to Badman: The Black Folk Hero in Slavery and Freedom.* Philadelphia: University of Pennsylvania Press.

Smith, Moira. 1984. "The Kernel Story: A New Conversational Genre?" *Folklore Forum* 17:199–207.

Stewart, Susan. 1991. "Notes on Distressed Genres." *Journal of American Folklore* 104:5–31.

Thompson, Stith. 1946. *The Folktale.* New York: Dryden Press.

———. 1955a. *Motif-Index of Folk-Literature: A Classification of Narrative Elements in Folktales, Ballads, Myths, Fables, Mediaeval Romances, Exempla, Fabliaux, Jest-Books, and Local Legends.* Bloomington: Indiana University Press.

———. 1955b. "Myths and Folktales." *Journal of American Folklore* 68:482–88.

Tompkins, Jane. 1992. *West of Everything: The Inner Life of Westerns.* New York: Oxford University Press.

Utley, Francis Lee. 1965. "Folk Literature: An Operational Definition." In *The Study of Folklore.* Ed. Alan Dundes. 7–24. Englewood Cliffs, N.J.: Prentice-Hall.

van Gennep, Arnold. 1960 [1928]. *The Rites of Passage.* Chicago: University of Chicago Press.

Wachs, Eleanor. 1982. "The Crime-Victim Narrative as Folkloric Genre." *Journal of the Folklore Institute* 19:17–30.

DEBORAH A. KAPCHAN

5   *Performance*

> If music affects snakes, it is not on account of the spiri-
> tual notions it offers them, but because snakes are long
> and coil their length upon the earth, because their bod-
> ies touch the earth at almost every point; and because
> the musical vibrations which are communicated to the
> earth affect them like a very subtle, very long massage;
> and I propose to treat the spectators like the snake-
> charmer's subjects and conduct them *by means of their
> organisms* to an apprehension of the subtlest notions.
> —Artaud
>
> What seems paradoxical about everything that is justly
> called beautiful is the fact that it appears.
> —Benjamin

To perform is a transitive verb. Grammatically, this means
that the verb *perform* takes a direct object, relating one element or property to another. One performs something, a theater piece (a drama, a
comedy, a farce, a tragedy), a musical score, a ritual, a critique, a sales
spiel. And this piece, this work, is performed by someone—an actor, a
man, a woman, an herbalist, a hermaphrodite, a queen, a slave. Relating
subject to object, to perform is also to facilitate transition. There is an
agentive quality to performance, a force, a playing out of identities and
histories. "Everything in human behavior indicates that we perform our
existence, especially our social existence," writes Schechner (1982:14).
To perform is to act in the fullest sense of the word.

Performance is not a text—or, rather, not *merely* a text. Performance
is so intricately bound up with the nonverbal attributes of sound, taste,
shape, color, and weight that it cannot be verbally mapped—only allud-

ed to, only invoked. It is apprehended by means of the organism, as Artaud proposes. Intricately connected to form, performance is the fullness of history as it is *shaped* in the moment. It is a materialization—of emotion, of mind, of spirit. What seemed to Benjamin "the wonder of appearance" may be also regarded as the wonder of performance.

Familiarity with such form reassures us. We know, for example, that the shepherd's play is performed every year at Christmastime (Flores 1994) or that on the day of the Great Feast (*'aid l-kabir*), every male head of household in Morocco will sacrifice a sheep when returning home from morning prayers at the mosque (Combs-Schilling 1989). Yet the seeming reliability of the form is a deception, promising repetition yet producing evanescence. For a performance is different every time it is enacted. Each performance emerges from different historical configurations (Bauman 1977); reading performances over time, we are also reading history.

As analysts, we want to seize performance, to make it stand still. We press to memorialize it, to document it for the record. In an act akin to murder, we transform performance into a text and display it as an object somehow out of time. We carve out its bounds and limits and thereby create "a historical moment." We become taxidermists, mounting, naming, and numbering it. Some would even like to breathe new life into the beast. But once a performance has been turned into a text, the original is, in fact, dead, its simulacrum fit only for a museum or a book.

Entextualizing Performances

WHY THE DESIRE TO CAPTURE AND POSSESS PERFORMANCE?

Transforming a performance into a text available for analysis involves its objectification. As objects, performances can be studied, interpreted, and, in an illusory sort of way, controlled. But there are other, less hegemonic reasons to render performances as texts. In their function as either preservers or reshapers of tradition, social performances are indexes of social transformation. Freezing the frames of such performative moments and comparing them to one another over time, it is possible to understand how individuals and collectivities create their local or national identities and how events such as civic celebrations, pageants, parades, and other crowd rituals define social movements (Abrahams 1987); it is also possible to perceive permutations in these modes of identity creation.

Some performances mark their own limits—fairy tales, for example, begin with "once upon a time" and end with "and they lived happily ever after." The oral tale can be lifted from its context of utterance and transported to other locations—a child's bedroom, a fireside, a theater—or it can be made into a text, "entextualized," to use the term of Bauman and Briggs (1990), and thus become available for other usages and interpretations. Other performances have fuzzier boundaries (Briggs 1988) and are more intimately linked to their context of utterance. Where does gossip begin and end, for example? How is the performance of gender identity enacted in daily life? As Briggs notes, "most of the meaning of performance would be lost if equal weight was not accorded to the manner in which performative and nonperformative modes intermingle as well as the way they are distinct" (Briggs 1988:17). Accordingly, Hymes devotes careful attention to moments within a text where there is a "breakthrough into performance" (1975). Understanding where, when, and why this breakthrough happens, we also understand important aspects of a culture's aesthetics.

Performances are not only verbal. Because of this, writing about performance brings us to the limits of representation. How represent a gesture in words? How represent desire or anger? "All true feeling is in reality untranslatable," notes Artaud (1970:71). "To express it is to betray it. But to translate it is to *dissimulate* it." Writing about performance is always a sort of fabrication, an attempt to recapture a presence forever lost (see Derrida 1978). "To report it back, to record and repeat it, is at once to transform it and to fuel the desire for its mimetic return. Writing is a substitute for the failure of this return [of performance]," says Phelan (1993a:19). The transcribed performance, then, provides only a systematized approximation, one that, like a musical score, operates on many levels, moves in many directions, but does not sing. Transcription is what Fine calls "inter-semiotic translation" (1984), emphasizing the shift from one system of meaning to another.

Transcriptions of performance, however, can *evoke* the original fairly closely, documenting certain cultural phenomena. Take, for example, the following transcription based on Tedlock's formulation of an "open text," a text that, although it cannot reproduce the performance it transcribes, nonetheless "captures a particular configuration of contour and timing that occurs just once in just one audible text" (1983:7). The text represents a sales spiel by a female herbalist-orator in the contemporary open-air marketplace in Morocco. Dressed conventionally in a djellaba and head scarf, she is seated on a small mat under an umbrella, her back against the side of an old car. A microphone is strapped to her wrist and her voice is magnified with the movements of her hand. Her audience consists of about twenty men and women, some squatting down next to her in a small semicircle and others standing behind them.

> This little bit that I'm going to give you
> what is it used for?
> BY GOD I won't tell you what it's used for until you ask "what?"
> > *What is it used for, alalla?*
> BY GOD I didn't hear you!
> > *What is it used for?*
> Listen to what I'm going to tell you
> and REMEMBER my words . . .
> First, give me the one that's going like this [she holds her side and
> > puts on a pained expression]
> And the one who has destroyed his own liver.
> He complains about his back bone.
> He's screaming about these [she motions to the groin area].
> Half of THIS has died on him [another arm motion to the lower
> > abdomen].
> He's sick and tired.
> Desire is dead.
> You're no longer a man.
> Remember what I'm saying
> well, I'M TALKING TO YOU!
> You get up four or five times a night.
> You can't hold your urine.
> Go ask about me in El Ksiba [a nearby mountain village]—
> lines from here to there.
> You spend the night going in and out.
> The woman with a stinking uterus.
> You're no longer a man.
> The prostitute owns you
> but your face is shy.
> If I let some doctor examine your body,
> between me and you,
> the one who we all share is the Messenger of God.
> *Prayers and peace be upon him.*
> You're a witness to God.
> You're a witness to God.
> You're a witness to God.
> You're a witness to God.
> You're a witness to God.
>
> had shwiya lli ghadi n-'ti-k lash y-liq?
> wa-llahi ma-n-gul li-kum lash y-liq hta t-gul-u ntuma "lash."
> *'lash y-liq alalla?*
> ULLAHI ma sma't-kum!
> *'lash y-liq?*

sma' ash ghadya n-gul w 'qal 'la klam-i . . .
l-ltwla 'ti-ni dak lli y-təm ghadi . . .
udak lli had b-l-idd dyal-u l-klawi.
y-t-shəka b-l-'amud l-fiqari.
had-u y-ghawət bi-hum.
n-nas hada mat 'li-h.
had-u zhaf bi-hum.
n-nafs matət.
ma bqitish rajəl.
'qal ash kan-gul, rani KAN-TKALLəM MA'K.
t-nud rub'a, khmsat l-marrat f-l-lilla.
l-bul ma t-shədi-h.
sir suwwəl 'liya f-l-had dyal l-qsiba,
rah s-sərbis ħna u ħna.
t-bat, dakhəl kharəj.
mra khanza li-ha l-walda.
ma bqitish rajəl
l-qaħba malka-k, as-sifa mərgat.
ila n-khali shi ṭ-ṭbib baqi y-kshəf 'la dat- ək,o
bin-i u bin-ək,lli mshark-na kamlin, huwa rasul ḷḷah.
ṣalla ḷḷah 'l-ih wa salləm.
sh-shahadat-ḷḷah.
sh-shahadat-ḷḷah.
sh-sh'ahadat-ḷḷah.
sh-shahadat-ḷḷah.
sh-shahadat-ḷḷah.

An open text, this stretch of discourse transcribes as much of the voice and sensory qualities of the performance as possible. Loudness, emphasis, rhythm, and phrasing are noted in punctuation. Textually marked pauses and changes in intonation evoke the jocularity of the performance. Phrasing emphasizes the parallel nature of the discourse, its artistry and rhythm. What is not captured, however, is the *history* that permeates these words, and the ways in which the performance breaks taboos.

Performing History

The Moroccan herbalist's performance exemplifies the limits of transcription. Although marketplace discourse is notoriously bawdy (subjects often revolving around the ills, excesses, and desires of the body), up until recently only men had social license to engage in it. Nothing in the transcribed performance indicates this, however. Without understanding the history of open-air performances in the public realm, we cannot fully appreciate the import of the herbalist's gestural vocabulary as she directs the attention of onlookers to different areas of their bodies, pointing to her own "lower bodily strata" instead of referring to body parts that are taboo. The herbalist *acts out* afflictions related to sexuality, using deictic markers that anchor the discourse in her body and in the sensations of her audience. We do not know from the textual rendition of this performance that the herbalist manages to break most of the rules that govern feminine behavior in the public domain. What we do know is that audience members not only participate verbally and vicariously in this performance but are made morally responsible for its later recounting, as the herbalist points to specific people and designates them "witnesses to God" (Islamic law requires twelve witnesses, or *shahid*, and their testimony to establish a fact). Requiring the participation of her audience (their co-performance), her discourse adds a new genre of feminine behavior into the repertoire of social practices (Kapchan 1996).

In a performed discourse such as the one above, only attention to the historical relations between performance texts (their intertextuality) reveals the density of their meaning. Whereas the herbalist has borrowed many strategies for establishing her public authority from extant texts in the male canon, she embodies, and revoices, these texts differently, effecting and responding to changes in *social practice* that lie outside the text. Examining the mimetic elements of a performance, such as reported speech or adopted formulas, and the use of parallelism, repetition, and other formal patterns (Sherzer 1990) reveals how performance traditions are both maintained and changed, or reinvented (Hobsbawm and Ranger 1983). Although transcription practices like the one advocated by Tedlock manage to document some of the more ephemeral and affective qualities of a performance, they must be supplemented by close attention not only to history but also to social conditions (like gender relations) that inform it.

Embodying Performance

Techniques such as those just described for verbal art have existed in music for a long time. And whereas musical notation has been criticized as a system that does not fully capture the affective quality of a composition, especially the improvisatory aspects of jazz and non-European musics, few would question its efficacy as a tool for analysis. Indeed, Farnell observes that although ethnographers are quite literate in linguistic and musical analysis, most are poorly schooled in the realm of movement. This state of affairs, she says, can be attributed to Western philosophical biases, which separate mind (language, audition, and visual objectification) from body (processual movement, gesture, dance). If the marketplace discourse transcribed above were accompanied by a record of the herbalist's movements, for example, the analysis would clearly show how her bodily positions and gesticulations break with those of other women in the public sphere and resemble those associated with men. "What is required," Farnell asserts, "is a script that will provide the means to become literate in relation to the medium of movement just as we have been able to achieve literacy in relation to spoken language and music. By 'literacy', I mean the ability to read and write movement so that translation into the medium of words is unnecessary for creating ethnographically appropriate descriptions of actions" (1990:937). Although several systems have been developed for the transcription of movement, Farnell employs Labanotation (a script written from the actor's perspective rather than from that of the viewer), asserting that it is the most nuanced means of documenting phenomena such as sign language, gesture, and the spatial orientation and import of performance more generally. "The breakthrough that is represented by a movement script . . . is that it provides the means to *think* and analyze in terms of movement itself" (ibid., emphasis added). For Farnell, understanding movement in ritual, dance, and daily life first requires the analyst to be aware of movement as a form of knowledge and then to have a system that can render this knowledge intelligible to oneself and to others.

> At the present time, it seems paradoxical that while many anthropologists, linguists and folklorists are engaged in the expansion of the parameters of what counts as language and grammar, encapsulated in the phrase 'breakthrough into performance' (Bauman 1977 [Hymes 1975]), those of us involved in an anthropology of human movement are at the same time attempting an equally exciting breakthrough from performance—into literacy. Also paradoxical is the fact that only in the process of encoding movement into a script, which removes it from the flow of 'real' time, can movement actually be retained in records rather than being lost in a no-man's-land through its depiction as successive, static positions. (Farnell 1990:965)

These techniques form part of the scientific move in anthropological analysis to objectify the subject being studied (even when that subject is one's own movement). Thus they participate in an ideology that holds objective truth or reality as a model and strives to translate that truth into another rational system with the goal of fully apprehending and, often, controlling it. Performance is rendered as text; movement becomes a graph of detailed symbols on a page or computer screen; music, likewise, is transcribed according to its own semiotic system, one that only trained "readers" can understand. And even in our everyday communications, media, speech, and movement must be placed at a distance, defamiliarized, if we are to fully appreciate them. Labanotation does for movement what Tedlock's system does for words—it translates one sign system into another so that the properties of one system, properties so naturalized in the case of speech and movement as to be virtually invisible, become manifest and open to analysis.

Another way of understanding a performance is to experience it viscerally (we rarely have the choice not to) and then reenact it on its own terms—that is, imitate it. Some scholars have called this the mimetic function (Taussig 1993), noting the important role it plays in cultural reproduction. Such a repetition of semiotic signs may involve a critical response to power relations; sometimes it is simply so excessive that it unintentionally mocks, or at least marks and throws into cultural relief, the object imitated. Mimesis, however, may also be an ethnographic tool (see K. Stewart 1996). "Mimeticism," notes Michael Jackson, "based upon a bodily awareness of the other in oneself, thus assists in bringing into relief a reciprocity of viewpoints" (1989:130). Conquergood echoes this sentiment, stating that "ethnography is an *embodied practice*; it is an intensely sensuous way of knowing. The embodied researcher is the instrument" (1991:180). Using his or her body as the medium for another kind of knowing, the ethnographer engages in a process Sklar calls "kinesthetic empathy" (1994; see also Foster 1995). Embracing the bodily dispositions—the gestures and postures—of others, we provoke emotions in ourselves that give us a better understanding of a different kind of lived experience.

Beyond the Text: *Performance Ethnography*

The work of performance ethnographer Joni Jones exemplifies this approach; for her, "performance ethnography is how the body does culture" (Jones 1996:132). Jones therefore translates her ethnographic experiences into plays, asking, "Can performance stand alongside print and film as ethnographic documentation? What does performance reveal that print may obscure, and vice versa?" (137). For Jones and other performance-oriented ethnographers influenced by the experimental theaters of Schechner (1982) and Victor Turner (1990), performance is a means to confront the complexity and often the contradictions of the ethnographic enterprise: "The initial ethnographic experience is a collision with the self," notes Jones, "an exercise in shifting the self from center to periphery. The ethnographer confronts the constructions of the other created prior to contact and the ways in which those constructions are intimately linked

with the construction of self. For me, as a Pan-Africanist African American ethnographer doing fieldwork in Africa, the cultural collision de-
railed both constructions" (Jones 1996:133).

> From the play *Broken Circles:*
> *Joni the Ethnographer:* And I had to ask myself,
> was I really making friends,
> or was I making deals?
> laughs How about this for my next article!
> *video footage begins that reads,*
> "'Cultural Exchange'
> by Dr. Joni Jones
> B.S., M.A., Ph.D., D.S.T.
> (Desperately Seeking Tenure)
> After three weeks of study
> among the Yoruba of
> Southwestern Nigeria
> I learned . . .
> How to get scholarly
> articles in refereed
> nationally recognized
> journals,
> the respect of my peers,
> and tenure;
> and they get
> a ticket to the land
> they think brings them
> easy material wealth."
> video footage ends
> *Joni the Ethnographer:* In this context, who were we to each other?
> Was he [Michael Oludare, Yoruba artist] merely the subject of my
>   American publish-or-perish ritual and an unwilling partner in
>   the dance of African American romanticizing
> of Africa?
> Was I merely his American meal ticket to the good life America
>   offers in his own
> romantic visions of America?
> In short, did we both see each other as a means to a financial end?
> Probably more so than I care to admit. (Jones 1996)

This short excerpt from Jones's work demonstrates the reflexive
nature of performance as well as its ability to negotiate the ambiguities
of cultural interaction. Jones does not become the Other simply because
she performs otherness; yet her embodiment of difference allows for a
more visceral understanding of the ethnographic project.

From the various perspectives on performance examined thus far, we may glean the following common denominators: (1) Performance is public; it needs an audience, whether that audience be a group of theatergoers, a single child, or an invisible spirit. Performance assumes community and communication. (2) Performance is set apart from practice. It is thus appropriable; unable to "speak" for itself because it is more than text, it is always interpreted or misinterpreted. (3) Performance is participative. Because of its public nature, performance engages its audience to varying degrees, depending on its context. (4) Performance is transformative; like metaphor, it moves its participants to another social or affective state (see Fernandez 1986).

PERFORMANCE IS PUBLIC

Performance is an element of many different genres of cultural behavior, from highly formalized ritual to improvisatory theater, from political speeches to laments. Each of these performance genres functions differently from the others, though all actively create social and individual identities in the public domain.

In ritual life, for example, performances encode and transmit the core values of society, implanting ideologies such as religion, patriarchy, and social hierarchy in the very bones of children, in their flesh and breath. In ritual both the public and the participative aspect of performance is highlighted. Rituals involve a repertoire of emotional and aesthetic phenomena, the understanding of which brings us to a deeper comprehension of what constitutes self and society. Indeed, many scholars see a correlation between different kinds of performance and different definitions, or experiences, of selfhood. Abrahams's theories of performance, for example, regard performance genres as existing on an arc, running the gamut from "the pole of interpersonal involvement [ritual] to that of complete removal [theatrical monologue], [wherein] the embodiment of movement becomes progressively formal and performer-oriented, more reliant upon symbol, imagination, and vicarious involvement of audience" (1976:207; see Fernandez 1986). Schechner in his early work also delineates genres of performance according to different subjective stances. What he calls the "self-assertive 'I'" (what might be referred to as the ego) inheres in the performance of *play*; the "social 'We'" dominates in *games, sports,* and *theater*; whereas the "self-transcendent 'Other'" is the domain of *ritual* (1969:86–87; see Urban 1989). Both scholars find inspiration in the work of Victor Turner, for whom all social drama exists on a continuum, beginning with ritual, which enacts "la vie sérieuse," often unconsciously (Durkheim, quoted in V. Turner 1974:64), and extending to self-conscious drama and play. As Sherzer has emphasized, attention to language *play* is a central concern insofar as the ludic contains a high level of metadiscourse and social critique (Sherzer 1993; see also Bateson 1972; Kirshenblatt-Gimblett 1975).

In ritual performances linguistic formalism "is combined with other types of formalism in which speech, singing, gesture and dance are bound together in a compositional whole. . . . An event which did not contain all these elements would probably not be described by anthropologists as ritual; it is these features taken together that are ritual's distinguishing mark" (Connerton 1989:60).

PERFORMANCE IS SET APART FROM PRACTICE

The notion of self-consciousness asserts itself over and over in the works of performance analysts (Bateson 1972; Babcock 1977b). Certainly, to examine genres marked as set apart from the flow of everyday life—or, as Goffman puts it, "framed" (Goffman 1974)—provides special insight into the system of aesthetics recognized by those who take part in it. Musical, dramatic, or theatrical performances in particular offer an aspect of reflexive distance that allows the actor and audience to step back from social experience in the very act of embracing it. Keeler, for example, notes the importance of studying aesthetic phenomena already marked as "art" or "performance": "An art form," he asserts, "provides us indigenously generated representations of people's lives while still constituting a part of those lives. Both observed and lived, and so both a representation of social life and an instance of it, a performance provides a commentary upon interaction and yet also exemplifies it" (Keeler 1987:262). Implicit in Keeler's astute rendering of the art form's double function is the observation that performance is not only a specular event but a way of inhabiting the world. Keeler proposes to analyze performance as a place where different forms of social relationships converge, where aesthetics, sociology, and ideology meet (17–18). Intercultural performances (those composed of the traditions of two or more cultures or those enacted by one culture and interpreted by another) require the analyst to acknowledge other ways of knowing and being and to understand how these epistemological and ontological practices are in turn interpreted by those who engage in them.

It is impossible to talk about performative and public identities without talking about genre, as the two depend on and define each other. Performances materialize and are recognized within generic bounds. Thus political oratory is distinguishable from a sales spiel because each genre employs conventionally appropriate rhetorical strategies, formulas, citations, and symbols within conventional temporal and spatial contexts of

locution. History, its categories and valuations, is embedded in the web
of sign relations that compose genre. As an institution (think of the State
of the Union address), genre is always informed by an ideology (if not
several), invoking the words of others in order to establish genre as well
as genealogical authority—that is, the authority of historical precedent
(Bakhtin 1984a; Bauman 1992; Gal 1990; Irvine 1982). The empirical reality of genre imposes itself in the world, as does its tendency to spin out
from itself, etiolating its own boundaries, feeding on its own excess, and
metamorphosing into other forms. Nonetheless, a genre is a social con-
tract (Jameson 1981) on the level of both form and content. It is in this
spirit that Bauman defined performance as "responsibility to an audience
for a display of communicative competence" (1977:11). This display,
however, need not always bow to the law; indeed, performance genres
are often in deliberate and flagrant breach of genre convention, mixing
frames and blurring boundaries so that tradition and authority are put into
question and redefined (Geertz 1983).

Frequently sites of political struggle, performance genres are intertextual fields where the politics of identity are negotiated (Caton 1990;
Feld 1990; Tsing 1993). Describing the South African performance genre
of *isicathamiya*, a capella choir singing, for example, Erlmann notes the
important relation between the temporal and spatial frame within which
performances occur and the content of the performances themselves:

> nighttime sets *isicathamiya* apart from the flow of ordinary events dur-
> ing daytime, which is largely shaped by forces outside the migrants' con-
> trol: train schedules, time clocks, pass laws that determine when one is
> allowed to be in a certain place and for how long, and so on. If daytime
> belongs to the realm of work and the exigencies of physical survival,
> nighttime is playtime. "Nightsong" performances, then, construct "priv-
> ileged operational zones" (Boon 1973), relatively unpatrolled and unmon-
> itored locations, which temporarily protect the participants from outside
> intervention by the hegemonic order while enabling the playful negoti-
> ation of alternative images of social order. (Erlmann 1992:693)

In situations where territory and its appropriation are contested, live
and mediated performance genres become particularly charged with political import as polyphonic symbols of identity and power. This is not
to celebrate performance as a mode of liberation, however. As Fabian
notes in his study of Zairean theater, "the kind of performances we find
in popular culture have become for the people involved more than ever
ways to preserve some self-respect in the face of constant humiliation,
and to set the wealth of artistic creativity against an environment of ut-

ter poverty" (1990:19). In such contexts, performance is resistance. Conversely, however, performance genres such as anthems, national dances, or state and religious rites may invoke metanarratives that idealize unity, purity, and freedom in the service of monologic discourses of oppression (Lyotard 1992). What studies such as Fabian's recognize is the intimate relation between performance and the creation of public worlds of influence. Attending to performance, we attend to the way social organization is effected—from the structures of selfhood to the structures of community, nation, and beyond.

Performance illuminates how material and discursive practices mediate the varying degrees of attraction or repulsion with which individuals and groups are invested within an "economy of performance" (Bruner and Kirshenblatt-Gimblett 1994) that is increasingly politicized as cultures and identities are appropriated, commodified, and essentialized, ultimately becoming objects of both disgust and desire.

PERFORMANCE IS PARTICIPATIVE

Performance relies on an audience; indeed, inherent in the concept of audience or audition is the sound wave, which, traveling invisibly, affects everyone with whom it comes in contact. No performance fails to resonate with its auditors in this fashion. As Artaud notes in the epigraph to this chapter, transmitted vibrations communicate the subtlest notions. But the waves do not travel in only one direction. Rather, they spiral in a dialogic dance of interactive forces.

Performance is always an exchange—of words, energy, emotion, and material. Phelan talks about this exchange as a relation of love and desire; performing our identities and longings, we seek an unattainable "Real Love"; writing our desires and their failures, we perform a sort of compensatory love song. "The challenge raised by the ontological claims of performance for writing," she notes, "is to re-mark again the performative possibilities of writing itself" (1993b:148).

For Flores, by contrast, performance emerges from a material exchange, the product of what he terms "the labor of performance" (Flores 1994:277). Building on Limon's insight that the oppositional quality of folklore inheres in the process of gift giving, Flores delineates performance as both a *gift* that obliges reciprocity and creates sociability and a *commodity* whose value resides in the material object alone, alienable from its producers and the process of its production. Flores convincingly demonstrates how different contexts of performance create different social relations. For their presentation of the *Los Pastores* shepherd's play before a local audience in the San Antonio, Texas, barrio, for example, the actors were paid little, but the performers and the audience gathered together after the show to share food in an atmosphere of mutual goodwill, creating a spontaneous community of performance that reposed on shared values. In a paid performance for tourists sponsored by the San Antonio Conservation Society, on the other hand, the same performers, though far better compensated for their labor, were highly dissatisfied with the nature of the short-term commodity exchange, which led to no enduring bonds of reciprocal obligation or sociability.

Although both performances of *Los Pastores* represented a form of exchange, the first one made the audience "co-participants" in the event to a much greater extent than did the second (Brenneis 1986; Duranti 1986). The exchange in the first instance was built on a mutual affection not bounded by the frame of the performance itself. Speaking of social life in the central Nepalese town of Bhatgaon, Brenneis remarks that performances often function as enactments of social coherence: "Public performance—verbal, musical, ritual—is an achievement," he says, "often allowing times of negotiated social order and sociability in an otherwise very flexible world" (1987:239). Indeed, there are times when the exchange between performers and audience goes so deep that no distinction can be made between them. As Noyes notes in a recent examination of the Patum festival of northern Spain's Berga, for example,

> communal action creates a shared reality, and over time, a fund of common experience: it makes mutual understanding at some level possible. Consensus, as James Fernandez has noted, is etymologically con-sensus, feeling together (1988:1–2). The Patum's intensity of performance brings the individual's senses into concert to receive strong impressions. Near-universal Patum participation in Berga guides the senses of the entire community in the same direction, obliges them to feel together in a way that their divided everyday experience can never foster. (Noyes 1993:138)

Turner called this consensus, this "feeling together," *communitas* and noted that it was most often experienced in liminal moments of transition from one symbolic domain to another, such as first marriage rites, when everyday rules give way to other, sometimes dramatically different norms, or "anti-structures" (V. Turner 1969; see Babcock 1977a).

PERFORMANCE IS TRANSFORMATIVE

To such liminal activity, which, although involving license and the suspension of normative codes of behavior (antistructure), eventually serves to reinforce social codes (structure), Turner has opposed "liminoid" events, ludic enactments characteristic of postmodernism, such as large-scale festivals, that actually have the power to subvert social structures. In light of this distinction, it is not surprising that much contemporary writing on the transformative power of performance concerns experimental and avant-garde theater (Carr 1993; Hart and Phelan 1993; Miller 1995; Schechner 1993). Since performance is agentive—that is, it either repeats or enacts change in the world—many pressing political actions are taken in the aesthetic domain of the avant-garde. As Grotowski notes, "Art is profoundly rebellious. Bad artists *speak* of rebelling; real artists *actually* rebel. They respond to the powers that be with a concerted act: this is both the most important and the most dangerous point. Real rebellion in art is something that persists and is competent and never dilettante" (1968). Thus it is no wonder that many scholars of contemporary performance are examining feminist and avant-garde performance art—self-conscious art forms that challenge conventional social practices and worn-out gender ideologies.

What is feminist performance? Where and how is it performed? And by whom? To begin with, feminist performance is imbricated in identity politics. Hart notes that identity is like "a prosthesis or an armor that one must wear in order to be understood. Identities are necessary if we are to live in reality, but they mask our desire. Feminist identities [by contrast] embrace the monstrous possibilities of acting out. Cutting ourselves off from 'reality' can be a way to escape our inundation in *a* masculine imaginary that passes as *the* symbolic order" (Hart and Phelan 1993:2). Feminist performance, in other words, accords women a space to rewrite themselves and the cultural texts that have defined them. And the feminist critique of performance brings the dominant cultural scripts to light, illuminating both how they oppress women and how women counter (or do not counter) that oppression. Studying feminist performance "is in part motivated by the desire to displace the dominance of text-based work in theater studies, to value the ephemerality of performance" (Hart and Phelan 1993:4). For the feminist critic Dolan, for example, "a feminist inquiry into representation as a form of cultural analysis [explores how a] given performance—the dialogue, choice of setting, narrative voice, form, content, casting, acting, blocking—deliver[s] its ideological message." Her intent, Dolan says, is "to uncover ideological meanings that otherwise go unnoticed and continue to perpetuate cultural assumptions that are oppressive to women and other disenfranchised social groups" (1988:17–18).

Time, Emergence, and the Performance of Ethnography

Performance has much in common with the enterprise of ethnography (Fabian 1990; Stoller 1994; Turner and Turner 1982). Both are framed activities concerned with giving meaning to experience. Both may use strategies of mimetic reproduction to create the illusion of a natural context that makes the audience forget the staging of artifice. Both may also break this facade in order to jar the audience into reflexive awareness. Both involve an exchange. Performance, like ethnography, is palpable, arising in worlds of sense and symbol. Ethnography, like performance, is intersubjective, depending on an audience, community, or group to which it is responsible, however heterogeneous its members may be (Bauman 1977; cf. Ben-Amos 1993; Hymes 1975). In its concern with a self-critical methodology that takes account of its effects in the world, ethnography is first and foremost performative—aware of itself as part of a dynamic process from which meaning is emergent, not preexistent and forever etched in stone.

Bauman noted the importance of the emergent in verbal art in 1977, stating that "completely novel and completely fixed texts represent the poles of an ideal continuum, and that between the poles lies the range of emergent text structures to be found in empirical performance" (1977:40). In his later work, "fixed" texts become those that try to closely imitate a historical precedent in what he calls, following Hymes, an act of "traditionalization" (Bauman 1992; see also Briggs and Bauman 1992). Texts that distinguish themselves from prior texts make a claim to novelty or hybridity (Kapchan 1993). The emergent in cultural phenomena, however, is what is unpredictable and indeterminate. Focusing on the emergent in situated expression means identifying the points at which performances challenge or play with tradition in order to inscribe a politics of difference onto the cultural landscape (Appadurai 1990).

Relating the concept to the process of ethnography, Marcus defines emergence as a "temporal dimension" of indeterminacy necessary for cultural analysis. Emergence becomes an imagined ethnographic space of hybridity:

> The time-space or chronotope in terms of which this imaginary is constructed in ethnography rests on evoking a temporal dimension of emergence in terms of which global-local processes, as objects of study, are unfolding as they are studied. Such a temporality guarantees a felicitous and liberating indeterminacy. Studying something emergent does not place the onus of prediction upon the scholar, nor does it imply futurism associated with strong utopic or dystopic visions, nor does it embed

perspective in an historical metanarrative in which the terms of description are largely given. In effect, emergence is precisely the temporal dimension that "hedges bets," so to speak, that guarantees the qualified, contingent hopefulness that, as noted, the cautious, critical moralism of work in cultural studies seeks. (1994:426)

The concept of emergence may be an ethnographic safety net of sorts but it need not erase history or its contingencies. Fabian (1983) has already noted the necessity of coevality in the joint production of ethnographic knowledge. For Fabian, ethnographies are coproduced performances that emerge "as a result of a multitude of actors working together to give form to experiences, ideas, feelings, projects" (1990:13). Ethnography, then, performs the analysis of the emergent. In an attempt to track social change, performance studies stand attentive to vagaries of cultural change.

Performing Analysis

A definition marks a boundary, an inside and an outside, a limit. Performances do the same; they say, this is X—a nation, a folk group, a human being, a woman, a jinn. But performances, like definitions, also challenge boundaries, speaking their contradictions into being. Thus performance is a form whose contents are as fluid as ether, as pliant as clay; like the body, performance is ever emergent, never fixed, yet it partakes of a shared real—odor, sound, density, shape—that is ultimately unrepresentable. Performances are cultural enactments (Abrahams 1977); they appeal to all our senses, recalling us not only to our bodies and selves, not only to the subjectivities of others, but to the perpetual task of limit making, where we balance on the edge of the imaginary and the real. It is the task of performance to pivot on this border and to pluck the tense string of difference between the two realms, sending sound waves out in all directions.

References Cited

Abrahams, Roger D. 1976. "Genre Theory and Folkloristics." *Studia Fennica* 20:13–19.
———. 1977. "Toward an Enactment-Centered Theory of Folklore." In *Frontiers of Folklore*. Ed. William Bascom. 79–120. Boulder, Colo.: Westview Press.
———. 1983. *The Man-of-Words in the West Indies: Performance and the Emergence of Creole Culture*. Baltimore: Johns Hopkins University Press.
———. 1985. "A Note on Neck-Riddles in the West Indies as They Comment on Emergent Genre Theory." *Journal of American Folklore* 98:85–94.

———. 1986. "Ordinary and Extraordinary Experience." In *The Anthropology of Experience.* Ed. Victor W. Turner and Edward M. Bruner. 45–72. Urbana: University of Illinois Press.

———. 1987. "An American Vocabulary of Celebration." In *Time Out of Time.* Ed. Alessandro Falassi. 175–83. Albuquerque: University of New Mexico Press.

Abu-Lughod, Lila. 1986. *Veiled Sentiments: Honor and Poetry in a Bedouin Society.* Berkeley: University of California Press.

———. 1993. *Writing Women's Worlds: Bedouin Stories.* Berkeley: University of California Press.

Anderson, Benedict R. O. 1983. *Imagined Communities: Reflections on the Origin and Spread of Nationalism.* London: Verso Press.

Appadurai, Arjun. 1990. "Disjuncture and Difference in the Global Cultural Economy." *Public Culture* 2 (2): 1–24.

———. 1991. "Afterword." In *Gender, Genre, and Power in South Asian Expressive Tradition.* Ed. Arjun Appadurai, F. J. Korom, and M. A. Mills. 467–76. Philadelphia: University of Pennsylvania Press.

Artaud, Antonin. 1970. *The Theatre and Its Double.* Trans. Victor Corti. London: John Calder.

Babcock, Barbara. A. 1977a. "Introduction." In *Reversible Worlds: Symbolic Inversion in Art and Society.* Ed. Barbara A. Babcock. 13–36. Ithaca: Cornell University Press.

———. 1977b. "The Story in the Story: Metanarration in Folk Narrative." In *Verbal Art as Performance.* Ed. Richard Bauman. 61–80. Prospect Heights, Ill.: Waveland Press.

———. 1980. "Reflexivity: Definitions and Discriminations." *Semiotica* 30 (1/2): 1–14.

———. 1994. "Pueblo Cultural Bodies." *Journal of American Folklore* 107:40–54.

Bakhtin, M. M. 1981. *The Dialogic Imagination.* Trans. Caryl Emerson and Michael Holquist. Austin: University of Texas Press.

———. 1984a. *Problems of Dostoevsky's Poetics.* Trans. Caryl Emerson. Minneapolis: University of Minnesota Press.

———. 1984b. *Rabelais and His World.* Trans. Helene Iswolsky. Bloomington: Indiana University Press.

Bateson, Gregory. 1972. *Steps to an Ecology of Mind.* San Francisco: Chandler Publishing.

Bauman, Richard. 1977. *Verbal Art as Performance.* Prospect Heights, Ill.: Waveland Press.

———. 1986a. "Performance and Honor in Thirteenth-Century Iceland." *Journal of American Folklore* 99:131–50.

———. 1986b. *Story, Performance, and Event: Contextual Studies of Oral Narrative.* New York: Cambridge University Press.

———. 1989. "American Folklore Studies and Social Transformation: A Performance-Centered Perspective." *Text and Performance Quarterly* 9 (3): 175–84.

———. 1992. "Contextualization, Tradition, and the Dialogue of Genres: Icelandic Legends of the Kraftaskald." In *Rethinking Context*. Ed. C. Goodwin and A. Duranti. 125–46. Cambridge: Cambridge University Press.

Bauman, Richard, and Charles L. Briggs. 1990. "Poetics and Performance as Critical Perspectives on Language and Social Life." *Annual Review of Anthropology* 19:59–88.

Bauman, Richard, and Joel Sherzer. 1989 [1975]. *Explorations in the Ethnography of Speaking*. New York: Cambridge University Press.

Ben-Amos, Dan. 1972. "Toward a Definition of Folklore in Context." In *Toward New Perspectives in Folklore*. Ed. Américo Paredes and Richard Bauman. 3–15. Austin: University of Texas Press.

———. 1993. "Context in Context." *Western Folklore* 52:209–26.

Benjamin, Walter. 1969. *Illuminations*. New York: Schocken Books.

Brenneis, Don. 1986. "Shared Territory: Audience, Indirection, and Meaning." *Text* 6 (3): 339–47.

———. 1987. "Performing Passions: Aesthetics and Politics in an Occasionally Egalitarian Community." *American Ethnologist* 14:236–50.

Briggs, Charles L. 1988. *Competence in Performance: The Creativity of Tradition in Mexicano Verbal Art*. Philadelphia: University of Pennsylvania Press.

Briggs, Charles L., and Richard Bauman. 1992. "Genre, Intertextuality, and Social Power." *Journal of Linguistic Anthropology* 2 (2): 131–72.

Bruner, Edward M., and Barbara Kirshenblatt-Gimblett. 1994. "Maasai on the Lawn: Tourist Realism in East Africa." *Cultural Anthropology* 9 (4): 435–70.

Carr, C. 1993. *On the Edge: Performance at the End of the Twentieth Century*. Hanover, Conn.: Wesleyan University Press.

Caton, Steve C. 1990. *"Peaks of Yemen I Summon": Poetry as Cultural Practice in a North Yemeni Tribe*. Berkeley: University of California Press.

Clifford, James, and George E. Marcus. 1986. *Writing Culture: The Poetics and Politics of Ethnography*. Berkeley: University of California Press.

Combs-Schilling, M. E. 1989. *Sacred Performances: Islam, Sexuality, and Sacrifice*. New York: Columbia University Press.

Connerton, Paul. 1989. *How Societies Remember*. Cambridge: Cambridge University Press.

Conquergood, Dwight. 1991. "Rethinking Ethnography: Towards a Critical Cultural Politics." *Communication Monographs* 58:179–94.

Csordas, Thomas J. 1993. "Somatic Modes of Attention." *Cultural Anthropology* 8 (2): 135–56.

Dégh, Linda. 1969. *Folktales and Society: Storytelling in a Hungarian Peasant Community*. Trans. Emily Schossberger. Bloomington: Indiana University Press.

Derrida, Jacques. 1978. "The Theater of Cruelty and the Closure of Representation." In *Writing and Difference*. Trans. Alan Bass. 232–50. Chicago: University of Chicago Press.

———. 1980. "The Law of Genre." *Glyph.* 202–32. Baltimore: Johns Hopkins University Press.

Dolan, Jill. 1988. *The Feminist Spectator as Critic.* Ann Arbor, Mich.: UMI Research Press

Douglas, Mary. 1982. *Natural Symbols: Explorations in Cosmology.* New York: Pantheon.

Dorst, John. 1983. "Neck Riddle as a Dialogue of Genres." *Journal of American Folklore* 96:413–33.

———. 1989. *The Written Suburb: An American Site, an Ethnographic Dilemma.* Philadelphia: University of Pennsylvania Press.

———. 1990. "Tags and Burners, Cycles and Networks: Folklore in the Telectronic Age." *Journal of Folklore Research* 27 (3): 179–90.

Duranti, Alessandro. 1986. "The Audience as Co-Author: An Introduction." *Text* 6 (3): 239–47.

Duranti, Alessandro, and Charles Goodwin, eds. 1992. *Rethinking Context: Language as an Interactive Phenomenon.* New York: Cambridge University Press.

Erlmann, Veit. 1992. "'The Past Is Far and the Future Is Far': Power and Performance among Zulu Migrant Workers." *American Ethnologist* 19:688–709.

Fabian, Johannes. 1983. *Time and the Other: How Anthropology Makes Its Object.* New York: Columbia University Press.

———. 1990. *Power and Performance: Ethnographic Explorations through Proverbial Wisdom and Theater in Shaba, Zaire.* Madison: University of Wisconsin Press.

Falassi, Alessandro. 1987. "Festival: Definition and Morphology." In *Time Out of Time: Essays on the Festival.* Ed. Alessandro Falassi. 1–10. Albuquerque: University of New Mexico Press.

Farnell, Brenda M. 1990. *Ethnographics and the Moving Body. Man* 29:929–74.

Feld, Steven. 1990. *Sound and Sentiment: Birds, Weeping, Poetics, and Song in Kaluli Expression.* Philadelphia: University of Pennsylvania Press.

———. 1995. "From Schizophonia to Schismogenesis." In *Music Grooves.* Ed. S. Feld and C. Keil. 257–89. Chicago: University of Chicago Press.

Fernandez, James W. 1986. *Persuasions and Performances: The Play of Tropes in Culture.* Bloomington: Indiana University Press.

———. 1988. "Isn't There Anything Out There We Can All Believe In?: The Quest for Cultural Consensus in Anthropology and History." Paper read at the Institute for Advanced Study School of Social Science, Princeton, N.J.

Fine, Elizabeth C. 1984. *The Folklore Text: From Performance to Print.* Bloomington: Indiana University Press.

Flores, Richard R. 1994. "'Los Pastores' and the Gifting of Performance." *American Ethnologist* 21:270–85.

Foster, Susan Leigh, ed. 1995. *Choreographing History.* Bloomington: Indiana University Press.

Gal, Susan. 1989. "Language and Political Economy." *Annual Review of Anthropology* 18:345–67.

———. 1990. "Between Speech and Silence: The Problematics of Research on Language and Gender." In *Gender at the Crossroads of Knowledge: Feminist Anthropology in the Postmodern Era.* Ed. M. DiLeonardo. 175–203. Berkeley: University of California Press.

Geertz, Clifford. 1973. *The Interpretation of Cultures.* New York: Basic Books.

———. 1983. "Blurred Genres: The Refiguration of Social Thought." *Local Knowledge.* 21–35. New York: Basic Books.

Goffman, Erving. 1967. *Interaction Ritual: Essays on Face-to-Face Behavior.* New York: Anchor Books.

———. 1974. *Frame Analysis: An Essay on the Organization of Experience.* New York: Harper and Row.

Grotowski, Jerzy. 1968. *Towards a Poor Theatre.* Holstebro, Denmark: Odin Tearet Forlag.

Gumperz, John J. 1982. *Discourse Strategies.* London: Cambridge University Press.

Hammoudi, Abdellah. 1988. *La victime et ses masques: Essai sur le sacrifice et la mascarade au Maghreb.* Paris: Editions du Seuil.

Hanks, William F. 1987. "Discourse Genres in a Theory of Practice." *American Ethnologist* 14:668–92.

Haring, Lee. 1992. "Parody and Imitation in West Indian Ocean Oral Literature." *Journal of Folklore Research* 29:199–224.

Hart, Lynda, and Peggy Phelan. 1993. *Acting Out: Feminist Performances.* Ann Arbor: University of Michigan Press.

Haviland, John. 1986. "'Con Buenos Chiles': Talk, Targets, and Teasing in Zinacantan." *Text* 6 (3): 249–82.

Hertzfeld, Michael. 1985. *The Poetics of Manhood: Contest and Identity in a Cretan Mountain Village.* Princeton: Princeton University Press.

Hobsbawm, Eric, and Terance Ranger, eds. 1983. *The Invention of Tradition.* Cambridge: Cambridge University Press.

Hymes, Dell. 1974. *Foundations in Sociolinguistics: An Ethnographic Approach.* Philadelphia: University of Pennsylvania Press.

———. 1975. "Breakthrough into Performance." In *Folklore: Performance and Communication.* Ed. Dan Ben-Amos and Kenneth Goldstein. 11–74. The Hague: Mouton.

Irvine, Judith T. 1982. "Language and Affect: Some Cross-Cultural Issues." In *Contemporary Perceptions of Language: Interdisciplinary Dimensions.* Ed. Heidi Byrne. 31–47. Washington, D.C.: Georgetown University Press.

Jackson, Michael. 1989. *Paths toward a Clearing: Radical Empiricism and Ethnographic Inquiry.* Bloomington: Indiana University Press.

Jakobson, Roman. 1960. "Closing Statement: Linguistics and Poetics." In *Style in Language.* Ed. Thomas A. Sebeok. 350–77. Cambridge, Mass.: MIT Press.

Jameson, Fredric. 1981. *The Political Unconscious: Narrative as a Socially Symbolic Art.* Ithaca: Cornell University Press.

Jones, Joni L. 1996. "The Self as Other: Creating the Role of Joni the Ethnographer for Broken Circles." *Text and Performance Quarterly* 16:131–45.

Kapchan, Deborah A. 1993. "Hybridization and the Marketplace: Emerging Paradigms in Folkloristics." *Western Folklore* 52:303–26.

———. 1994. "Moroccan Female Performers Defining the Social Body." *Journal of American Folklore* 107:82–105.

———. 1996. *Gender on the Market: Moroccan Women and the Revoicing of Tradition.* Philadelphia: University of Pennsylvania Press.

Keeler, Ward. 1987. *Javanese Shadow Plays, Javanese Selves.* Princeton: Princeton University Press.

Kirshenblatt-Gimblett, Barbara. 1975. "A Parable in Context: A Social Interactional Analysis of Storytelling Performance." In *Folklore: Performance and Communication.* Ed. D. Ben-Amos and K. Goldstein. 105–30. The Hague: Mouton.

———. 1989. "Authoring Lives." *Journal of Folklore Research* 26 (2): 123–50.

Kirshenblatt-Gimblett, Barbara, ed. 1976. *Speech Play: Research and Resources for Studying Linguistic Creativity.* Philadelphia: University of Pennsylvania Press.

Kratz, Corinne A. 1994. *Affecting Performance: Meaning, Movement, and Experience in Okiek Women's Initiation.* Washington, D.C.: Smithsonian Institution Press.

Lavie, Smadar, Kirin Narayan, and Renato Rosaldo, eds. 1993. *Creativity/Anthropology.* Ithaca: Cornell University Press.

Lyotard, Jean-François. 1992. *The Postmodern Explained to Children: Correspondence, 1982–1985.* Trans. and ed. Julian Pefanis and Morgan Thomas. London: Turnaround.

MacAloon, John J. 1984. "Cultural Performances, Culture Theory." In *Rite, Drama, Festival, Spectacle.* Ed. J. J. MacAloon. 1–15. Philadelphia: Institute for the Study of Human Issues.

Marcus, George E. 1994. "General Comments." *Cultural Anthropology* 9:423–28.

Mauss, Marcel. 1973 [1934]. "Techniques of the Body." *Economy and Society* 2:70–88. Paris: Presses Universitaires de France.

McDowell, John H. 1985. "The Poetic Rites of Conversation." *Journal of Folklore Research* 22:113–32.

Merleau-Ponty, Maurice. 1962. *Phenomenology of Perception.* Trans. Colin Smith. London: Routledge.

Miller, Lynn C. 1995. "'Polymorphous Perversity' in Women's Performance Art: The Case of Holly Hughes." *Text and Performance Quarterly* 15:44–58.

Mills, Margaret A. 1991. *Rhetorics and Politics in Afghan Traditional Storytelling.* Philadelphia: University of Pennsylvania Press.

Noyes, Dorothy. 1993. "Contesting the Body Politic: The Patum of Berga." In *Bodylore.* Ed. Katharine Young. 134–61. Knoxville: University of Tennessee Press.

Perloff, Marjorie. 1992. *Postmodern Genres.* Norman: University of Oklahoma Press.

Phelan, Peggy. 1993a. "Reciting the Citation of Others; or, A Second Introduction." In *Acting Out: Feminist Performances.* Ed. Lynda Hart and Peggy Phelan. 1–31. Ann Arbor: University of Michigan Press.

———. 1993b. *Unmarked: The Politics of Performance.* London: Routledge.

Ricoeur, Paul. 1979. "The Model of the Text: Meaningful Action Considered as Text." In *Interpretive Social Science.* Ed. Paul Rabinow and William Sullivan. 73–102. Berkeley: University of California Press.

Rose, Dan. 1993. "Ethnography as a Form of Life: The Written Word and the Work of the World." In *Anthropology and Literature.* Ed. Paul Benson. 192–224. Urbana: University of Illinois Press.

Schechner, Richard. 1969. *Pubic Domain: Essays on the Theatre.* Indianapolis: Bobbs Merrill.

———. 1977. *Essays on Performance Theory.* New York: Drama Books Specialists.

———.1982. *The End of Humanism: Writings on Performance.* New York: PAJ Publications.

———. 1985. *Between Theater and Anthropology.* Philadelphia: University of Pennsylvania Press.

———. 1988. "Playing." *Play and Culture* 1:2–19.

———. 1993. *The Future of Ritual: Writings on Culture and Performance.* London: Routledge.

Scott, James C. 1985. *Weapons of the Weak: Everyday Forms of Peasant Resistance.* New Haven: Yale University Press.

Sherzer, Joel. 1987a. "A Discourse-Centered Approach to Culture." *American Anthropologist* 89:295–309.

———. 1987b. "A Diversity of Voices: Men's and Women's Speech in Ethnographic Perspective." In *Language, Gender, and Sex in Comparative Perspective.* Ed. Susan U. Philips, Susan Steele, and Christine Tanz. 95–120. Cambridge: Cambridge University Press.

———. 1990. *Verbal Art in San Blas: Kuna Culture through Its Discourse.* Cambridge: Cambridge University Press.

———. 1993. "On Puns, Comebacks, Verbal Dueling, and Play Language: Speech Play in Balinese Verbal Life." *Language in Society* 22:217–33.

Silverstein, Michael. 1976. "Shifters, Linguistic Categories, and Cultural Descriptions." In *Meaning in Anthropology.* Ed. K. Basso and H. Selby. 11–55. Albuquerque: University of New Mexico Press.

Sklar, Deirdre. 1994. "Can Bodylore Be Brought to Its Senses?" *Journal of American Folkore* 107:9–22.

Slyomovics, Susan. 1987. *The Merchant of Art: An Egyptian Hilali Oral Epic Poet in Performance.* Berkeley: University of California Press.

Spivak, Gayatri Chakravorty. 1993. *Outside in the Teaching Machine.* London: Routledge.

Stallybrass, Peter, and Allon White. 1986. *The Politics and Poetics of Transgression.* Ithaca: Cornell University Press.

Stewart, Kathleen. 1991. "On the Politics of Cultural Theory: A Case for 'Contaminated' Cultural Critique." *Social Research* 58:395–412.

———. 1996. *A Space on the Side of the Road: Cultural Politics in an "Other" America.* Princeton: Princeton University Press.

Stewart, Susan. 1978. *Nonsense: Aspects of Intertextuality in Folklore and Literature.* Baltimore: Johns Hopkins University Press.

———. 1984. *On Longing: Narratives of the Miniature, the Gigantic, the Souvenir, the Collection.* Baltimore: Johns Hopkins University Press.

———. 1991a. *Crimes of Writing.* New York: Oxford University Press.

———. 1991b. "Notes on Distressed Genres." *Journal of American Folklore* 104:5–31.

Stoeltje, Beverley. 1988. "Gender Representations in Performance: The Cowgirl and the Hostess." *Journal of Folklore Research* 25:219–41.

Stoller, Paul. 1989. *The Taste of Ethnographic Things: The Senses in Anthropology.* Philadelphia: University of Pennsylvania Press.

———. 1994. "Ethnographies as Texts/Ethnographers as Griots." *American Ethnologist* 21:353–66.

Taussig, Michael. 1993. *Mimesis and Alterity: A Particular History of the Senses.* London: Routledge.

Tedlock, Dennis. 1983. *The Spoken Word and the Work of Interpretation.* Philadelphia: University of Pennsylvania Press.

Todorov, Tzvetan. 1990. *Genres in Discourse.* Cambridge: Cambridge University Press.

Trawick, Margaret. 1986. "Iconicity in Paraiyar Crying Songs." In *Another Harmony: New Essays on the Folklore of India.* Ed. A. K. Ramanujan and S. Blackburn. 294–344. Berkeley: University of California Press.

Troin, Jean-Francois. 1975. *Les souks marocains: Marches ruraux et organisation de l'espace dans la moitié nord du maroc.* Aix-en-Provence: Edisud.

Tsing, Anna Lowenhaupt. 1993. *In the Realm of the Diamond Queen: Marginality in an Out-of-the-Way Place.* Princeton: Princeton University Press.

Turner, Edith. 1993. "Experience and Poetics in Anthropological Writing." In *Anthropology and Literature.* Ed. Paul Benson. 27–47. Urbana: University of Illinois Press.

Turner, Victor W. 1967. *The Forest of Symbols.* Ithaca: Cornell University Press.

———. 1969. *The Ritual Process.* Chicago: Aldine.

———. 1974. "Liminal to Liminoid in Play, Flow, and Ritual: An Essay in Comparative Symbology." *The Anthropological Study of Human Play.* Rice University Studies. 53–91. Houston: Rice University Press.

———. 1982. "Dramatic Ritual/Ritual Drama: Performative and Reflexive Anthropology." *From Ritual to Theatre.* 89–101. New York: PAJ Publications.

———. 1987. "Carnival, Ritual, and Play in Rio de Janeiro." In *Time Out of Time: Essays on the Festival.* Ed. Alessandro Falassi. 76–89. Albuquerque: University of New Mexico Press.

———. 1988. *The Anthropology of Performance.* New York: PAJ Publications.

———. 1990. "Are There Universals of Performance in Myth, Ritual, and Drama?" In *By Means of Performance: Intercultural Studies of Theatre and Ritual.* Ed. R. Schechner and W. Appel. 8–18. New York: Cambridge Unversity Press.

Turner, Victor W., and Edith Turner. 1982. "Performing Ethnography." *Drama Review* 26:2 (Summer): 33–50.

Turner, Victor W., and Edward Bruner, eds. 1986. *The Anthropology of Experience.* Urbana: University of Illinois Press.

Urban, Greg. 1989. "The 'I' of Discourse." In *Semiotics, Self, and Society.* Ed. Benjamin Lee and Greg Urban. 27–52. Berlin: Mouton de Gruyter.

———. 1991. *A Discourse-Centered Approach to Culture: Native South American Myths and Ritual.* Austin: University of Texas Press.

van Gennep, Arnold. 1960. *The Rites of Passage.* Chicago: University of Chicago Press.

Volosinov, V. N. 1973. *Marxism and the Philosophy of Language.* Cambridge, Mass.: Harvard University Press.

Webber, Sabra J. 1991. *Romancing the Real: Folklore and Ethnographic Representation in North Africa.* Philadelphia: University of Pennsylvania Press.

Young, Katharine. 1993. "Still Life with Corpse: Management of the Grotesque Body in Medicine." In *Bodylore.* Ed. Katharine Young. 111–33. Knoxville: University of Tennessee Press.

———. 1994. "Whose Body?: An Introduction to Bodylore." *Journal of American Folklore* 107:3–8.

6   Context

Context has not drifted far from its Latin root, contexere, "to weave together, interweave, join together, compose," meanings whose spirit is retained in vernacular terms such as "spinning yarns," "weaving lies," and "fabricating tales." Context contains the word text, which stems from texere, "to weave." Like textile weavings, texts are coherent, detachable, importable items with careers of appearance in different contexts. We tend to think of the text as the fixed component and of contexts as the variable settings into which the text can be placed. The relationship between context and text is far more complex than such a nested model suggests, however. To say that something has been "taken out of context" is in fact to say that a prior context has been usurped by a later one (Young 1985:119). What is of interest in contextual analysis is not simply the mechanics of inserting old texts into new situations but the strategic ways in which performances weave together contexts of all sorts, including the contexts for folklore and ethnography.

Frames, Frameworks, and the Making of Meaning

At close range, context is a frame of reference created in order to constitute and interpret an object of attention. Viewed more broadly, contexts model the master frameworks that relate nature and society. Implicit here is the concept of framing, which Erving Goffman developed into a powerful tool for exploring the interrelations of alternative domains and everyday life. As adapted by folklorists, this concept draws on Goffman's synthesis of Gregory Bateson's theory of metacommunication and Alfred

Schutz's phenomenological sociology (Goffman 1974:2–8). The basic metaphor is that of a picture on a wall. The frame around the picture distinguishes the picture from its surroundings, invoking a different set of interpretive rules for what is inside the frame. Deploying this metaphor, analysts have looked at how expressive forms are first set apart from and then related to the flow of ordinary events.

A performance begins with an act of framing that separates it from the surrounding flow of events, opening onto a conjured imaginary realm. Frames can take the form of physical boundaries, like the curtains on a stage or the covers of a mystery novel. Or frames can be conceptual in nature, enclosing a performance, for instance, by identifying it as a fairy tale ("Once upon a time") or a game of make-believe ("Let's pretend").

Performers construct performance by shifting attention back and forth between the frame and the imaginary world enclosed within it. I once watched in fascination as my six-year-old daughter and two of her friends conjured and inhabited an imaginary animal hospital, framing it as an alternative realm through repeated use of the word "pretend." "Pretend you're my two puppies," said my daughter to her friends. "Ruff! Ruff! Ruff!" responded one puppy. "Pretend I'm the animal doctor now to help you guys because you're sick," my daughter said. "Pretend you carry me out of this corner because it was dangerous to me," replied the other, who then draped herself across a chair, wearing goggles. "Pretend your eyes didn't work," said the vet, hammering on the goggles with a felt mallet.

Noticing me, the puppy undergoing treatment said, "Would you please go away?"

"Why?" I asked.

"Because it will feel more like a real game," she explained.

As I rose to leave, the other child offered, "You can watch us, but don't let us see you."

"You can go in the other room and sneak and spy," supplied my daughter. But the first child held her ground. "Just go away completely," she insisted.

Note that there are two objects of attention here: an imagined alternate domain (the animal hospital) and a frame that marks the alternate domain as "make-believe"—"a game," as one little girl said. Together these resemble the two events that Mikhail Bakhtin has identified as making up the novel: "We have before us two events: the event that is narrated in the work and the event of narration itself (we ourselves participate in the latter as listeners or readers); these events take place in different times (which are marked by different durations as well) and in different places, but at the same time these two events are indissolubly united in a single but complex event that we might call the work in the totality of all its events" (Bakhtin 1981:255). This principle of "double-grounding" (Bauman 1986:112) works for any object of interpretation, whether the object is a novel, a folktale, an artifact, or a game of make-believe.

The children's "game" pivots between the immediate situation of three youngsters playing a game in one child's bedroom (the "event of narration") and the alternate time and space of the animal hospital (the "narrated event"). Through a series of repeated utterances ("Pretend . . ."), the three children mark off the boundaries of an imaginary world, transforming themselves and their surroundings into puppies in an animal hospital being treated by an animal doctor. The production in its entirety is sustained by a shifting of attention from the imaginary to its framing devices and back. Set off from the ordinary flow of events, the imaginary grounded in the game is held open by the command "pretend." Its occupants are six-year-olds become puppies and an animal doctor. My attention to their game as a detached observer impeded the children's absorption in their imaginary, however. They addressed this crisis of attention by shifting their focus to the game and negotiating the conditions under which spectatorship might be acceptable.

One might be tempted to see the game (the event of narration) as the context for the animal hospital (the narrated event), but in fact the narrated event itself can be viewed as providing a remote context for the specific occasion of interpretation that occurs in each event of narration (Young 1985). In other words, the relationship between a text and its context is more complex and dynamic than scholars once believed.[1] There is, as Goodwin and Duranti write, an "intricate and subtle relationship between the interpretive frames we use in everyday life . . . and the implicit power relations that each frame implies, exploits, and, at the same time helps reproduce" (Goodwin and Duranti 1992:31). Of special interest to our analysis here is the relationship between the event of narration (in this case, the game) and the domain it anchors (the animal hospital). The remote context of the animal hospital playfully models what Goffman termed a "primary framework" (1974), a widely accepted conceptual apparatus for relating nature to society. Here a time of healing unfolds in the space of the animal hospital, where a licensed practitioner acts upon the body.[2]

When we frame social processes and structures of power and authority through game and narrative, we hold them at a distance for inspection. This framing is essential for making the meanings that situate us in a social world that is already the effect of primary frameworks. Schutz argues that meaning is available to the reflective glance alone, a glance that can be cast only on experiences framed and set in the past. We cannot reflect on the flow of events in which we are absorbed (1970:63). The capacity to shift our attention from absorption in a conjured world (the animal hospital) to abstract reflection on how we produce that world (the game) is central to our ability to frame experience and thus imbue it with meaning. This ability to shift between states of consciousness enables us not only to frame our imaginaries ("Pretend . . .") but to map our imaginaries onto nature and society.

Context, then, is a means of relating an alternative domain to the occasion of its conjuring, whether through performance, exhibition, or written or verbal analysis. How does this concept of context align with distinctions folklorists make among kinds of context? Dan Ben-Amos, for example, describes two types of context: contexts of situation and contexts of culture. The context of situation is "the narrowest, most direct context for speaking folklore." The context of culture, on the other hand, constitutes "the broadest contextual circle which embraces all other possible contexts," including "the reference to, and the representation of, the shared knowledge of speakers, their conventions of conduct, belief systems, language metaphors and speech genres, their historical awareness and ethical and judicial principles" (Ben-Amos 1993:215–16).

Situating "context of situation" within "context of culture" has been a key practice of contextualism.[3] This practice is evident in the emerging arena of heritage tourism, where folklorists work explicitly to develop "cultural context" for interpreting local history and lifeways to the public. For instance, the Pennsylvania State Heritage Park Program defines "cultural context" as "a body of information drawing on ethnographic and historical sources about a region's settlement patterns, social organization and folklife. A cultural context will provide information about the daily patterns of activity experienced by people of different social groups at particular periods of time, covering such elements as occupational, domestic, religious, and social life; sense of place, and attitudes toward, and interaction with the built and natural environment" (Commonwealth of Pennsylvania 1991).[4] While admitting to the practical necessity of such definitions, many scholars acknowledge a risk in first reifying "culture" and then obscuring its status as a bounded entity imagined and defined by the ethnographer (Marcus 1989). The problem occurs when we begin to operate in what Victor Turner calls the indicative mode (1981). Here the subjunctive "pretend" drops out of view and "culture" is reified into a whole that exists apart from domains such as science (within which ethnographers have historically operated), technology, politics, economics, and other spheres of endeavor that powerfully shape a hegemonic order. What disappears from our awareness is the fabricated nature of the frameworks separating these domains—and with it, the possibility of alternatives.

Everyday speech is saturated with interpretive frames that mediate our understandings of nature and society. Such interpretive frames contextualize the situations in which we find ourselves, enabling us to hold the world of daily life at a distance for inspection and evaluation. We may invoke a sports or game metaphor to cast an inchoate situation in terms of an organizing totality set in an alternative time. A person who promises more than he delivers may be said to be "all windup and no pitch"; someone who cheats may be said to be "touching the ball in the rough"; a dupe may "swallow the bait—hook, line, and sinker"; an arbitrator may "finesse" a deal. As my daughter and her friends enchanted their surroundings, transforming themselves into puppies, a chair into an operating table, goggles into the sign of disease, we fleetingly use proverbs to map remote contexts onto immediate situations. Motorists making a long journey may disagree on whether to take the time to patch a tire or simply rely on the spare to get them more quickly to their destination. "A stitch in time saves nine," declares the traveler who prefers to patch the tire. "But we've got to make hay while the sun shines," counters the impatient companion. The two proverbial expressions conjure competing narrative contexts for the situation they gloss, even as the situation contextualizes the proverbs. Here each saying appeals to a remote context, with the goal of placing an object of attention within a larger narrative whole. Invoking the remote context is a way of enchanting the world, if only for a moment.

We might see such speech acts as efforts to recover a larger context, to place events within a stock sequence that justifies our actions here and now. The repeated recourse to such artful expressions helps constitute reality and its premises, ensuring that dominant imaginaries maintain their hold on the world, shaping society and culture. Proverbs create meaning not so much by setting a present experience in the past as by placing it within an alternate temporal and narrative framework that implies a given outcome.

Situating spaces and players within forms of time, stock temporal sequences, such narrative frameworks render an inchoate world coherent. Bakhtin used the term "chronotope"—time-space—to describe the conjunction of forms of time with particular spaces (1981). Forms of time—those predictable sequences such as biography, the career, the calendar year, the journey, or the daily round—are associated with certain spaces (places of birth and burial, the sites of morning and evening

rituals, seasonal activities). In literature, particular forms of time unfold
in specific settings; quest narratives or picaresque novels, for example,
take place on the road. In the life of a nation such as the United States—
a "collective individual" (Handler 1988)—time takes its shape from the
notion of progress, a sequence of economic and individual development,
of continual advancement away from primitive conditions toward more
civilized ones. The "path of progress" metaphor represents this sequence
as a journey through space. This powerful narrative structure rational-
izes the disparity between rural poverty and urban wealth as a natural
relationship between cities, those "developed" centers of progress, and
the "developing" hinterlands on the margins.

The American narrative of progress provides a remote context for a
wide variety of texts and performances that work the way proverbs do,
bringing remote contexts to bear on the here and now. The national
media, for instance, appeal to the narrative of progress in accounts of
Appalachia as an enclave of poverty in a land of plenty, a destitute region
in dire need of outside assistance—from industry, the government, and
a host of charitable groups. David Whisnant has identified an "allegory
of loss and rescue" as the primary legitimizing narrative for missionary
work in the mountains—one that, by failing to address the underlying
causes of poverty, helps to sustain the status quo (1989).

How do the contexts of culture that folklorists, heritage workers, and
other ethnographers create relate to this master framework of progress?
Do they simply replicate it, through allegories of loss and rescue, or do
they hold the framework out for critical inspection?

Folklore emerged as both discipline and disciplinary object in tandem with the Enlightenment's project of supplanting traditional authority by the authority of enlightened reason (Bauman 1992b). As Max
Horkheimer and Theodor Adorno argue (1972 [1944]), the hegemonic
order sustained by Enlightenment principles relies on a process of disenchantment that strips the world of traditional meanings. Through the
mathematical, absolute modes of measure that displace mimetic, rela-
tional modes, the world is then reenchanted as the embodiment of Enlightenment categories. Having "extinguished any trace of its own self-
consciousness," as Horkheimer and Adorno put it, the Enlightenment
frustrates the effort to discern and critique the context of culture—a context made up of (and by) the Enlightenment and its disenchantment-based
practices of domination.

Contextualism emerged over the course of the twentieth century
alongside a growing awareness of the Enlightenment's process of mastering parts of the world by isolating them and recontextualizing them ac-

cording to a logic of classification. Viewed in terms of this history, contextualism in folklore could be seen as a practice of reenchanting a panoply of texts, artifacts, and practices. Along with this effort comes the practice of folklore as the retrieval of the meanings people create, through performance, in response to the Enlightenment and its particular ways of modernizing the world and its Others.

The concept of culture itself is a legacy of the Enlightenment's separation of modernity's cultural aspect from its economic aspect (which Marshall Berman characterizes as a split between moder*nism* and moder*nization*).[5] Raymond Williams and other cultural critics have observed that in tandem with the Enlightenment's reconfiguration of knowledge and the Industrial Revolution's literal displacement of people, a romantic structure of feeling came into vogue, "the assertion of nature against industry and of poetry against trade; the isolation of humanity and community into the idea of culture" (R. Williams 1973:79). What was left over after science carved up the world became the domain of antiquarians, forerunners of folklorists who dealt initially with a special kind of part—such fragments of vanishing culture as ballads, folktales, and superstitions. Over the past century such fragments have repeatedly been lifted out of originary "contexts" and recontextualized within imaginaries that pit culture against commerce and the coherence of preindustrial lifeways against the fragmentation of modernity. Appalachia, for example, has long provided fodder for one American imaginary as a locus of preindustrial culture (Batteau 1990). Though such imaginaries have flexed with the times, their continuing role has been to mark the eternal and the immutable under chronic conditions of upheaval (Harvey 1989:18).

Contextualism in Folklore Studies: From Evoking Atmosphere to Launching Critique

As the Enlightenment placed the production of knowledge and wealth within an unfolding story of nations on the path of progress, it spatialized progress itself. The Enlightenment's master narratives created a disciplinary "field," populated by peasants or other "Others," for the collection and documentation of folklore, conferring significance on the rescue of cultural fragments as part of a continuing struggle against the fragmentation, ephemerality, and chaotic flux endemic to capitalism. Underlying the nineteenth-century collection of texts was the premise that cultural fragments were windows onto earlier stages of civilization. In keeping with the narrative of evolutionary anthropology, for instance, the Bureau of American Ethnology documented Indian culture as "a window onto the savage phase of a people's evolution" (Brady 1988:40).

"Context," a twentieth-century insight, has several aspects that we can distinguish in general terms as modernist and postmodernist. In what might be seen as an early modernist manifesto for contextualist studies, Bronislaw Malinowski complained about the anthropological practice of detaching cultural expressions from their originating milieus (a practice, we might note, that assisted the Enlightenment's disenchantment of the world): "The stories live in native life and not on paper, and when a scholar jots them down without being able to evoke the atmosphere in which they flourish he has given us but a mutilated bit of reality" (1946 [1923]: 104; cited in Kirshenblatt-Gimblett 1975:105 and in Bascom 1965 [1954]). In its modernist aspect, contextualism supplanted the evolutionary narrative with "a relativist apparatus in which all frames and concepts could be seen as 'culture bound' and dependent on 'context' and 'perspective'" (Stewart 1996:25).

"Atmosphere" notwithstanding, in the decades that followed, culture remained "an object of analysis that was whole, bounded, and discrete" (Stewart 1996:25). The value of building knowledge through the collection of ethnographic data went unquestioned. The practice was still one of detachment from the time-space of the ethnographic encounter and insertion into the time-space of civilization on the path of progress. During the New Deal, folklorists working for the Federal Writers Project (FWP) of the Works Progress Administration (WPA) rejected the model of folklore as a window onto the past, conceiving it rather as mirror of the present. As Jerrold Hirsch points out, whereas antimodernists such as John Lomax had seen diversity and change as antithetical to "real" American folklore, modernists like Benjamin Botkin saw folklore as a means of developing American identity by linking it with cultural diversity (Hirsch 1988:54). Thus Federal Writers Project state guidebooks allowed Americans riding in their automobiles to become connoisseurs of cultural pluralism, one of America's definitive features (Hirsch 1988:53). The guides offered middle-class tourist-readers a transcendent view of picturesque poverty and American folk culture. As Hirsch argues, "The FWP was unable to face the issue of whether the revitalized American culture they hoped for could be created without changes in social and economic arrangements" (1988:52).

A more postmodern contextualism emerged in a climate of increasing discomfort with the transcendent narratives legitimizing such efforts as those of the FWP and other culture workers. Writing of the disjuncture between the historical creation of museum displays and the contemporary reception of them, Robert Cantwell argues that "the impulse to contextualize suggests that the force of the display no longer resides in a kind of admiration for the deeds and powers that brought the specimen or artifact into the museum—an admiration that implies a willingness to tolerate an overt assertion of class distinction" (1993:63).

The 1960s and 1970s, exploding with "rage against humanism and the Enlightenment legacy" (Harvey 1989), challenged such overt assertions of class. Various disciplines—from philosophy and linguistics to architecture and urban planning—mounted efforts to situate meanings locally and historically, to draw inspiration from the vernacular, to decenter the Enlightenment's fixed point of view (Harvey 1989). In folklore Richard Dorson noted the emergence of a "contextual movement" distinguished by its "insistence that the folklore concept apply not to a text but to an event in time in which a tradition is performed or communicated. Hence the whole performance or communicative act must be recorded" (1972:45–46).

In its postmodernist aspect, contextualism retains the emphasis on the situated and contingent and dwells on how texts and objects are deployed to create meaning. Here folklore is neither culture's residue nor its reflection. Rather, folklore, like any other cultural production, powerfully constitutes reality. In this vein, Bauman distinguishes between "outside in" and "inside out" approaches to the study of performance. The "outside in" approach constructs "a kind of contextual surround for the folklore forms and texts under examination." The inside-out approach, by contrast, uses "the text itself as a point of departure," "allowing it to index dimensions of context as the narrator himself forges links of contextualization to give shape and meaning to his expression" (1992a:142). In effect, the text becomes a tool, pivoting between the remote and immediate contexts it ties together.

This inside-out perspective radically recasts folklore's relationship to culture as constitutive and productive. We deploy folklore in the production of alternative domains that effect outcomes in everyday life. From classic examples of such scholarship: A woman in Canada uses a parable to model and defuse a volatile family situation (Kirshenblatt-Gimblett 1975). Conversationalists in Devon, England, produce and co-inhabit their locale through a series of stories (Young 1987). Elders in New Mexico constitute "las platicas de los viejitos de antes," the talk of the elders of bygone days, as a domain by speaking it (Briggs 1988). Fox hunters in southern New Jersey engender a world of the chase and arrange society and history around it (Hufford 1992). In each instance, people shape society through performances of folklore. An individual performing a parable clarifies the course a man should take to restore harmonious relations with his family. Friends telling stories in conversation order themselves into tellers and hearers of stories that bear on their social standing. The genres performed by New Mexican elders—proverbs, legends, scriptural allusions, hymns, prayers, and jests—powerfully produce the context within which their younger audiences form their social identities. Chasing foxes and telling stories about fox chases, working-class men in New Jersey continually create and re-create a society uniquely grounded in Pine Barrens history and spaces.

Thinking of folklore as constitutive, we render suspect the ideal of "decontaminated critique" (Stewart 1996)—an ideal that upholds a fiction of the scientist as detached, unbiased observer. Yet close examination of how people produce meaning through performance in particular situations makes it clear that the ethnographic event is a cultural production in its own right. As coproducers of ethnographic knowledge, ethnographers not only help to shape the content and structure of the ethnographic event (Haring 1972, Hymes 1975) but contribute stories to imaginaries under construction (Young 1987, Briggs 1988), becoming both subjects and objects in the production of local imaginaries (Stewart 1996).

Contextualism offers a way of relating folklore and folklore scholarship—as aspects of modernity—to continuing processes of modernization. As the twenty-first century begins, social *contexts* are implicated in the shifting times and spaces of capitalism lurching from one "crisis of overaccumulation" to another (Harvey 1989). The forms folklorists study are outcroppings not of vanished civilizations but of what John Dorst terms "the vast and pervasive cultural formation of advanced consumer capitalism" (1999:9). Poised on the cusp of the declining nation-state and the rising global economic order, scholars are turning their attention to how folklore produces locality as a context impinged on by the contexts of region, nation, and globe (Appadurai 1996). Context itself has become an object of study.

Enclosures, Scientific Enclaves, and the Soul of the Nation-State

What is the relationship between situated cultural productions conjured in everyday life and larger domains such as "Art," "Science," "America," and "Appalachia," imaginaries naturalized as if they were independent givens existing in the world "out there"? Like six-year-old girls conjuring a make-believe animal hospital, we use language to conjure reality, inscribing it onto our surroundings. A crucial difference between fictive and nonfictive domains resides in the conjurers' inclination to expose their shaping hand ("Pretend . . .") or to conceal it, imputing the way things are to nature or the market or some other power beyond anyone's control. Removing the markers of human agency, we lose sight of the possibility of alternatives.

The children's imaginary animal hospital grants a peep at a realm in which science is authoritative, magically vested with the power to improve on an imperfect creation. But when the children conjure their domain, their use of the word "pretend" reminds us that this is one possibility among many. Somewhat analogously, we conjure the domains of scientific knowledge through a continual process of enclosure. Through acts that "replace real space and time with classificatory, tabular spaces" (Stewart 1996:71), we create science's physical and conceptual clearings. Enclosure supplies an apt metaphor for the decontextualization against which contextualists rebelled. The metaphor of enclosure keeps in view the link between decontextualized cultural fragments and the "relentless displacement" that Dan Rose says gives rise to the global marketplace's "pure product." Chronic displacement "of traditions, beliefs, values, and natural objects" is accomplished through language that "endlessly reconfigures the planetary landscape and reunifies the human species within a highly differentiated frame of frames that lies concealed from us and, alternately, openly defies us to understand it" (Rose 1991:112). Revealing the "frame of frames" that relentlessly transforms and encloses the world is one challenge for contextualism and for public folklore.

We produce and distribute knowledge and wealth through a similar process of enclosure, which Cantwell terms "the parent of Culture" (1993). Harvey divides this process of decontextualizing and recontextualizing into three stages: de-territorialization, a stripping away of prior significance, and re-territorialization (1989:264). In the early stages of industrial capitalism and the Enlightenment, a still-ongoing process of enclosure began whose object was the commons—the "commons" of shared knowledge as well as shared land (R. Williams 1973, Cantwell 1993). The anthropologist Keith Thomas has shown, for instance, how an enclosed system of scientific discourse was erected in the eighteenth century through the systematic assessment of common knowledge (Thomas 1983). Botanists canvassed popular knowledge about plants and reordered it using the Latin terminology that indexed its new context. Linnaeus reinscribed with Latin names plants whose common names indexed local histories, personages, seasonal rounds, and healing practices. He thereby incorporated the plants into an international domain of knowledge. What the Latin names in fact indexed was the community of scientists now arrayed around this domain of knowledge, with great influence at the political centers of emerging nations. One historian terms this process "the gentle conquest" (Revere 1993).[6]

Those whose knowledge was newly marginalized complained of being closed out of the scientific discourse. Thomas writes, "A [late-eighteenth-century] contemporary protested that to give plants hard Latin names when they already had easy English ones would mean that in the future only learned botanists would be able to identify them: 'to class them botanically . . . so that nobody but a botanist can find them out, appears . . . something like writing an English grammar in Hebrew. You explain a thing by making it unintelligible'" (Thomas 1983:86).[7] The common names continue to be used locally, of course, even as rational planning girds the natural world in a classificatory grid that marginalizes the common names and knowledge. Local perspectives are preempted by a master framework that reduces complex landscapes to "resources," renaming them in relation to a project of progress through development. For example, in the Appalachian coalfields, land used as commons for hunting and gathering is routinely described as "overburden" in permit applications for mineral extraction. Reinscribing the land in relation to the underlying coal, the term *overburden* detaches the land from its historical social context and reduces it to one thing only: an obstacle to be removed. Kathleen Stewart theorizes that in response to "a felt enclosure which excludes a local real," counterdiscourses in the coalfields create "room for maneuver." Residents of West Virginia's coal camps continually reinscribe upon the officially designated world their own local names, stories, and counterhistories (Stewart 1996:128). Stewart notes that such local narratives and ways of speaking, associated with marginal spaces, thought of as threatened, and celebrated in festivals and coal-heritage sites, have emerged historically as ways of dealing with domination, as ways of reenchanting a world continually disenchanted by Enlightenment ways.

The ideological work of early folklorists was to take the meanings stripped from physical nature and contextualize them within the narrative of the developing nation-state. As Bill Readings argues, the development narrative underlying the production of knowledge is a nationalist narrative of *Bildung,* "the Kantian narrative of enlightenment that characterizes the knowledge process itself in modernity" (Readings 1996:147). Nation-states on the rise had a stake in the project of producing knowledge, not only for the sake of what needed to be "known" in order to manipulate the physical world, but because the narrative of *Bildung* was the medium for producing subjects of the nation-state.

Text-centered collections of folklore helped construct the nation-state as a powerful imaginary, which in turn formed the remote context for building knowledge through scientific collections. "It is our firm belief," wrote Jakob and Wilhelm Grimm in the introduction to their collection of German legends, "that nothing is as edifying or as likely to bring more joy than the products of the Fatherland." As plants renamed in Latin stood guard outside a domain in which scientific reason preempted traditional authority, artifacts and tales inscribed as products of the Fatherland helped tether emerging nations to bounded territories.

While advancing techniques of scientific measurement made it possible to assess and redistribute natural resources and to relocate populations deemed "in the way," folklore scholarship and public folklore productions may inadvertently play a key role in constituting, and stabilizing relations between, national centers and marginal spaces.

Of interest here is the relationship between productions that conjure the nation (or any seat of power and authority) and the "other" spaces that define what it is not, productions that conjure, for instance, America on the one hand and Appalachia on the other. As anthropologists helped to build empire by producing knowledge about exotic peoples, folklorists helped build nation-states by locating disappearing culture among the "backward" populations of the interior. This work helped to constitute a "soul" for nations emerging as collective individuals on the world scene (Handler 1988).[8] Displaying this soul could be a way for nations to demonstrate their true nationhood, insofar as having what Cantwell terms an "ethnoetic plenum" indicates cultural wealth (Handler 1988, Cantwell 1993).

In the globalizing society of the late twentieth century, transnational corporations are becoming more powerful than nation-states. David Harvey links this changing socioeconomic context with an emerging "regime of flexible accumulation." He argues that this regime consists of "new systems of production and marketing, characterized by more flexible labour processes and markets, of geographic mobility and rapid shifts in consumption practices" (Harvey 1989:124). Since 1973 this flexible accumulation has supplanted the Fordism (with its totalizing, paternalistic social vision) that was firmly implanted during the New Deal. The upheavals of global restructuring send us scurrying to find new holdfasts in the academy and the public sector. With the nation-state in decline, what is our frame of reference? How does the ideological labor of inventing heritage and situating it in a "cultural context" relate to the system of flexible accumulation? If this is the context in which "heritage" makes sense, how shall we reimagine folklore and ethnography?

Public Culture, Heritage, and the Critical Void

As "folklore" appeared in tandem with the rise of the nation-state, "heritage" seems to mark pathways of globalization (Abrams 1994, Corner and Harvey 1991). In the context of the decline of the nation-state and the rise of the transnational corporation (being brought about by such instruments as multinational trade agreements),[9] heritage proliferates. "Heritage discourse," writes James Abrams, "is formulated during and after periods of significant social transformation, and it functions as an act of cultural redefinition and repair. Migration, economic dislocation, and a sense of generational discontinuity are a few stimuli that provoke intense feelings of loss, absence, and yearning, conditions that heritage projects attempt to assuage by recovering memories and traditions presumed emblematic of a group's desired continuity" (1994:25).

Corner and Harvey elucidate the tight fit between heritage and enterprise. Mediating the shift between old and new orders, heritage seems to be a way of simultaneously keeping local identity from being swallowed up by corporate investment while offering that investment a distinctive place to locate its operations (Corner and Harvey 1991). But heritage can be as readily staged from the political right as from the left. On the one hand, the unreflective celebration of a heritage of nineteenth-century entrepreneurship can provide a remote context for a new round of exploitation. But on the other, critically staged social history could anchor a critique of socially irresponsible free-market enterprise (Corner and Harvey 1991:41).

Relating this to context, we face the question of how structures of power are replicated through the interpretive frames of public culture, including art and heritage. To deal with this issue we have to move beyond the notion "context of culture" to explore the meaning of structural similarities among domains that are considered cultural (heritage, art, folk art) and domains that are not (economics, science).

America and a Heritage of Fine Art

In his study of the Brandywine River Museum in Chadd's Ford, Pennsylvania, John Dorst finds that Wyeth art, three generations of which are displayed there, is contextualized by a narrative of transcendence that ratifies dynastic wealth and the authority of "anonymous, portable expertise." This transcendent narrative, related from an omniscient perspective, looks down from above and is not attached to any specific locale. It ignores the roots of Wyeth art in historical, localized conditions and anchors in Wyeth art and the Brandywine Valley a story of national artistic heritage. Andrew Wyeth's art, as the work of "America's greatest living artist," becomes a way to map the domain of America onto the Brandywine Valley, and to position Chadd's Ford as a leading actor on the national stage. The museum's exhibit tells the story of art in the valley. In the beginning there was an eclectic set of amateur painters whose work was the product of a particular time and place. Their eventual descendants were a dynasty of fine artists whose familial genius became the Brandywine Valley's crowning heritage. Here Dorst identifies a narrative glorifying a dynastic art paralleling the dynastic wealth of the DuPont family that had settled in the valley to manufacture gunpowder shortly after the turn of the nineteenth century. In a manner consistent with the principles of flexible accumulation, transcending the historical particulars of time and place, this narrative ratifies and naturalizes the mobility of expertise and capital on which the valley's managerial class of DuPont employees depends (Dorst 1989).

Countless other productions afford a similar view of America. If the ideological work of such cultural and artistic displays is to manufacture consensus, how do they do so? Mary Douglas theorizes that meaning leaks along the boundaries of disjunct domains via similarities in rule structures (1968:13).[10] The manufacture of consensus works, then, as Dorst observes, through a kind of sympathetic magic: if the public agrees to this social arrangement in the domain of art, it will accept it in the domain of economics (Dorst 1989).

In Dorst's analysis, a narrative of dynastic wealth and its tenure in the Brandywine Valley provides the context for understanding the valley's heritage of fine art. The valley itself forms an enclave protected from the processes of social displacement and environmental degradation inherent in the regime of flexible accumulation. In this enclave, artistic talent, like Dupont wealth, runs in families and ensures a position of economic and cultural leadership in America. Ironically, this exhibit in effect sanctions the processes disrupting lives and environments elsewhere (for example, in the town of Dupont in southern West Virginia's Chemical Valley), processes from which the valley remains sheltered. Missing in the display is any reflexive discourse on the making of the enclave itself. As such an enclave, the valley and its interpretive centers fit within the Enlightenment's enduring legacy of landscape gardens. Dorst's analysis, which repositions the valley in the history of landscape gardens, provides an alternative context for gaining an understanding of places like Chadd's Ford.

Appalachia and a Heritage of Folk Art

Robert Cantwell argues that modern enclaves of heritage were anticipated by landscape gardens created around the ruins of English common life
in the wake of the seventeenth and eighteenth centuries. Like those landscape gardens, our modern equivalents—national parks, deep suburbs,
heritage corridors, and golf courses, to name a few—embody the thinking
that pits "nature against industry . . . poetry against trade," and collapses
"humanity and community into the idea of culture" (R. Williams 1973:79).
Parks and heritage sites in Appalachia offer a breathtaking view of the
continuing tradition of landscape gardens in the context of modernization.

Appalachia as a place out of time has been produced and reproduced,
invested with material reality, for more than a century by the national
media, economic and environmental policy, and scholarly and industrial
practice (Batteau 1990, Whisnant 1989). This Appalachia, which Dorson
once termed "folklore's natural habitat" (1964:163), is conjured as such a
space through myriad interpretive acts. Each one—a film, a joke, a ballad
collection, a newspaper article, an exhibit, an outdoor museum—like Bakhtin's narrative, is doubly grounded. In tourist productions, this double
grounding opens Appalachia to outsiders and insiders alike as a domain of
preindustrial culture, a rite "performed to social differentiation" (McCannell 1989 [1976])—distinguishing, that is, between tourist and "native."
Appalachia, in effect, provides spaces to which urbanites may symbolically
"return" to redeem the fragmentation of modern life, while realizing themselves to be modern, in contrast to "natives" (Kostlin 1997).

Conjured in tourist destinations throughout the region, Appalachia
occupies a time and space "other" to America. A 1989 newsletter issued
by the National Park Service at the New River Gorge National River in
southern West Virginia offers an exemplary "interpretive frame":

> By 1900 the folk culture typical of the Appalachians was submerged un-
> der an enormous transition to the exploitation and transportation of coal.
> Handicrafts were replaced by cheap manufactured products from stores or
> mail order houses; live music was replaced by phonograph records and
> eventually radio. . . . Popular American traditions of the industrial age were
> a pervasive force which eroded the traditional culture rapidly. . . . As tour-
> ism grows and people earn an income from restoring the older customs,
> there will be more opportunity for visitors to experience them through
> fairs, festivals, and craft shops. (National Park Service 1989:1)

Here, in the modern landscape garden of the National Scenic River, is a
nineteenth-century artifact—an antimodernist view of folk culture

threatened by commerce and industry. Ironically, this view is framed within a narrative of development ("As tourism grows") commercializing aesthetic production. Here tourism is the inevitable next stage for America's deindustrialized spaces. Imagining two populations, "visitors" and "[local] people," this text distinguishes and relates these populations around a tourism in which people at leisure will consume the heritage produced by Appalachian workers. Heritage thus pivots between preindustrial and modern contexts. The interpretive text distinguishes Appalachia from America, designating Appalachia as an inappropriate site for "popular American traditions," hence constituting Appalachia as an "other" space—which is essential for setting up the contrast on which the rites of tourism depend (McCannell 1989 [1976]). The economic system that tainted mountain culture (with "cheap manufactured products," "phonograph records," and "radio") will now help to restore it by creating a demand for the "older customs."

The context for crafts in this text is the development of tourism, which the text anchors in the New River Gorge National River. Though the narrative of the scenic river contains the trope of the rescue of nature from industry, it is nonetheless a narrative of development that lays out an inevitable economic progression from extractive industry to heritage tourism. In a remarkable example of historical flattening, vernacular culture produced under the reign of the coal industry is discounted. Here is a denial not only of the chaotic exploitation and literal fragmentation of the mountains in surrounding counties but also of the way in which vernacular practices come to terms with it.

The site's interpretive plan frames the New River Gorge as "a microcosm of the industrial revolution," a framework that lifts the locale from the particulars of its history in order to make it a point of entry into a generalized narrative of economic growth and decline. As historian Ken Sullivan argues in *New River Gorge,* a video, "In the New River Gorge you can find within close confines . . . a lot of history that in other parts of Appalachia occupied a lot more space both geographically and in time. So New River makes a nice case history in industrialization: how it happens, how it stops" (Panorama International Productions 1996). Rather than critique free-market enterprise, the complementary texts of interpretive plan and video naturalize it.

At risk under conditions of advanced consumer capitalism is the critical function of art. "Esthetic production," writes McCannell, "which in an earlier time might have provided a critique of capitalism, has become fully integrated with commodity production. This integration disrupts the dialectic of surface and depth on which we could once depend for alteration of social and economic relations from within" (1989 [1976]:ix-x). Similarly, Dorst sees in postmodern idioms like "vignette" and "veneer"—depthless surfaces with indeterminate frames—a capacity to dodge or stymie critique (1989).

The mirroring provided by the Brandywine River Museum and the New River Gorge National River does not, like the interpretive frames examined earlier, hold the world of everyday life out for critical inspection. Like the one-way mirrors typical of postmodern architecture, it confounds efforts to see what is behind the reflection. Behind the images of the industrial revolution and the replication of preindustrial culture, the regime of flexible accumulation and the logic legitimating dislocation remain hidden. It is the context of interpretation that conjoins or tears asunder the domains of economy and culture. Evoking flexible accumulation as a context, heritage sites could foster critical thinking about the processes underlying the proliferation of heritage and its concomitant experience of exile. In the vernacular discourses folklorists study, and particularly in the discourse of those who find themselves excluded, we find the recovery of context through critique.

Of interest here are the scholarly efforts of folklorists and others to recover context by recovering the perspectives of the disenfranchised, exiled, or otherwise displaced. Just down the road from the Wyeth gallery in Chadd's Ford, for example, is the Christian C. Sanderson Museum, where an eclectic collection of everyday memorabilia from a common man's life has been labeled and placed on display. Here one finds everything from matches used for lighting candles on a sixtieth-birthday cake to pieces of a raincoat worn at the 1957 presidential inauguration, arranged according to a logic alien to the nearby tourist displays. Dorst views the Sanderson artifacts as an implicit critique of Chadd's Ford's postmodern modes of cultural production. Kathleen Stewart locates critique in the speech acts of those living in "doubly-occupied places"— spaces that, like central Appalachia, have long been colonized and controlled from without (1996). There speech ways that place speakers "within the entire historical dynamics of their society" constitute "graphic theoretical models" (Stewart 1988:238, 80). Likewise Charles Briggs writes that "the creative capacity of tradition to provide a critical perspective on changing experience . . . frequently stands as a central asset of communities that have been stripped of their natural resources and of control over their own destinies" (1988:375).[11]

Briggs's grounding of critical perspective in tradition has implications for public folklore, especially for public folklore practiced in "doubly-occupied" or "othered" spaces such as Appalachia and many of the early ethnographic settings. Othered spaces have been produced and reproduced through a variety of hegemonic narratives and productions, from ethnography to the WPA's American Guide series to heritage corridors. Responses to "othering" shaped from within such spaces suggest ways of opening up the landscape gardens that aid and abet the process of containing and controlling cultural difference.

Jockeying for position in the spaces onto which the dominant conception of Appalachia is mapped are countless local domains constructed from within, designated as "here" or "the mountains" or "Coal River" and the like. "The mountains" is a social imaginary anchored in contested space. Locally, "the mountains" has functioned for centuries as an informal commons, where surrounding communities have for generations exercised fructuary rights; nationally and officially, the mountains are owned by absentee corporations acting in accordance with the national narrative of fueling (with coal and timber) the nation on a path of progress while battling poverty in the hinterlands.

This condition of "double occupancy" (Stewart 1996) gives rise to a kind of double-voiced discourse that Stewart terms "backtalking" (1990). Double-voicing is a special order of framing, in which a prior utterance is contained in a response that cannibalizes it (Bakhtin 1981). Two voices, the informal and the formal, are locked in a struggle over meaning, and the informal triumphs. This backtalking is grounded in a style of speaking riddled with quoted speech. Quotation, which always entails framing, is an efficient means of holding out experience for critical inspection.[12] Framing one's speech in the past implies the presence of interlocutors. It has the effect of populating and democratizing an imaginary.

Backtalking thoroughly permeates discourse on southern West Virginia's Big Coal River, the New River's next-door watershed, where I conduct fieldwork. On Coal River, anecdotes and parodic sayings humorously recast the dominant narrative of progress and development (an official context of culture) as a narrative of undevelopment, displacement, and exile (an unofficial, subversive context of culture). Consider the "lie" offered by Danny Williams to an audience including his neighbor, John Flynn (a journalist and forest activist), Lowell Dodge (coordinator of a scientific study of the Central Appalachian forest), myself (a federal employee assessing the cultural implications of forest species decline), and Gregory, Danny's brother, on whom the lie was told.

> JF: Tell me a good story, Danny
> DW: What do you want to hear? A lie?
> JF: No, I want to hear a good Danny Williams story. A fairly clean story.

DW: I told you about the Volkswagen. (pauses) I'll tell you one. Me and Gregory

GW: Now he's gonna tell a lie

DW: and that son of mine was out ginsenging in the mountains, and we set down to rest, we were setting there. And Gregory got hurt. He got his hand cut off and they sewed it back. And we was settin there resting. (To GW) Now don't get mad at me!

GW: He's gonna tell a lie

DW: and Gregory was settin there restin, and we looked, and here come a man walkin round the side of the hill. It was Jesus. And he walked up to us, we was setting there restin, he looked at DJ, he said, he said, "DJ," he said, "Do you believe?"

DJ said, "Well," said, "Lord," said, "Sometimes I do," said, "Sometimes I don't," said, "I just don't know sometimes."

He [the Lord] said, "Is there anything bothers you?"

DJ said, "Yes," said, "My arm bothers me a lot."

The Lord reached down, he touched his arm, He said, "Well you're healed." And DJ twisted that arm around, up and down, [DW flexes his arm] said, "I believe," he said, "That arm ain't never felt that good."

He looked over at me, he said, "Do you believe?" I said, "Well," I said, "I'm like DJ. Sometimes I do, and," I said, "Sometimes I don't." I said, "I don't know."

He said, "Well, you got anything that bothers you?" I said, "My legs bother me," I said, "They hurt all the time." He reached over and he touched my legs, and he said, "They're healed." They quit hurtin, I got moving them around [DW flexes his legs] settin there.

He looked at Gregory. Looked at Gregory, said, "Gregory," said "You believe?"

He said, "Hold it right there, Lord," said, "Don't come no closer."

Said, "I'm on compensation!" (Laughing) He didn't want healed. (Laughter)

GW: Told you he was gonna tell a big'n, now didn't I? (Laughter)

DW: Said, "Hold it right there, Lord, don't come no closer. I'm on compensation."

GW: (with chagrin) Shee-it.

JF: Greg, do you think this forest is in trouble?

GW: Ah, "sometimes it is, sometimes it ain't." (Laughter).

This transcript illustrates many of the points I've made here about framing and the creation of context—context that replicates structures of power and authority—through performance. DW's "lie" is an interpretive frame that opens up a domain (an aborted time of healing in the space of the mountains) relating Appalachia to America in the presence of two federal employees. (In addition to me, Lowell Dodge also worked at the time as general counsel for the Government Accounting Office.) The story models the process of the informal attacking the formal (Douglas 1968). Danny uses reported speech to establish a pattern that is reversed through the punch line. The punch line of reported speech ("Don't come no closer, I'm on compensation") dramatizes the inversion of the American narrative of development in an othered space conceived, owing to its dependence on federal programs, as one that "could never grow up."[13] As a critique, this inversion repudiates (in the form of a "lie") the hegemonic Kantian ideal of the autonomous and complete individual.

The punch line shows that a taken-for-granted master framework ("progress"), linking the ideal of the individual as a completed, autonomous being with economic development, does not apply to this part of the world. The punch line effectively shatters an official "context" of culture (and economy). The laughter this punch line elicits registers "the satisfaction that comes with fragmenting a felt enclosure which excludes a local real" (Stewart 1996:128).

In the conversational realm, the narrated world becomes a resource for creating meaning, which, as we have seen, leaks across the borders of disjunct domains (Douglas 1968:13). Here the narrated world is superimposed upon the narrative event through the replication of a trick. Gregory's trick on the Lord in the narrated world is paralleled in the narrative event—the context of situation—by Danny's use of the story to victimize Gregory with words. Gregory then replicates the pattern with a verbal trick on John Flynn ("Sometimes it is, sometimes it ain't"). These tricks are played through the establishing of worlds within boundaries that temporarily redefine social relations. Gregory's quotation calls attention to the context of situation (the event of narration) for which the story (the narrated event) now serves as a context.

Gregory's trick maps the social arrangement of the narrated world onto the ordinary world of the conversation, modeling the way in which remote contexts are used to structure society and nature. This structure replicates power relations constituted in other hegemonic narratives. In his essay on the foundation of settlement schools in the mountains, David Whisnant examines the "allegory of loss and rescue" presiding over the establishment of those schools (1989). The same structure underlies the master narrative in which environmentalists seek, through a process of conversion, to heal ecosystems fallen from grace.

Meaning leaks through other boundaries as well: the narrative's troubled human limbs recall the diseased tree limbs snapping off and injuring woodcutters that were mentioned earlier in the conversation. Where laborers are treated as appendages of a shifting system that incorporates them not as persons but as "hands," it is significant, too, that the lie makes the fragment of the hand the site on which power relations are played out (Foucault 1984:159). In the othered space where few jobs are available, disability is what makes it possible to remain. If compensation is for being "cut off," as they say, from work, integrity is what's at issue in the lie. The body's transformation into a commodity betokens a loss of integrity at multiple levels. Labeling this as a "lie" calls attention to the fictitious underpinnings of the dominant order, and subversively raises the specter of alternatives. Kathleen Stewart argues that the logic of putting back together "what is always falling apart" deeply informs cultural practice in the doubly occupied space of the southern West Virginia coalfields (1988). On the Big Coal River, mountaintop removal—carefully rendered invisible from the New River Gorge—has recently displaced communities and closed off large portions of "the mountains." People rummage through ruins on the brink of enclosure for fragments to suture into new contexts for fathoming the experience of exile. A chapel is dismantled and divided among community members. Rosebushes and grape arbors are transplanted from the site of a future coal refuse impoundment to other hollows. One man built a log cabin out of the oak timbers that for sixty years spanned the river at the evacuated place of Edwight, a once populous coal town. "A lot of trucks have driven over this house," he quipped when he took me to see it. He built the chimney by reassembling the rocks from the homestead of a founding settler at the head of a hollow now behind locked gates. And he filled the cabin with artifacts from places now emptied of people. After the fashion of the memory quilt, each artifact recalls a particular person or event or place or kind of activity: the fiddle played by his grandfather; the drawknife an uncle used to make hickory chairs; the elaborately tooled leather hunting pouch made by another grandfather, a skilled craftsman. "Now they shot him in the back for making moonshine," he commented, evaluating America's reception of that mode of craftsmanship. Ascending the slope behind the cabin are patches of ramps (wild plants somewhat like onions) and ginseng, started from plants in the hollows now closed off.

A narrative of *undevelopment* and displacement serves as the context for this cabin and its contents. In contrast to the New River narrative, told from the rescuer's perspective, the narrative of the oak-timber cabin unfolds from a perspective of exile (Stewart 1988). Like Danny's lie, the cabin dismantles hegemonic time to expose an othered space where time flows in reverse. Interpreting the log cabin, its maker implicitly refutes the testimony given by scientists (Dorst's "anonymous, portable expertise" [1989:5]) working for coal companies and accepted by the state that "there are no historic artifacts" in the region. As "graphic theoretical models," to think with (Stewart 1996:80), the lie and the cabin illuminate clashes in forms of time. In the discourse of national progress, industrial time is a time of "growth." But growth is a form of time suppressed throughout the othered spaces of the central Appalachian region. "This place could never grow up," said a man, attributing this condition to the fact that most of the land is owned by land companies that will lease but will not sell (90 percent of the land on the Appalachian plateau). Where a place can't grow up, neither can its inhabitants. Biographical time on Coal River includes a period of outmigration that precludes "growing up around here." Shorty Bongalis summarized this time in a parodic saying: "They taught the three R's here in the school for a long time: 'Reading, 'Riting, and the Road to Akron.'" In that period, people traveled "hillbilly highways" northward to find work. "Now they go south, to North Carolina." Here past, present, and future are linked in a saying that highlights exile as collective time in an othered space.

The parodic saying here recasts the Enlightenment formula for developing the autonomous, educated individual. Like proverbs that map their own contexts, the parodic saying remaps its context while revoking the original map. The domain conjured by "Reading, 'Riting, and 'Rithmetic" *is* the context evoked and cannibalized by the parody. The parody is recontextualized in this conversation to illuminate a new spatial orientation—facing south instead of north—in what is not a new time. Appalachian time, in other words, flows counter to American time.

During the 1980s, the economic regime of flexible accumulation implanted itself on Coal River through practices of union busting, downsizing, subcontracting, evacuation, and temporary employment. In the 1990s, when schools were being closed, the commons enclosed, and the valleys vacated, to be filled with rubble and "reclaimed" as wildlife refuges and tourist resorts, a new three R's was coined: "Remove, Remove, Reclaim." This saying, spoken by survivors in a place in the process of emptying out, depicts the evolution of an aphorism that was once a transcendent formula for self-development (Reading, 'Riting, and 'Rithmetic), then was modified to address the contingencies attendant on industrial colonization (Reading, 'Riting, and the Road to Akron), and has now come to fully expose the relentless transformation of a post-Fordist territory by transnational corporations. It compresses a century of domination into three words.

Context is a historically contingent framework that we generate, shape, contest, and critique through our cultural productions. Contextualism's strong suit is its capacity to illuminate the framing conventions that allow or disallow shared—and sometimes socially disparate—meanings in public discourse. Ways of speaking that articulate the boundaries between local and hegemonic frameworks suggest modes of representation as well. James Abrams imagines such a mode: "If the concept of heritage is to be reimagined as a shifting terrain of debate intersected by a variety of voices in dialogue about the past, we need to position ourselves on the borders between cultures where these voices can be heard" (1994:34).

Fashioning our alternative domains at the borders both in public and in the academy, we constantly reimagine the context for the objects of our attention. In this "shifting terrain," our own frameworks become modulating hybrids, like the vernacular forms of backtalk that so artfully illuminate political abuses of time (Fabian 1983). As folklore's history shows full well, celebrating community art forms and aesthetic values can become a way of enhancing the "ethnoetic plenum" (Cantwell 1993), but it can also be a way of enhancing local resistance, of modeling the competition among imaginaries anchored in the same material world and holding it out for critical inspection.[14]

"Shifting" is key here. As Jerrold Hirsch observes, the New Deal folklorists' radical celebrations of democracy and diversity "became in a more conservative time a shibboleth easily repeated, while realities of discrimination and inequality were not confronted" (1988:63). In the emerging world of flexible accumulation, cultural representation has become a high-wire act. Do our representations, brimming as they are with quotation, grounded as they are in shared time, open up an alternative domain for engagement, or do they assist hegemonic practices of containment and exclusion? Like backtalk, each production we stage bears the possibility of revealing "the frame of frames that lie concealed from us" (Rose 1991:112) and of transforming that framework, if only to keep it visible and thereby negotiable.

Notes

1. In the 1970s and early 1980s a debate known as the "text/context controversy" arose over the primacy traditionally assigned to texts over their contexts (Young 1985:115). As Katharine Young observes, "formalists" tended to concentrate on the relationship between stories and the events they are about, while performance theorists (i.e., contextualists) began to look at events that stories are about as remote contexts for the storytelling occasion itself. It also was becoming clear that "some of the content of the story comes not from the events it is about but from the occasion on which it is told." The text, Young points out, happens to be that aspect of the storytelling event

that lends itself to transcription; paring away tracings of social interaction in the transcript, we arrive at what appears to be a fixed text. But even these fixed texts "display contextual influences in changes formalists grapple with as versions and variants, which have the peculiar virtue of lodging contextual considerations inside texts" (Young 1985:119).

2. It is within such historically contingent frameworks that children form identities, as Fernandez theorizes, by "taking the animal other." Imitating animals, children symbolically reproduce frameworks for constituting and relating nature and society, holding these frameworks out for investigation (Fernandez 1986:32–35).

3. For instance, symmetry and asymmetry in folk art, or tenets of hound breeding, have been linked with egalitarian and hierarchical social structures (Pocius, Hufford), while genres of children's folklore have been linked with cognitive and social development (Sutton-Smith, McDowell, Fernandez).

4. For related definitions and discussion, see Staub 1994.

5. The problem with context of culture relates to an insight of Marshall Berman's. Berman queries a split between modernism—as the social and cultural side of modernity—and modernization, the economic and historical process undergirding modernity. Both sides are driven by narratives of development—whether of self on the one hand or economy on the other.

6. Linnaeus incorporated the names of many biological explorers into his Latin binomials. Consider, for instance, the Asiatic dayflower, which has three petals, two of which are fully developed and one that is poorly developed. Linnaeus named its genus *Commelina* after the three Commelina brothers, two of whom were distinguished botanists, and one of whom died young without making a significant contribution to science. Thus the Latin name anchored the history of botanical discovery in a physical world stripped of associations with local places, people, seasons, and uses encoded in vernacular names (Runkel and Bull 1987 [1979]:201).

7. The scientific creation of fragments exemplifies the practices of enclosure involved in the production of knowledge. The symbolic violence of replacing history with classification was not lost on Wilhelm Heinrich Riehl, a folklorist in mid-nineteenth-century Germany, who compared the collectors and classifiers of isolated narratives to specimen hunters "who set out with a tin can to . . . gather superficial folk antiquities . . . in order to place them, properly pressed, dried and classified, into a Germanic herbarium . . . who try to catch unknown folk song specimens, in order to pin them in categories, well spread out, in a collection" (cited in Linke 1990:122).

8. *Washington Post* journalist Richard Harrington keeps this view open in a 1997 article about Alan Lomax: "Over the course of seven decades, Lomax—writer, folklorist, ethnomusicologist—has single-mindedly pursued the notion that folk culture can be a picture window onto the soul of a nation, but that unless someone opens the blinds, elemental truths and ancient histories will disappear and die in the darkness" (1997:G4).

9. Specifically the General Agreement on Tariffs and Trade (GATT), the North American Free Trade Agreement (NAFTA), and the European common market and currency.

10. With respect to riddles, Alan Dundes points out that "the structure of the context (social situation) . . . is paralleled by the structure of the text used in that context" (1980:25).

11. In the same vein, K. Stewart notes that those exercising this same creative capacity to "retain and continuously redeem conventional cultural discourses . . . are on the one hand romanticized as those who can (still) speak and on the other hand coldly judged and dismissed because they speak 'incorrectly' and 'inefficiently'" (1988:228). Edward Said provides a rationale for the emergence of critique out of the experience of exclusion. "Only to those who are excluded from the social nexus," he writes, "comes the idea of raising a question about the limits of human nature because they need a human that includes them" (1984).

12. "Laminator verbs" (such as say, tell, call, dream, and name) "frame enclaves as a different order of event from the events around them and mark one boundary of the events so named" (Young 1985:226; see also Goffman 1974:505).

13. In Appalachia over the past century, independence has given way to dependence, systematically codified through government policy (Salstrom 1994).

14. For examples of frameworks that could underpin public presentation with critique, see Dorst's analysis of the competing narrative constructions of Devil's Tower, produced by Native Americans and the National Park Service (Dorst 1999); Michael Ann Williams's portrayal of Great Smoky Mountains Folklife (M. Williams 1996); and Joseph Sciorra's work on the Casitas of New York City, structures for which City Lore has advocated (Sciorra 1996).

References Cited

Abrahams, Roger D. 1977. "Toward an Enactment-Centered Approach to Folklore." In *Frontiers of Folklore*. Ed. William R. Bascom. 79–107. Boulder, Colo.: Westview Press.

———. 1993. "Phantoms of Romantic Nationalism in Folkloristics." *Journal of American Folklore* 106:3–37.

———.1994. "Powerful Promises of Regeneration; or, Living Well with History." In *Conserving Culture: A New Discourse on Heritage*. Ed. Mary Hufford. 78–93. Urbana: University of Illinois Press.

Abrams, James. 1994. "Lost Frames of Reference: Sightings of History and Memory in Pennsylvania's Documentary Landscape." In *Conserving Culture: A New Discourse on Heritage*. Ed. Mary Hufford. 24–38. Urbana: University of Illinois Press.

Appadurai, Arjun. 1996. *Modernity at Large: Cultural Dimensions of Globalization*. Minneapolis: University of Minnesota Press.

Bakhtin, Mikhail M. 1981. *The Dialogic Imagination*. Trans. Caryl Emerson and Michael Holquist. Austin: University of Texas Press.

———. 1986. "The Problem of Speech Genres." In *Speech Genres and Other Late Essays*. Trans. Vern McGee. Ed. Michael Holquist and Caryl Emerson. 60–102. Austin: University of Texas Press.

Bascom, William R. 1965. "Four Functions of Folklore" (1954). In *The Study of Folklore*. Ed. Alan Dundes. 279–98. Englewood Cliffs, N.J.: Prentice-Hall.

Bateson, Gregory. 1955. "A Theory of Play and Fantasy." *Psychiatric Research Reports* 2:39–51.

Batteau, Allen. 1990. *The Invention of Appalachia*. Tucson: University of Arizona Press.

Bauman, Richard. 1986. *Story, Performance, and Event: Contextual Studies of Oral Narrative*. Cambridge: Cambridge University Press.

———. 1989. "American Folklore Studies and Social Transformation: A Performance-Centered Perspective." *Text and Performance Quarterly* 9:175–84.

———. 1992a. "Contextualization, Tradition, and the Dialogue of Genres: Icelandic Legends of the Kraftaskald." In *Rethinking Context: Language as an Interactive Phenomenon*. Ed. Charles Goodwin and Alessandro Duranti. 125–45. Cambridge: Cambridge University Press.

———. 1992b. "Folklore." In *Folklore, Cultural Performances, and Popular Entertainments: A Communications-Centered Handbook*. Ed. Richard Bauman. 29–40. New York: Oxford University Press.

———. 1993. "The Nationalization and Internationalization of Folklore: The Case of Schoolcraft's 'Gitschee Gauzinee.'" *Western Folklore* 52:247–70.

Bauman, Richard, and Charles L. Briggs. 1990. "Poetics and Performance as Critical Perspectives on Language and Social Life." *Annual Review of Anthropology* 19:59–88.

Ben-Amos, Dan. 1993. "Context in Context." *Western Folklore* 52:209–26.

Berman, Marshall. 1982. *All That Is Solid Melts into Air: The Experience of Modernity*. New York: Simon and Schuster.

Brady, Erika. 1988. "The Bureau of American Ethnology: Folklore, Fieldwork, and the Federal Government in the Late Nineteenth and Early Twentieth Centuries." In *The Conservation of Culture: Folklorists and the Public Sector*. Ed. Burt Feintuch. 35–45. Lexington: University Press of Kentucky.

Briggs, Charles. 1988. *Competence in Performance: The Creativity of Tradition in Mexicano Verbal Art*. Philadelphia: University of Pennsylvania Press.

———. 1993. "Metadiscursive Practices and Scholarly Authority in Folkloristics." *Journal of American Folklore* 106:387–434.

Cantwell, Robert. 1993. *Ethnomimesis*. Chapel Hill: University of North Carolina Press.

Commonwealth of Pennsylvania. 1991. *Commonwealth of Pennsylvania Heritage Parks: A Program Manual*. 3d ed. Harrisburg, Pa.: Department of Community Affairs.

Corner, John, and Sylvia Harvey, eds. 1991. *Enterprise and Heritage: Crosscurrents of National Culture*. London: Routledge.

Dorson, Richard M. 1964. *Buying the Wind: Regional Folklore in the United States*. Chicago: University of Chicago Press.

————. 1972. "Introduction: Concepts of Folklore and Folklife." In *Folklore and Folklife: An Introduction*. Ed. Richard M. Dorson. 1–50. Chicago: University of Chicago Press.

Dorst, John. 1983. "Neck-Riddle as a Dialogue of Genres." *Journal of American Folklore* 96:413–33.

————. 1989. *The Written Suburb*. Philadelphia: University of Pennsylvania Press.

————. 1999. *Looking West: Forays into a Discourse of Vision and Display*. Philadelphia: University of Pennsylvania Press.

Douglas, Mary. 1968. "The Social Control of Cognition: Some Factors in Joke Perception." *Man* 3:361–76.

Dundes, Alan. 1980. "Text, Texture, and Context." *Southern Folklore Quarterly* 18:251–65.

Fabian, Johannes. 1983. *Time and the Other: How Anthropology Makes Its Object*. New York: Columbia University Press.

Fernandez, James. 1986. *Persuasions and Performances: The Play of Tropes in Culture*. Bloomington: Indiana University Press.

Foucault, Michel. 1984. *The Foucault Reader*. Ed. Paul Rainbow. New York: Pantheon.

Goffman, Erving. 1974. *Frame Analysis: An Essay on the Organization of Experience*. New York: Harper Colophon Books.

Goodwin, Charles, and Alessandro Duranti. 1992. "Rethinking Context: An Introduction." In *Rethinking Context: Language as an Interactive Phenomenon*. Ed. Charles Goodwin and Alessandro Duranti. 1–42. Cambridge: Cambridge University Press.

Handler, Richard. 1988. *Nationalism and the Politics of Culture in Quebec*. Madison: University of Wisconsin Press.

Haring, Lee. 1972. "Performing for the Interviewer: A Study of the Structure of Context." *Southern Folklore Quarterly* 36:383–98.

Harrington, Richard. 1997. "The Ballad of Alan Lomax: A Man and His Tape Recorder, Immersed in the Sounds of America's Backwaters." *Washington Post*, June 29, sec. G.

Harvey, David. 1989. *The Condition of Postmodernity*. Cambridge, Mass.: Blackwell.

Hirsch, Jerrold. 1988. "Cultural Pluralism and Applied Folklore: The New Deal Precedent." In *The Conservation of Culture: Folklorists and the Public Sector*. Ed. Burt Feintuch. 46–71. Lexington: University Press of Kentucky.

Horkheimer, Max, and Theodor Adorno. 1972 [1944]. *Dialectic of Enlightenment*. New York: Herder and Herder.

Hufford, Mary. 1992. *Chaseworld: Foxhunting and Storytelling in New Jersey's Pine Barrens*. Philadelphia: University of Pennsylvania Press.

————. 1995. "Context." *Journal of American Folklore* 108:528–49.

Hymes, Dell. 1975. "Breakthrough into Performance." In *Folklore: Performance and Communication*. Ed. Dan Ben-Amos and Kenneth S. Goldstein. 11–74. The Hague: Mouton.

Jones, Michael Owen, and Robert Georges. 1995. *Folkloristics: An Introduction*. Bloomington: Indiana University Press.

Kapchan, Deborah A. 1993. "Hybridization and the Marketplace: Emerging Paradigms in Folkloristics." *Western Folklore* 52:303–26.

Kirshenblatt-Gimblett, Barbara. 1975. "A Parable in Context: A Social Interactional Analysis of a Storytelling Performance." In *Folklore: Performance and Communication*. Ed. Dan Ben-Amos and Kenneth S. Goldstein. 105–30. The Hague: Mouton.

———. 1988. "Mistaken Dichotomies." *Journal of American Folklore* 101:140–55.

Kostlin, Konrad. 1997. "Passion for the Whole: Interpreted Modernity or Modernity as Interpretation." *Journal of American Folklore* 110:260–76.

Labov, William. 1972. "The Transformation of Experience in Narrative Syntax." In *Language in the Inner City: Studies in the Black English Vernacular*. Ed. William Labov. 354–96. Philadelphia: University of Pennsylvania Press.

Linke, Uli. 1990. "Folklore, Anthropology, and the Government of Social Life." *Comparative Studies in Society and History* 32:117–48.

Malinowski, Bronislaw. 1946. "The Problem of Meaning in Primitive Languages" (1923). In *The Meaning of Meaning*. Ed. C. K. Ogden and I. A. Richards. 293–336. New York: Harcourt, Brace and World.

Marcus, George. 1989. "Imagining the Whole: Ethnography's Contemporary Efforts to Situate Itself." *Critique of Anthropology* 9:7–30.

Marcus, George, and Michael Fischer, eds. 1986. *Anthropology as Cultural Critique*. Chicago: University of Chicago Press.

McCannell, Dean. 1989 [1976]. *The Tourist: A New Theory of the Leisure Class*. New York: Schocken.

National Park Service. 1989. *New River Gorge Newsletter* (Glen Jean, W.Va.) 9 (2).

Panorama International Productions. 1996. *New River Gorge*. Burbank, Calif. 30 mins.

Readings, Bill. 1996. *The University in Ruins*. Cambridge, Mass.: Harvard University Press.

Revere, James. 1993. *The Gentle Conquest*. Washington, D.C.: Library of Congress.

Roberts, Warren. "Fieldwork: Recording Material Culture." In *Folklore and Folklife: An Introduction*. Ed. Richard M. Dorson. 431–44. Chicago: University of Chicago Press.

Rose, Dan. 1991. "Worldly Discourses: Reflections on Pragmatic Utterances and on the Culture of Capital." *Public Culture* 4:109–27.

Runkel, Sylvan T., and Alvin F. Bull. 1987 [1979]. *Wildflowers of Iowa Woodlands*. Ames: Iowa State University Press.

Said, Edward. 1984. "The Mind of Winter: Reflections on Life in Exile." *Harper's* 269:49–55.

Salstrom, Paul. 1994. *Appalachia's Path to Dependency: Rethinking a Region's Economic History, 1730–1940*. Lexington: University Press of Kentucky.

Schutz, Alfred. 1970. *On Phenomenology and Social Relations.* Ed. Helmut Wagner. Chicago: University of Chicago Press.

Sciorra, Joseph. 1996. "Return to the Future: Puerto Rican Vernacular Architecture in New York City." In *Re-presenting the City: Ethnicity, Capital, and Culture in the Twenty-first-Century Metropolis.* Ed. Anthony D. King. 60–92. London: Macmillan Press.

Sommers, Laurie. 1996. "Defining 'Folk' and 'Lore' in the Festival of American Folklife." *Journal of Folklore Research* 33:227–31.

Staub, Shalom. 1994. "Cultural Conservation and Economic Recovery Planning: The Pennsylvania Heritage Parks Program." In *Conserving Culture: A New Discourse on Heritage.* Ed. Mary Hufford. 229–44. Urbana: University of Illinois Press.

Stewart, Kathleen. 1988. "Nostalgia: A Polemic." *Cultural Anthropology* 3:227–41.

———. 1990. "Backtalking the Wilderness: 'Appalachian' En-genderings." In *Uncertain Terms: Negotiating Gender in American Culture.* Ed. Faye Ginsburg and Anna Lowenhaupt Tsing. 43–56. Boston: Beacon Press.

———. 1996. *A Space on the Side of the Road: Cultural Poetics in an "Other" America.* Princeton: Princeton University Press.

Thomas, Keith. 1983. *Man and the Natural World: A History of the Modern Sensibility.* New York: Pantheon Books.

Turner, Victor. 1981. "Social Dramas and Stories about Them." In *On Narrative.* Ed. W. J. T. Mitchell. 137–64. Chicago: University of Chicago Press.

Ulmer, Greg. 1983. "The Object of Post Criticism." In *The Anti-Aesthetic: Essays on Postmodern Culture.* Ed. Hal Foster. 83–110. Port Townsend, Wash.: Bay Press.

Whisnant, David. 1989. "Old Men and New Schools." In *Folklife Annual, 1988–89.* Ed. James Hardin. 74–85. Washington, D.C.: Library of Congress.

Williams, Michael Ann. 1996. *Great Smoky Mountains Folklife.* Oxford: University of Mississippi Press.

Williams, Raymond. 1973. *The Country and the City.* New York: Oxford University Press.

Young, Katharine Galloway. 1985. "The Notion of Context." *Western Folklore* 44:115–22.

———. 1987. *Taleworlds and Storyrealms: The Phenomenology of Narrative.* Dordrecht: Martinus Nijhoff.

7 *Tradition*

Accept, to begin, that tradition is the creation of the future out of the past. A continuous process situated in the nothingness of the present, linking the vanished with the unknown, tradition is stopped, parceled, and codified by thinkers who fix upon this aspect or that, in accord with their needs or preoccupations, and leave us with a scatter of apparently contradictory yet cogent definitions. More important, I believe, than erecting and polishing a new definition, which would but stand as a monument to the worries of our unmemorable era, is developing an understanding of the concept in the breadth of its semantic extent. Widening into an embrace of the many ways people convert the old into the new, tradition spreads into association with adjacent, related, equally indispensable terms. Our understanding begins as we refine tradition in conjunction with history and culture.

History

History is not the past; it is an artful assembly of materials from the past, designed for usefulness in the future. In this way, history verges upon that idea of tradition in which it is identified with the resource out of which people create. History and tradition are comparable in dynamic; they exclude more than they include and so remain open to endless revision. They are functionally congruent in their incorporation of the usable past. But the terms cannot be reduced, one to the other.

Overtly, histories are accounts of the past. Their authors, acceding to the demands of narration, customarily seek change, the transformations by which they can get their story told. Change and tradition are commonly coupled, in chat and chapter titles, as antonyms. But tradition is the opposite of only one kind of change: that in which disruption is so complete that the new cannot be read as an innovative adaptation of the old. Discovering one variety of pottery lying above another in the silent earth, the archaeologist is tempted to interpret the site as the record of invasion. Undisturbed, the people would have continued to alter their old pottery, driving their ceramic tradition through a sequence of linked stages, but a clean break followed by novelty implies replacement, hints of violence; one tradition has gone, another has come.

If tradition is a people's creation out of their own past, its character is not stasis but continuity; its opposite is not change but oppression, the intrusion of a power that thwarts the course of development. Oppressed people are made to do what others will them to do. They become slaves in the ceramic factories of their masters. Acting traditionally, by contrast, they use their own resources—their own tradition, one might say—to create their own future, to do what they will themselves to do. They make their own pots.

The point at which traditions die, at which one tradition replaces another, might be described by the historian as the moment in which a superior force replaces an inferior. The superior, the active agent of the tale, is granted volition, made human, while the inferior is converted into circumstance, like climate and topography, reduced to a complicating factor in the context of progress. The folklorist might see the same moment as one in which a will, inferior in power, though perhaps superior in virtue, was conquered, the conqueror being reduced to a destructive circumstance—environmental like a cyclone—in the local context of creation. History is ill served by dichotomizing human beings into angelic and bestial, active and passive, victors and victims—some blessed with volition, others the creatures of circumstance. A better history would speak of the engagement of wills, of the interaction among traditions, each fraught with value, all driving toward their several visions of the future.

Historians need tradition. For one thing, it would wean them from their obsession with rupture, free them from the need to segment time into trim periods, and enable them to face the massive fact of continuity (Glassie 1994a:963–68; cf. Braudel 1980:29–34, 67–69; Evans 1973:1–17; Levi 1991 [1947]:135–41; Zimmer 1946:170). Not only in the cool, nonliterate society or the cyclical Eastern society, but also in the hot, progressive societies of the West, life goes on, people are born, they love and work and pass away. Most of that which makes up life, and makes it endurable, is neglected in history because it cannot be gracefully assimilated into hearty narratives of violent change. You can witness the struggle as the great Fernand Braudel, striving to limn the structures of everyday life, lapses into an ethnocentric evolutionism to bring order into his story (e.g., Braudel 1992:193–94, 205–6, 286, 304–11, 313, 323–24, 423, 495–97, 548). What Braudel needed was a tough, pliable idea of tradition that would have allowed him to collect continuity and revolution into a useful approximation of the past.

One boon tradition holds for history is that it would help historians handle the massive matter of continuity, perhaps guiding them to discriminations among the disparate occurrences jumbled under the rubric of change. For another thing, the big events, the instances of raucous conflict that punctuate the tale, would return to human scale and grow in interest if they were imagined as times when traditions—distinct styles of volitional, temporal action—met, merged, recoiled, or hardened into antagonism.

Since Herodotus, the eastern Mediterranean has been pictured in the West as the division between continents, the borderland between people complete in their difference. War, then, from Troy to the Persian Gulf, seems inevitable. But how much subtler it is to view that terrain as a place where people interlock in continuous conflict because, as Bernard Lewis argues, they share such similar theological traditions, while, as John Keegan argues, they hold such different traditions of warfare (Lewis 1993:3–15, 25, 79, 86, 134; Keegan 1993:188–217, 332).

Or consider the American Civil War. The mind numbs with lists of causes and balks at notions of mere difference between the North and South. The southern adventure in romantic nationalism created rival claimants to the American heritage; Herman Melville was disturbed to find Robert E. Lee to be—as he contrived to be—the new Washington (Anderson and Anderson 1989:572). The big pattern in the eastern theater becomes clearer when it is realized that the leaders of both sides were trained in the same tradition, that they adhered to the same culture of war, and that men in the ranks in both armies shared a tradition of political order. The result was stalemate, as every invasion of alien territory ended in defeat. Then the theory of command shifted in the North. The North did not defeat the South; the West defeated the East (cf. Churchill 1985 [1958]:7). The westerner Lincoln, willing to suspend the Constitution in his righteous cause, gathered western generals, willing to suspend the accepted rules of warfare. The new leaders, acknowledging number and acting out of the trans-Appalachian tradition of pragmatism that had made the western theater so unlike the eastern, pressed on, reeling from defeat to defeat, wasting land and lives, until victory had been won.

The simple story dissolves into a mixed welter of conflict. Slavery was the issue, but Pat Cleburne, a Confederate general fated for death at the battle at Franklin in Tennessee, was surprised to learn it from the response he received to his proposal that African American men be enlisted; and the Emancipation Proclamation precipitated mass desertion from the Union army (Foote 1963:631–38, 953–55). Boredom, diarrhea, religiosity, and ethnic prejudice, in humor and assault, unified the men at war. Class difference, reified in insignia, cut across the line drawn at the front, as men hid their fraternization from their leaders, and made young officers the butts of their jokes and old officers into objects of patriarchal veneration. And what of the gendered war: the women who clamored for secession at the convention where Jubal Early, who would lead his troops to the suburbs of Washington and watch them wither in the Valley of Virginia, spoke for union; the woman on the road to Appomattox who asked an officer for her man because it was time to plow (Osborne 1992:34–52; Wheeler 1989:140–43)?

A history of traditions unfolding out of different presuppositions into different visions of the future, and therefore often into conflict, undermines the clarity war demands, making it seem fortuitous that the right result was achieved in 1865. That it might have been different is proved by the subsequent period in world history, marked by spatial fragmentation in Ireland, the Balkans, the Middle East, India, Korea, Vietnam, and the Soviet Union. The student of the aftermath of the Civil War—or, in terms to fit this essay, the student of the Confederate tradition nurtured in reminiscence—might find it interesting to ponder the degree to which the process of fragmentation, segregating people deemed to be irreconcilably different into different countries, thereby kindling an era of dirty little wars, was advanced in the day of the League of Nations by Woodrow Wilson, a child of old Virginia, and, in the vigorous, simple-minded language of our time, a racist. At least, the wars of our days, like the Civil War, are not to be understood as simple and inevitable instants of pure conflict, but as moments of the mad convergence of different styles of creating the future. Tradition, a key to historical knowledge, is to be understood as a process of cultural construction.

Culture

Tradition and culture share vulnerability to superorganic conceptualization. Both are, at times, assigned deterministic roles in human affairs. But existential reformulation in the social sciences, now in its third or fourth generation and so far from its source as to require a new name—postmodernism—has properly inspired us to relocate power in people. There were distractions while structural, then poststructural, vocabularies were developed to clothe our thought, but culture and tradition are alike in that, today, we understand them both to be created by human beings going through life. The fact that cultures and traditions are created, invented— willfully compiled by knowledgeable individuals—seems a surprise to scholars who cling to superorganic concepts and who invent, in order to sharpen spurious contrasts, uninvented, natural traditions (see Hobsbawm 1992; e.g., Moeran 1984:122–24, 133–35, 166–67, 178, 213–14, 232), much as the ethnographers of an earlier day, surprised by the impurity of their field sites, drifted into dreams of a mythic time before change, and invented natural, static, functionally pat cultures. But culture and tradition, we have come to accept, are created by individuals out of experience. They have reasons for their actions, and their actions entail change.

Recognizing existentialism at the root of our thought, we should recall, in these days of intolerance toward the ancestors, that existentialism, if now metamorphosed into postmodernism, was once the dangerous philosophy of modernism. Carried back to the dawn of modernism, to the beginnings of the anthropology and folklore we still practice, we find two scientifically inclined men heading west to discover traditions that were clearly distinct from those dominant in the period. Boas among the Kwakiutl and Synge on the Arans described what they saw—the winter ceremonial, the festival of thatching—as old ideas newly enacted by real people with real names, in accordance with values that set them apart, distinguished them collectively, from the people among whom the observer usually lived (Boas 1966:179–208; Synge 1911:121–23, 149–54). We could drop back another century to find Johnson and Boswell on their westward search for alternative traditions (Pottle and Bennett 1936:3, 55, 63, 99–100, 135, 151–52, 186, 212–14, 221, 228, 263, 322, 326, 384) or continue to peel time away and follow Ibn Battuta or Marco Polo eastward, but it is enough to say that culture and tradition are alike in that they are constructed by individuals and in that they are constructed differently by people who, as a consequence of interaction within different environments, develop ways that, being shared to a degree of mutual comprehension, serve to draw them together, while distinguishing them from others.

Though they approach synonymy, culture and tradition remain distinct for reasons that made culture the modern term when tradition seemed fusty, and that make tradition, despite its detractors, better suited for use today. Tradition is a temporal concept, inherently tangled with the past, the future, with history. Culture comprises synchronic states of affairs. Overreacting to the excesses of evolutionism, anthropologists stripped culture of history and shaped it to fit the scientific fashion prevalent in the period from 1910 to 1960. But once acculturation became an anthropological focus, the need for history became obvious. Promising neoevolutionary arguments were advanced (Harris 1968; Hymes 1972). Culture began to be resynthesized by the half-step of diachronic analysis, in which steady states are compared with each other but the subdiscipline of ethnohistory remains peripheral, cultural history has not matured, change still titillates, and culture remains resistant. Culture is derived historically, of course; it owns no existence beyond temporal process, but history is not yet integral to the concept of culture. Culture resists time—tradition is a temporal concept. Now define tradition as culture's dynamic, as the process by which culture exists, and it emerges as the swing term between culture and history, the missing piece necessary to the success of a cultural history that would bring anthropology and history, with folklore as the mediating agent, into productive alliance.

In that scientistic time when *culture* was preferred to *tradition* for its ahistorical—nonhumanistic—properties, it was also valued for its comprehensive, systemic nature. Tradition seemed fragmentary, ad hoc, resistant to systematization. There is a way to talk about tradition that pushes it toward culture; we might speak of a "French tradition." In doing so, however, we seem not to imply a totalizing system but a historical linking of select, peculiarly French traits, and it feels more comfortable to speak more particularly of a French tradition in cuisine, or even a Western tradition of philosophy. Interest groups coalesce, people teach, learn, innovate, and teach again, and culture becomes a concatenation of diverse efforts to construct it. Politicians, priests, and poets, all French perhaps, do it differently, maintaining distinct styles of cultural construction, different traditions. We need not, then, think of culture as a consistent whole within which deviant versions are shaped by the rich or the poor, children or old folks, women or men. Instead of commencing with a comprehensive concept, we can move inductively, attentive to detail and disjunction, bit by bit working toward an unachievable completeness, learning how people, each of them individual, all of them social, use the resources within their command to create. Then we can note the ways in which their actions and interpretations align or conflict with what others do and say they do. Culture need not be abandoned. It can remain one of the goals toward which we work while speaking of the interactions among traditions. Another of the goals is history.

Folklore

Tradition shadows the effort to define folklore. More than a sign of academic insecurity, the argument over folklore's definition enwraps our moral stance and incorporates our concern for authenticity (Glassie 1983). If that which is folklore is that which is authentic, there is reason aplenty to be concerned with what folklore is and what it is not.

When folklore was distinguished by phenomenal patterning, authenticity was signaled by the simultaneity of the paradoxical traits of continuity and variability. Tales and houses were qualified as "folk" if antecedents could be arrayed behind them and uniqueness discerned within them. Alike and not alike, the objects of folklore were products of tradition, a process momentarily in the control of an individual whose peculiar presence was exhibited in variation, whose submission to the collective's need for order was displayed in an effort at continuity. It followed that tradition would be construed as a vehicle to authenticity, a means for achieving at once individual and social success. How could one accomplish the self without recourse to conventional media, learned in social experience, like language? How could society cohere without the compliant, consensual acts of individuals? And it followed that the inauthentic, the nonfolkloristic, was that which lacked tolerance for individual expressiveness, breeding alienation, or that which blocked continuity, begetting oppression.

When, as a result of the existentialization of the discipline during the paradigmatic crisis brought on by intensification of field research (e.g., Leach 1963), we folklorists shifted our attention from arrays of objects to people in action, and authenticity became situated in artistic communication in small groups. Arguing for his new definition of folklore, Dan Ben-Amos explicitly excluded tradition (Ben-Amos 1972:13–14; cf. Oring 1994:221). That fit the mood a quarter of a century ago, but Ben-Amos did not banish tradition from the discipline. He is the author of the one article on the subject that must be read (Ben-Amos 1984; cf. Rappoport 1989:79–100; Williams 1976:268–69). And his definition gained quick acceptance and remains, for me at least, adequate because it captured old virtues in new words (Glassie 1989c:24–35).

Folk and lore link people and expression in a functional circle. Epic and nation, myth and society, custom and community—all conjoin communications and groups. The group exists because its members create communications that call it together and bring it to order. Communications exist because people acting together, telling tales at the hearth or sending signals through computerized networks, develop significant forms that function at once as signs of identity and forces for cohesion.

To define folklore as communication within groups might have seemed satisfactory at the time. Dan Ben-Amos, however, added qualifiers that maintained the discipline's humanistic strain, provided continuity in a time of change, and welcomed the return of tradition by whatever name it would bear in the future. There might be communications that do not depend upon tradition; maybe the smile or the wail of sorrow issues from our genetic makeup. But communications qualified as "artistic" imply selections, formations, expectations, and evaluations that require time to pass, standards to be shared, and styles of creation and interpretation to shape into processes that are least cumbersomely named traditions. There are certainly groups that are not traditional—people gathered into units by police sweeps, statistical convenience, or sheer chance—but the group called "small" is only as large as it can be while it continues to be constituted by the artistic communications of its shifting membership.

The "small group" is like the "traditional society," a human aggregate assembled by customary conduct. Its order derives from powers held among its members that remain theirs to enact, modify, or discard in the moment. The opposite of the traditional society is the society governed by codified law and controlled by powers vested in the state. So radicals view traditional society as the authentic order, while liberals see it as a retarded stage on the evolutionary path to the state, old-time nationalists work in vain for the unification of custom and law, and bourgeois deconstructionists undermine both, inviting the war of all against all in which the victory of their class will be secured through unbridled economic competition. In daily life, people sometimes shift easily between customary and legal spheres, now gathering with friends for tea and conversation, now operating a licensed vehicle within the speed limit on a national highway, made wide and smooth for military movement. At other times, as E. P. Thompson has shown for eighteenth-century England, custom and law come into conflict as governments, serving the interests of property, seek to expand the province of law, while the people respond with the revival and consolidation of custom (E. P. Thompson 1975, 1991:9–10, 86–87, 110, 160–79, 336–39, 460, 530; cf. Burke 1988 [1978]:176, 243–48, 281–82). Our way, once casual and familiar, becomes formalized—traditionalized (Hymes 1975:353–56)—in resistance.

Accepting artistic communication in small groups as their definition, folklorists are not directed to the study of all of life. They come to focus on its moments of authenticity, when individual commitment brings social association. Their realm of the inauthentic, then, would contain nonartistic actions, the coerced or the perfunctory, and social orders so scaled that cohesion is trivial or merely legal.

Definitions of folklore by phenomenal patterning or artistic communication share anxieties about the survival of authenticity in the contexts of technological elaboration and the rise of the nation state. Both definitions shape programs of research that begin in reality and urge folklorists to abandon stratified concepts of society and learn to work from the inside out, from the place where people have the power to govern their own lives to the spaces in which their powers evaporate. The discipline's mission becomes balancing and complicating history's linear tale of sequential triumphs by attention to real people—women at the loom, men on the battlefield—operating in terms of their own limited capacity to construct the future.

Tradition in Performance

Inspired by Dell Hymes and Richard Bauman, we folklorists are apt to call the instances during which people create their own lives "performances" (see Bauman 1978, 1986; Hymes 1974:92–117, 128–34, 1981:79–259). It is a virtue of the theory of performance, a reason for its longevity as a central concept, that it accommodates the spirit of both the phenomenal and the communicational definitions of folklore. The dynamic of the phenomenal definition is transmission. When it conditioned our effort, we asked people where they learned their songs and in doing so worked to draw lines of transmission running vertically in time from source to singer. The communicational definition emphasizes horizontal exchange between singer and audience. But performance occurs in time, and within it acts of transmission and communication coincide. One audience member hears, enjoys, forgets; another absorbs the song, becomes a performer and a link in the chain of transmission.

Unifying transmission and communication, education and entertainment, performances are shaped differently by their participants to include, for example, greater or lesser degrees of interaction. And, in line with their interests, scholars can place the stress differently, featuring the vertical or horizontal, the historical or social, dimensions of a performance. But the performer is positioned at a complex nexus of responsibility. Taking command in the events out of which the future will rise, performers must, at once, keep faith with the past, with their deceased teachers, and with the present, the mumbling members of the audience who seek engagement now and might act later upon what they learn. Then, as the "variability" component of the phenomenal definition and the "artistic" component of the communicational definition suggest, performers must keep faith with themselves. Let me clarify these abstractions with real cases.

In the early 1960s, I often visited N. T. Ward of Sugar Grove, North Carolina. He knew many ancient ballads and several unusual local songs, and had even recast an old song into an account of the rough lifestyle he adopted after his wife's death. My intention in those days, when we accepted the obligation of documentation, was to record Tab Ward's entire repertory (cf. Abrahams 1970:147–60; Goldstein 1964:134–38). We spent hours with the tape recorder, and I was fortunate to hear him perform frequently for his neighbors in his kitchen and in the local store where the musicians gathered. The best I ever heard him play was one day when, seeing his orange pickup in the lane, I knew he was home and walked up on the porch. He was inside, singing "The Merry Gold Tree," accompanying himself on the plywood fretless banjo he had made. I stood and listened. The quality of his performance, the full volume of his voice, the energy in his hands, suggested he was playing for a valued and knowledgeable audience. He was. I entered and found him completely alone. I like to play, Tab Ward told me, and I like to hear the old songs. I remembered Wesley Sharp, a banjo picker from farther down the Blue Ridge, who played only for himself, after chores, on the back porch. Wes Sharp was one of the best musicians I have ever met, but he told me that he would not play in public for five dollars a day; he played, he said, only for his own amazement. Tab Ward would play anywhere, any time, but he played best for himself.

My grandmother, Alice Chichester Poch, was born in a log cabin and raised on a hardscrabble farm in the Piedmont. The baby of a big family, she was vain enough to alter her birthdate in the family Bible, and I recall her as the embodiment of elegance, pulling thin kid gloves onto her tiny hands, filling one pocket of her wasp-waisted jacket with shells, and lifting her own bright, slender shotgun from the wall in the hall. An hour alone on the hill, four pops, four hits, and at day's end she would bring the rabbit stew to the kitchen table that continues to define excellence in food for me. I was a sickly child, and she filled feverish nights with marvelous stories. Once I had become a folklorist, I realized those tales had Aarne-Thompson numbers, and I asked her to put them on tape. She remembered that she had learned them in her own childhood, and she might still know them, she told me, but she could not tell them to an adult. It was not until my children were old enough to listen that she could lie back, close her eyes, and let the stories roll out, faultlessly, one

after another. To her they were not folktales; they had no existence outside of the particular performative scene in which little children are fright-
ened and delighted, excited, calmed, and readied for sleep.

When I asked Peter Flanagan, a master of the violin, flute, and tin
whistle and the musical star of the Irish community of Ballymenone, why
he performed, he replied that he had nurtured his gift from God and his
talented parents for a reason loftier than getting free drinks in public
houses. His music, he said, could help people find the right road through
life. His claim, which allowed us to compare his gift of music to the
priest's gift of the body and blood of Christ at mass, was founded upon
the local view of life. Life is bad, and since it is bad, short, and hard, if
you slip into contemplation, you will become depressed, sucked toward
despair, the deadliest of the deadly sins. So it is our obligation to prevent
others from thinking too much. Peter Flanagan's music, like the tea that
his brother served, like the chat that circled their hearth, he called entertainment. Peter Flanagan defined entertainment as that which you do
for others in order to do them good. He fiddled to entertain, to lift people out of themselves and into social engagement, to keep his neighbors
safe from the terrors of meditation and moving on the right road through
life (Glassie 1982:96–97, 181–83, 467–73).

Lars Andersson's interest in pottery began in the big city, where he
took lessons and became a teacher of ceramics. Wishing to learn more
about the practice peculiar to his region—Skåne, in Sweden—he began
visiting Hugo Anderberg, old master of the pottery at Raus. Hugo had
determined to let the pottery close, rather than sell it to someone who
might not maintain his standards, but Lars Andersson impressed him.
Slowly a relationship grew, which Lars likened to that of grandfather and
grandson, and before Hugo was killed in a motorcycle accident, he had
taught Lars all the tricks of the kiln. Today, Lars has built a museum in
the factory, setting stern models from the past before him. Hugo's picture
hangs on the wall, the workshop is unchanged, and Lars works at the wheel
and kiln to make salt-glazed stoneware precisely in Hugo's manner. Lars
is pleased that his customers are pleased and numerous. But, as Peter
Flanagan said of the people in his audience, their ability to discriminate
is slight, and they will gladly accept less than the best; only another artist can begin to understand. To create the best requires upholding personal
standards, and for Lars Andersson that means making new pots of which
Hugo Anderberg would approve (Glassie 1994c:3; see Von Friesen 1976).

Yusuf Sezer describes his life's duty as passing his art unspoiled to
the future. Born to be a farmer in a mountain village in northern Turkey,
Yusuf encountered the art of calligraphy by chance. It changed his life.

Seeking deeper masters, he moved to Istanbul and received his *icazet-name*, the diploma empowering him to sign his works, from Hattat Hamid Aytaç, the greatest calligrapher of his generation, who had come, like Yusuf, from Anatolia to Istanbul for training (see İnal 1970:122–26; Ülker 1987:90–91). Through Hattat Hamid Bey, Yusuf Sezer connects to an unbroken succession of teachers and learners, stretching back to the great master of the sixteenth century, Şeyh Hamdullah. Proud to belong to this noble genealogy, Yusuf says it is his duty to practice correctly and bequeath a robust art to the future. But, he argues, he would not serve his art if he restricted himself to reproduction. Instead, weathering criticism from connoisseurs, he feels he must adapt and innovate, making changes to suit the times. Otherwise the new people of a new age, the girls and boys he teaches, would not be inspired to learn the art and carry it forward. Yusuf believes calligraphy was a special gift made by God to the Turks. Its enactment involves the measured inscription of God's very word. No art is more important, and Yusuf Sezer must make changes in it to keep history moving smoothly toward the future (Glassie 1993:130–37, 813–14).

In an endless ring of fire, the Lord Shiva dances. His left foot is lifted delicately from the earth; his right foot tramples the dwarf of ignorance. In one of his right hands, he holds the drum that sets the rhythm of universal life. In one of his left hands burns the flame that will consume the world, now in the fourth of its four phases—that time when people neglect the sacred and become obsessed with possessions, when teachers descend to vulgarity, the old attempt to seem young, and the young lack enthusiasm (Coomaraswamy 1971 [1913]:17–22; Zimmer 1946:15, 36, 152–75). The iconic form was established a thousand years ago in South India, but this image in brass, gleaming like gold, is a month old. It owes its existence to Rashida Musharraf, in Dhamrai, Bangladesh, who commands the men who model in wax, shape the clay mold, and cast the image in a stream of molten metal. Ananda Pal, sculptor of the enormous, terrifying image of Kali that occupies a new temple on the other side of Dhamrai, prayed and formed the model in accord with Hindu precept, but Rashida, a Muslim, directed its casting into permanence. She is pleased to help her Hindu neighbors, pleased to carry on the difficult craft of her deceased husband, but she is emphatic: it is her work, this god of other people, and she has made it because she is a woman of power (Glassie 1997:438–47).

It begins when the earthen egg of the crucible is cracked, when the lips part, the lump of clay is centered on the wheel. Yusuf Sezer touches black ink to white paper, Peter Flanagan lifts the bow to the strings. They take control, and they are performing when their multiplex responsibilities fuse in the heat of creation. Isolating within performance its valence of historical responsibility, without which it could not be, we have come again upon tradition.

Patterns of Historical Responsibility

Simple definitions dismiss tradition from serious consideration. One person, feeling tradition deserves no place in the brave new world of legal procedure, characterizes it as static. Another, favoring diversity, asserts a place for tradition in modern life by calling it fluid and shoving it into the maelstrom of negotiation and emergence. But tradition can be static, and it can be fluid; it can whirl in place, revolving through kaleidoscopic transformations, or it can strike helical, progressive, or retrograde tracks through time (Glassie 1994b:249–55).

Change, as William Morris observed over a century ago, is the natural state of tradition (Morris 1898 [1882]:157–58). Drifting through endless, numberless changes so subtle as to provide an illusion of stability, traditions stream into continuity. Wills collide and converge in new situations; continuity permutes through elaboration or compression, and stages emerge in history (e.g., Coffin 1961; Glassie 1974:181–88, 205–17, 225–31; Watanabe 1974:169–73). Or, since traditions exclude as well as include, they can be pressed toward progress (cf. Williams 1977:115–20). In progress, we bring certain aspects of life into sharp focus, dismissing others—though they continue—into the irrelevance of a dead past. A progressive tradition, old but still alive in our days, is that called modernization. In modernization the individualistic, the material, and the international claim attention and drive the planner. But the dramatic changes of modernization depend upon the simultaneity of continuity, and they are countered by revival, by efforts to revitalize the perduring collective, spiritual, and local dimensions of human existence (cf. E. P. Thompson 1994:72–74, 245–52; see Alver 1992; Burrison 1995 [1984]:xiv–xvii; Coe 1986:17–18, 39–44; Macnair et al. 1984:72–73, 85–143; Oring 1992:78–80; R. F. Thompson 1984:90–91; Webster 1991). Civic festivals, new versions of old works of art, and especially the consolidation of oppositional religious ideologies, when taken together, make, through revival, a feature of the contemporary world as pervasive and powerful as modernization. One tradition is continuous; running quietly at the edge of thought and beneath common life, this is the inner dynamic of Braudel's pattern of the long duration (Braudel 1973 [1949]:735–51, 773–76, 1241–45, 1980:11–12, 26–52, 202–17). Another, noisy and conspicuous, is modernization. A third tradition is built of recursive work as people plunder the past to confect new things. All of these traditions blend and contend in our world, and we are apt to congratulate ourselves for enduring in times of such complexity, times when traditions dedicated to stability, progress, and revival meet in confusion. But no golden age of integration lies in the past (cf. Williams 1973:9–12). It was ever thus.

All objects are traditional, in the sense that everything is created, however surprisingly, out of precedent. The spectrum of action is narrower. At one end lie routine behaviors during which people confront little problems within a stable field of old solutions, bearing down on the matter at hand while accepting the aid of the dead in the conduct of daily life (cf. Yanagi 1989 [1972]:135–36). At the other end lie energetic quests for novelty that eventuate in the creations that George Kubler named prime objects (Kubler 1962:39–61). The prime object, recognized as new and worthy of replication (the first image of Shiva, Lord of the Dance, for instance), requires a risky, valiant stretch during which tradition is reformulated, revitalized, or replaced. The question of authenticity arises, and the range of tradition is narrowed further by attitude. In my world, spun by the rapid changes necessary to capitalism, a scholar will alter a word or two in a tired formula and proclaim a new theory that will liberate us from the dead hand of tradition. In Rayer Bazar, the old pottery district of Dhaka, the capital city of Bangladesh, Mohammed Ali uses a new kind of clay and new tools and techniques to make new kinds of objects, yet stresses the traditionality of his effort.

People meet their historical responsibilities through modes of volitional, temporal action that their practitioners consider traditional. One such mode is repetition. A perfect instance is hadith. Literally "reports" or "accounts" and often translated "traditions," hadith are extra-Koranic revelations or sayings of the Prophet, sometimes set in narrative frames. Before they were written down, hadith were memorized for verbatim repetition, and those judged most reliable are accompanied by fastidious statements of their chains of transmission. It is logical that sacred words holding the force of law would be committed to memory. But in my days of collecting folksongs in the rural United States, I found singers frequently declaring that they were repeating an old song exactly, word for word, as they had received it. In 1962, Paul Clayton Worthington and I recorded the ballads that Ruby Bowman Plemmons had sung for Arthur Kyle Davis 30 years before. Separated by three decades, the texts contained changes in only 20 out of 276 lines. All were minor, and though all exemplified the variability of oral performance, only one was purposeful. When Ruby Bowman was a young woman from the mountains of Virginia, singing for a handsome young collector, she gentled one line in "Little Massey Groves." As a mature woman, she restored the original, more explicit words (Glassie 1970:31–33; see Davis 1960:172–75; cf. Mackenzie 1917:167–70). The songs were hers, but they had come from her dear mother, and while, of course, she met the scene of performance with her own spirit as a singer, at the heart of things she relied on her memory to hold and repeat the lyrics exactly.

With repetition the goal, people create and adopt aids to memory. Performers write texts down for preservation (e.g., Carey 1976:13–20; Dégh 1989 [1962]:264–85; Morton 1973:10; Scarborough 1937:15–16; H. W. Thompson 1958:xv–xvi). In Appalachia and in Ireland, I met singers who kept and traded manuscript "ballats." People refresh their memories from books and recordings until the songs learned from their parents become textually identical with those on paper or wax. Reference to external authority is not limited to late, literate, or technologically elaborated scenes. In medieval Ireland, as in the recent Irish past, and in widely separated parts of Africa, most notably Somalia, the roles of poet and singer separate, and the singer honors the poet through memorization and repetition (Bergin 1970:5–10; Finnegan 1970:106; Glassie 1982:696–99, 705–11). Traditions of creation are often accompanied by traditions of criticism designed to check creative excess. Russian painters of icons and Hindu sculptors of images were directed not only by the masters of their craft but also by priestly critics who evaluated new works in the hard light of religious stricture (Başeğmez 1989:13–16; Michell 1988 [1977]:54–55). When Peter Cassidy and James Owens mustered young Peter Flanagan and his comrades into the Ballymenone mumming squad, they taught them the text of the drama, and they taught them "the mummers' rule" that provided options, set limits, and established firm norms for performance (Glassie 1975:25–27, 48, 136–37).

For certain genres, among certain people, the technique is memorization and the goal is repetition (e.g., Ives 1978:396–401; Johnson 1974:12–15, 178–80). From such situations, folklorists learn to emphasize transmission and to think of traditions as things, items, as song texts and quilt patterns passed from generation to generation.

In Ballymenone, where singers feel they should repeat the words of the poets with care, where the young men memorized their lines and submitted to the mummers' rule on their rowdy ramble from house to house at Christmas, Hugh Nolan, the community's revered historian, told me that narrators must, at once, hold to the truth and use words of their own (Glassie 1982:36–40, 47–48, 69–70, 113, 118–19, 144–47, 699–705). To hold to the truth, Hugh Nolan said, one must tell the whole tale, and to do that, one must hear and evaluate every rendition. Sometimes the

wish is to reconstitute the creation of a particular composer of stories—
"composer," not "teller," was his word—after the manner of a singer
putting a poem into performance. But when accounts differ, as they generally do in the legends that he considered most important, the teller's
task is, in Hugh Nolan's words, to gather up and rehearse, synthesizing
the truest version. Then cleaving to that version, a creation of the responsible self, the teller is obliged, owing to the limitations of memory and
the peculiar needs of every audience, to use words of his own.

Some matters are nonnegotiable. Upholding a personal commitment
to truth that filled his body with pleasure, while shaping tales to delight
and instruct the people assembled at the small fire in his black house,
Hugh Nolan discriminated between what was essential and what was
expendable in the tales he had heard. He reduced the past to features
worthy of preservation—events in sequence, key quotations—then held
them ready at hand to be shuffled, combined, and strung together when
he invented a story to fit the flickering moment. Comparably, potters in
the United States make distinctions, attentively preserving certain aspects of old practice while releasing others into the realm of interactive
innovation. The women at Acoma and the men in north Georgia both
call their pottery traditional if its technology, in particular its technology of shaping and firing, follows received procedure. In form and orna-
ment, they feel freer to experiment (Glassie 1999:36–56). Performers who
establish a hierarchical relation between the variable and the invariant
become capable of expansive new creations (cf. Chomsky 1971:50–51; e.g.,
Buchan 1972:158, 166–67; Haring 1994:24–25, 42–43, 57; Holbek 1987:205,
407; Jones 1989 [1975]:245; Lord 1960:88–123, 230–31; Ramanujan 1992:
25, 44–46; Vlach 1992 [1981]:88–93). Artists who merge preservation and
experimentation in performance guide folklorists into understanding
tradition as a dimension within every creative act.

In one dynamic, the whole is repeated. In another, entities are dis-
membered and essences are preserved. In a third, what is preserved is a
general tone, a sound, a look, a certain spirit. Turkish artisans have a word
for tradition, *gelenek*, but they do not envision the traditional, the *gele-
neksel*, as requiring a struggle to memorize or preserve. They see it as the
ineluctable consequence of human experience, the result of growth
among unavoidable influences. They were trained by a master in an ate-
lier. But their training involved little by way of formal instruction. Instead, the master established a climate of discipline within which, the
artisans tell me, they worked, watched, tried, and, at last, taught themselves (Glassie 1989a:34, 37–38, 1989b:16–19, 1989c:92–106, 1993:201–
9, 527–30, 669–77, 701–3, 813–19, 830–32, 862–69; cf. Coomaraswamy

1956 [1943]:76–77; Frykman and Löfgren 1987:45; Saga 1990:216–17, 235–37). Then aspiring toward perfection, stretching for adult status, they simultaneously accomplished personal success and the incarnation of tradition in new things.

Mehmet Gürsoy, a leading potter in Kütahya, a city in western Turkey where forty thousand people work in the ceramic trade, employed Sufi metaphor to put it like this: In youth, while learning, you breathe in the air of experience. The air circulates within, mingling with the breath of your own soul. Then in creation you exhale and your works emit a certain *hava*, an air that they inevitably share with works created by others who inhale and exhale within the same atmosphere. Mehmet's creations, brought out of his own body, are exactly like no others in the world. Yet he has shaped them out of life in a particular time and place, and so they must, in some measure, resemble those of his colleagues and competitors—Ibrahim Erdeyer, Nurten Şahin, Saim Kolhan, Sıtkı Olçar—as well as those of the masters in the generation before them, Hakkı Ermumcu and Faruk Şahin. And so they will seem both fresh and familiar to the buyers in the market who matured in the same cultural environment. Artists in Kütahya are not obliged to memorize or preserve. They can do whatever they want to do—closely copying antique masterpieces, cleverly blending the models around them, boldly inventing original designs—because, being suspended in the alembic of collective experience, when they act authentically, their creations will necessarily, nonchalantly, radiate the aura of tradition. From such examples, folklorists learn to understand tradition as a process, an integrated style of creation.

Things vary with need and circumstance, by genre and culture. The more secure, the less embattled the actor, the freer the action. But when actions are shaped sincerely, tradition will be present.

Volitional, Temporal Action

At the end it is customary to repeat for clarity. While agreeing with Rabindranath Tagore that clarity is not the highest purpose in communication (Tagore 1980 [1917]:73), I will comply with tradition, as one should in an essay on the topic, and repeat that tradition is the means for deriving the future from the past and then define tradition, once again, as volitional, temporal action. Spanning from the routine to the inventive, tradition is characterized diversely as a result of scholarly interest and—and this is more important—as a result of differences among cultures. In different situations, tradition can be identified with the products, whether casual or canonical, of historical action, or as the historical axis within creative acts, or as the style of historical construction peculiar to a culture. As resource and process, as wish for stability, progress, or revitalization, tradition—or something like it with another name—is the inbuilt motive force of culture. History need not be seen as circumstantial to culture, as an external power that causes changes in synchronic states. It can be seen as an integral component of culture, its adaptive urge to becoming. Nor must history and culture be ranged beyond the reach of men and women. The big patterns are the yield of small acts. History, culture, and the human actor meet in tradition.

References Cited

Abrahams, Roger D. 1970. *A Singer and Her Songs: Almeda Riddle's Book of Ballads.* Baton Rouge: Louisiana State University Press.

Alver, Brynjulf. 1992. "The Making of Traditions and the Problem of Revitalization." In *Tradition and Modernisation.* Ed. Reimund Kvideland. 65–71. Turku: Nordic Institute of Folklore.

Anderson, Nancy Scott, and Dwight Anderson. 1989. *The Generals: Ulysses S. Grant and Robert E. Lee.* New York: Vintage.

Başeğmez, Şinasi. 1989. *Icons.* Trans. Victoria Taylor Saçlioğlu. Istanbul: Yapı Kredi Yayınları.

Bauman, Richard. 1978. *Verbal Art as Performance.* Rowley, Mass.: Newbury House.

———. 1986. *Story, Performance, and Event: Contextual Studies in Oral Narrative.* Cambridge: Cambridge University Press.

Ben-Amos, Dan. 1972. "Toward a Definition of Folklore in Context." In *Toward New Perspectives in Folklore.* Ed. Américo Paredes and Richard Bauman. 3–15. Austin: University of Texas Press.

———. 1984. "The Seven Strands of *Tradition:* Varieties in Its Meaning in American Folklore Studies." *Journal of Folklore Research* 21:97–131.

Bergin, Osborn. 1970. *Irish Bardic Poetry: Texts and Translations Together with an Introductory Lecture.* Dublin: Institute for Advanced Studies.

Boas, Franz. 1966. *Kwakiutl Ethnography.* Ed. Helen Codere. Chicago: University of Chicago Press.

Braudel, Fernand. 1973 [1949]. *The Mediterranean and the Mediterranean World in the Age of Philip II.* Trans. Sian Reynolds. New York: Harper and Row.

———. 1980. *On History.* Trans. Sarah Matthews. Chicago: University of Chicago Press.

———. 1992. *The Structures of Everyday Life: The Limits of the Possible.* Trans. Sian Reynolds. Berkeley: University of California Press.

Buchan, David. 1972. *The Ballad and the Folk.* London: Routledge and Kegan Paul.

Burke, Peter. 1988 [1978]. *Popular Culture in Early Modern Europe.* Aldershot, U.K.: Wildwood House.

Burrison, John. 1995 [1984]. *Brothers in Clay: The Story of Georgia Folk Pottery.* Athens: University of Georgia Press.

Carey, George C. 1976. *A Sailor's Songbag: An American Rebel in an English Prison, 1777–1779.* Amherst: University of Massachusetts Press.

Chomsky, Noam. 1971. *Problems of Knowledge and Freedom: The Russell Lectures.* New York: Vintage.

Churchill, Winston S. 1985 [1958]. *The American Civil War.* New York: Fairfax Press.

Coe, Ralph T. 1986. *Lost and Found Traditions: Native American Art, 1965–1985.* New York: American Federation of Arts.

Coffin, Tristram P. 1961. "Mary Hamilton and the Anglo-American Ballad as an Art Form." In *The Critics and the Ballad.* Ed. MacEdward Leach and Tristram P. Coffin. 245–56. Carbondale: Southern Illinois University Press.

Coomaraswamy, Ananda K. 1956 [1943]. *Christian and Oriental Philosophy of Art.* New York: Dover.

———. 1971 [1913]. *The Arts and Crafts of India and Ceylon.* New Delhi: Today's and Tomorrow's Printers and Publishers.

Davis, Arthur Kyle. 1960. *More Traditional Ballads of Virginia: Collected with the Cooperation of Members of the Virginia Folklore Society.* Chapel Hill: University of North Carolina Press.

Dégh, Linda. 1989 [1962]. *Folktales and Society: Story-telling in a Hungarian Peasant Community.* Trans. Emily M. Schossberger. Bloomington: Indiana University Press.

Evans, E. Estyn. 1973. *The Personality of Ireland: Habitat, Heritage, and History.* Cambridge: Cambridge University Press.

Finnegan, Ruth. 1970. *Oral Literature in Africa.* Oxford: Clarendon Press.

Foote, Shelby. 1963. *The Civil War: A Narrative, Fredericksburg to Meridian.* New York: Random House.

Frykman, Jonas, and Orvar Löfgren. 1987. *Culture Builders: A Historical Anthropology of Middle-Class Life.* Trans. Alan Crozier. New Brunswick, N.J.: Rutgers University Press.

Glassie, Henry. 1970. "'Take That Night Train to Selma': An Excursion to the Outskirts of Scholarship." In *Folksongs and Their Makers.* Ed. Ray B. Browne, Henry Glassie, Edward D. Ives, and John F. Szwed. 1–68. Bowling Green, Ohio: Bowling Green University Popular Press.

———. 1974. "The Variation of Concepts within Tradition: Barn Building in Otsego County, New York." In *Man and Cultural Heritage: Papers in Honor of Fred B. Kniffen.* Ed. H. J. Walker and W. G. Haag. 177–235. Baton Rouge: School of Geoscience, Louisiana State University.

———. 1975. *All Silver and No Brass: An Irish Christmas Mumming.* Bloomington: Indiana University Press.

———. 1982. *Passing the Time in Ballymenone: Culture and History of an Ulster Community.* Philadelphia: University of Pennsylvania Press.

———. 1983. "The Moral Core of Folklore." *Folklore Forum* 16:123–53.

————. 1989a. "Master of the Art of Carpet Repair: The Life of Hagop Barın—Part I." *Oriental Rug Review* 9 (6): 32–38.

————. 1989b. "Master of the Art of Carpet Repair: The Life of Hagop Barın—Part II." *Oriental Rug Review* 10 (1): 16–22.

————. 1989c. *The Spirit of Folk Art.* New York: Harry N. Abrams and Museum of International Folk Art.

————. 1993. *Turkish Traditional Art Today.* Bloomington: Indiana University Press.

————. 1994a. "The Practice and Purpose of History." *Journal of American History* 81:961–68.

————. 1994b. "The Spirit of Swedish Folk Art." In *Swedish Folk Art: All Tradition Is Change.* Ed. Barbro Klein and Mats Widbom. 247–55. New York: Abrams and Kulturhuset.

————. 1994c. "Values in Clay." *Studio Potter* 22 (2): 2–7.

————. 1997. *Art and Life in Bangladesh.* Bloomington: Indiana University Press.

————. 1999. *The Potter's Art.* Bloomington: Indiana University Press.

Goldstein, Kenneth S. 1964. *A Guide for Field Workers in Folklore.* Hatboro, Pa.: Folklore Associates.

Haring, Lee. 1994. *Ibonia: Epic of Madagascar.* Lewisburg, Pa.: Bucknell University Press.

Harris, Marvin. 1968. *The Rise of Anthropological Theory: A History of Theories of Culture.* New York: Thomas Y. Crowell.

Hobsbawm, Eric. 1992. "Introduction: Inventing Traditions" (1983). In *The Invention of Tradition.* Ed. Eric Hobsbawm and Terence Ranger. 1–14. Cambridge: Cambridge University Press.

Holbek, Bengt. 1987. *Interpretation of Fairy Tales: Danish Folklore in a European Perspective.* Helsinki: Suomalainen Tiedeakatemia.

Hymes, Dell. 1972. "The Use of Anthropology: Critical, Political, Personal." In *Reinventing Anthropology.* Ed. Dell Hymes. 3–79. New York: Pantheon.

————. 1974. *Foundations in Sociolinguistics: An Ethnographic Approach.* Philadelphia: University of Pennsylvania Press.

——. 1975. "Folklore's Nature and the Sun's Myth." *Journal of American Folklore* 88:345–69.

————. 1981. *"In Vain I Tried to Tell You": Essays in Native American Ethnopoetics.* Philadelphia: University of Pennsylvania Press.

İnal, Mahmud Kemal. 1970. *Son Hattatlar* [The last calligraphers]. Istanbul: Milli Eğitim Basımevi.

Ives, Edward D. 1978. *Joe Scott, the Woodsman-Singer.* Urbana: University of Illinois Press.

Johnson, John W. 1974. *Heellooy Heelleellooy: The Development of the Genre Heello in Modern Somali Poetry.* Bloomington: Research Center for the Language Sciences, Indiana University.

Jones, Michael Owen. 1989 [1975]. *Craftsman of the Cumberlands: Tradition and Creativity.* Lexington: University Press of Kentucky.

Keegan, John. 1993. *A History of Warfare.* New York: Knopf.

Kubler, George. 1962. *The Shape of Time: Remarks on the History of Things.* New Haven: Yale University Press.

Leach, MacEdward. 1963. "What Shall We Do with 'Little Matty Groves'?" *Journal of American Folklore* 76:189–94.

Levi, Carlo. 1991 [1947]. *Christ Stopped at Eboli.* Trans. Frances Frenaye. New York: Farrar, Straus and Giroux.

Lewis, Bernard. 1993. *Islam and the West.* New York: Oxford University Press.

Lord, Albert B. 1960. *The Singer of Tales.* Cambridge, Mass.: Harvard University Press.

Mackenzie, W. Roy. 1917. *The Quest of the Ballad.* Princeton: Princeton University Press.

Macnair, Peter L., Alan L. Hoover, and Kevin Neary. 1984. *The Legacy: Tradition and Innovation in Northwest Coast Indian Art.* Seattle: University of Washington Press.

Michell, George. 1988 [1977]. *The Hindu Temple: An Introduction to Its Meaning and Forms.* Chicago: University of Chicago Press.

Moeran, Brian. 1984. *Lost Innocence: Folk Craft Potters of Onta, Japan.* Berkeley: University of California Press.

Morris, William. 1898 [1882]. *Hopes and Fears for Art: Five Lectures, Delivered in Birmingham, London, and Nottingham, 1878–1881.* London: Longmans, Green.

Morton, Robin. 1973. *Come Day, Go Day, God Send Sunday: The Songs and Life Story, Told in His Own Words, of John Maquire, Traditional Singer and Farmer from Co. Fermanagh.* London: Routledge and Kegan Paul.

Oring, Elliott. 1992. *Jokes and Their Relations.* Lexington: University Press of Kentucky.

———. 1994. "The Arts, Artifacts, and Artifices of Identity." *Journal of American Folklore* 107:211–33.

Osborne, Charles C. 1992. *Jubal: The Life and Times of General Jubal A. Early, C.S.A., Defender of the Lost Cause.* Chapel Hill, N.C.: Algonquin Books.

Pottle, Frederick A., and Charles H. Bennett, eds. 1936. *Boswell's Journal of a Tour to the Hebrides with Samuel Johnson, LL.D., Now First Published from the Original Manuscript.* New York: Literary Guild.

Ramanujan, A. K. 1992. "Three Hundred *Rāmāyanas:* Five Examples and Three Thoughts on Translation." In *Many Rāmāyanas: The Diversity of a Narrative Tradition in South Asia.* Ed. Paula Richman. 22–49. Delhi: Oxford University Press.

Rappoport, Amos. 1989. "On the Attributes of 'Tradition.'" In *Dwellings, Settlements, and Tradition: Cross-Cultural Perspectives.* Ed. Jean-Paul Bourdier and Nezar Alsayyad. 77–105. Lanham, Md.: University Press of America.

Saga, Junichi. 1990. *Memories of Silk and Straw: A Self-Portrait of Small-Town Japan.* Trans. Garry O. Evans. Tokyo: Kodansha.

Scarborough, Dorothy. 1937. *A Song Catcher in Southern Mountains.* New York: Columbia University Press.

Synge, J. M. 1911. *The Aran Islands.* Boston: John W. Luce.

Tagore, Rabindranath. 1980 [1917]. *Reminiscences.* New Delhi: Macmillan India.

Thompson, E. P. 1975. *Whigs and Hunters: The Origin of the Black Act.* New York: Pantheon.

———. 1991. *Customs in Common: Studies in Traditional Popular Culture.* New York: New Press.

———. 1994. *Making History: Writings on History and Culture.* New York: New Press.

Thompson, Harold W. 1958. *A Pioneer Songster: Texts from the Stevens-Douglas Manuscript of Western New York, 1841–1856.* Ithaca: Cornell University Press.

Thompson, Robert Farris. 1984. *Flash of the Spirit: African and Afro-American Art and Philosophy.* New York: Vintage.

Ülker, Muammer. 1987. *Başlangıçtan Günümüze Türk Hat Sanatı* [Turkish calligraphic art from the beginning to our days]. Ankara: Türkiye İş Bankası Kültür Yayınları.

Vlach, John Michael. 1992 [1981]. *Charleston Blacksmith: The Work of Philip Simmons.* Columbia: University of South Carolina Press.

Von Friesen, Otto. 1976. *Krukan från Raus* [Crocks from Raus]. Stockholm: Nordiska Museet.

Watanabe, Yasutada. 1974. *Shinto Art: Ise and Izumo Shrines.* Trans. Robert Ricketts. New York: Weatherhill.

Webster, Gloria Cranmer. 1991. "The Contemporary Potlatch." In *Chiefly Feasts: The Enduring Kwakiutl Potlatch.* Ed. Aldona Jonaitis. 227–48. Seattle: University of Washington Press.

Wheeler, Richard. 1989. *Witness to Appomattox.* New York: Harper and Row.

Williams, Raymond. 1973. *The Country and the City.* New York: Oxford University Press.

———. 1976. *Keywords: A Vocabulary of Culture and Society.* New York: Oxford University Press.

———. 1977. *Marxism and Literature.* Oxford: Oxford University Press.

Yanagi, Sōetsu. 1989 [1972]. *The Unknown Craftsman: A Japanese Insight into Beauty.* Ed. Bernard Leach. Tokyo: Kodansha.

Zimmer, Heinrich. 1946. *Myths and Symbols in Indian Art and Civilization.* Bollingen Series, no. 6. Ed. Joseph Campbell. New York: Pantheon Books.

ROGER D. ABRAHAMS

8 *Identity*

> If you hear a word often enough, you'll forget what it
> means fairly quickly.
> —Brooks Hansen, *The Chess Garden*

Identity has become the encompassing term for cultural, social, and spiritual wholeness. It also emerges in discussions of territorial
integrity, often as a rhetorical ploy in struggles for establishing and maintaining domain. As such, it references many of the most central fictions
of our time. Such fictions invite questions, not of their truth value but
of their usefulness. *Identity* invokes a conception of individual and social life that has become ubiquitous but that causes more confusion and
confrontation than it designates meaningful social states of being.

The term presumes the uniqueness of each named whole (Köstlin 1997)
even as it draws on typical, even stereotypical, patterns that compromise
its value as a descriptive or analytic concept. Yet there is no more important key term in the vocabulary of cultural discussions; so it must surely
be useful to anatomize the body of this particular beast. This wholeness
is a longed-for state of being that emerges in a continuation of romantic
rhetoric and the invocations of nostalgia. Like authenticity, it rests on ideas
of the real and the enduring that do not bear up well under the investigation of everyday practices or extraordinary experiences (Bendix 1997).

In the body of this essay, I spell out some of the dimensions of identi-
ty-formation as argued by a variety of disciplinarians. I underscore the
dynamic and sometimes disturbingly contradictory features of conflating
democratic theories of self-realization with the politics of national or ethnic identifications. I conclude with the problems of confusing the two
modes of asserting identity through the argument pursued when using lib-

eral democratic norms to discuss conditions in what used to be called the Third World, including the Balkans, the Middle East, Southeast Asia, or Subsaharan Africa—wherever one hears the "Why do those people act that way?" question presuming that ancient tribalism is being resurrected.

Identity seems to be built on notions of an ideal life-plan or an archetypal map of the actual world. No sense of play is manifested in discussions of identity, nor is there any recognition of the historical ironies that hover around deliberations of national, social, or individual identities. The discourse on identity carries this burden because it emerges from perceptions of social and cultural difference, seemingly arguing that bounded wholeness can be maintained in a culturally plural environment.

Claims for the uniqueness of these markers of difference overwhelm the commonsense notion (borne out by genetic research) that human beings are more alike throughout the world than otherwise.

Difference observed along these parameters emerges within cosmopolitan and nation-state settings. Distinctions are made, for social and political purposes, on geographical, linguistic and lifestyle perceptions, sometimes by the group so identified and sometimes by those in power about others who are within their ambit or at its borders. It is difficult to discuss identity without invoking deep stereotyping of those designated as stranger or enemy. One way or the other issues of power, segregation, and often subjugation become an outcome of such discussions.

Observations of social and cultural identification and difference come to a head in vigorous connotations that act as magnets for diverse and highly mobilized peoples. But just how important these observations are in marketplace exchanges needs to be problematized. For at such centers, observations of cultural difference surely exist, especially with regard to differences arising from styles of interactions. But social leveling occurs at the moment of exchange, as well; within the marketplace, identity is subordinated to the power of the goods and the services being exchanged. Moreover, in the marketplace, the assuming of roles, even disguises, is taken for granted. This commonplace rehearsal of cultures, which appears to be built into commercial sites of exchange, has produced a popular literature on the different *types* of figures found at these crossroads, documents that both celebrate diversity and attempt to give it order. In the form of national and occupational stereotypes and conventional stage-figures, a map of the marketplace has been projected since the beginnings of early modern Europe.[1]

These are early responses to the dispersal of peoples driven by economic necessity or desire. Such "trade diasporas" (Cohen 1971; see also Curtin 1984) present an inventory of life-choices based on the observed stylistic differences dramatized at points of exchange between different peoples. This willing movement must be contrasted with the many displacements of whole populations during war.

Ethnographers concerned with expressive culture attempt to understand more subtly the concerns about achieving and maintaining identities within the polities in which the various diasporic peoples find themselves. The questions relating to the maintenance or disappearance of cultural forms, or the invention of new forms of expression, are highlighted in situations of both the host and guest and with the creation of isolated sites in which the dispersed peoples are interred: ghettos, prisons, concentration or internment camps, those "neutral" zones so often found at the border between polities at war.

The dispersals that arise in response to market forces are being reexamined by cultural critics, though often in league with terms such as *postcolonial* which draw on the rhetoric of victimhood. *Cosmopolitanism* is now replaced in the main by the less socially marked *creolization* and *hybridity* (Canclini 1995; Hannerz 1992; Kapchan and Strong 1999; Baron and Cara 2002). The question that arises from this altered perspective is whether one can conceive of a creole, a hybrid, even a diasporic identity.

Terms upon Terms

Identity also has been drawn into discussions of other loosely employed key terms: folklore, ethnicity, tradition, authenticity, heritage, and even culture and context. All have been designated as inventions in the sense used by cultural critics: socially constructed concepts, with the hint that they are used to mystify rather than clarify in public debates. Additionally, all have undergone extensive tugs and pulls as the tourist and the spectacle-seeker have come to dominate our modern condition and as the inventions of popular culture have caused us to rethink the very nature of vernacular creativity.

Identity-seeking is not a new concept. Rather it involves renaming and a recasting of older notions: of genius as it was employed in the Renaissance, and of race, blood, and national and personal character as understood in the eighteenth and nineteenth centuries. Identity was used as a way of discussing the basic features of an individual or a people negotiating social or national boundary markings (Dundes 1983:236–37). Identity carries the burden of these earlier terms and usages even as they have been displaced in contemporary debates. The ghosts that lie hidden in the ideological arguments of identities, nationalities, ethnicities and the other related terms need revealing, as my colleagues and I have argued.[2]

Identity, in one or another of its formulations, has entered discussions of the public sphere at the postmodern moment in which increasing urbanization and its by-product cosmopolitanism have undermined the foundations on which social, occupational, and political identities have been constructed in the past (Hall 1996:1–36). Cosmopolitanism is an epiphenomenon of globalization. The changing nature and speed of information storage and transfer, accompanied by the alterations in cross-cultural market exchanges, have brought stylistic differences in music, dance, and other display forms to the notice of the commercial world.

In the main, this expansion has been regarded as a threat to traditional cultures. Many politically engaged social scientists embrace the approach of the antimoderns through the rubric of cultural conservation (Lears 1981; Hufford 1994). For folklorists and other analysts of expressive culture, the raised level of recognition of how these global processes impact specific populations underscores the fragility of inherited traditions.

For many psychiatrists and sociologists, as well as folklorists, one's identity emerges from the stories one tells on oneself or one's community. The sum of these stories constitutes the life-history of the individual or the group. Each incident, each report of past experience, is transformed as an emblem of both the uniqueness of the individual—insofar as they replay an experience unique in its time and place of occurrence—and a badge of group membership.

Identity, in its primary present formulation, emerged during an era in which the Freudian narrative of the guilt-inspired family romance was being displaced by the psychosocial narrative put forward by Erik Homburger Erikson. A psychoanalyst turned social psychologist and psychobiographer, Erikson described a life development pattern of eight stages in which individual identities were constantly being reformulated in the face of the characterological problem, which he called an identity crisis, of an age-related stage (Erikson 1964). Erikson worked out his ideas through conversations not only with other analysts (he studied with and was analyzed by Anna Freud) but with cultural anthropologists such as Margaret Mead and Gregory Bateson (Friedman 1999).

The discussion of life stages initiated by Erikson described the transitional periods in crisis terms, a rhetoric totally in tune with the social and political ambience of the 1960s.[3] At each stage he underscored the possibilities of personal renewal in the face of the crisis.

After the popular acceptance of Erikson's progressive scheme, the term *identity* was so widely accepted, as it focused on one or another kind of life transition point, that by 1972, fellow psychiatrist and public intellectual Robert Coles could say that both *identity* and *identity crisis* had become "the purest of cliches" (Gleason 1983:463). To the extent that identity has been given over to the discourse on race or ethnicity, it has produced much discomfort.

Given the cataclysmic developments of world events and the use of racial or ethnic identity as reasons for massive displacements and military engagements, ethnicity and the process of purification and cleansing have once again raised the specter of genocide. On the more positive side, however, ethnic identities have been used in more benign political environments as the basis of official attempts to achieve political, social, and cultural equities in plural societies (Dundes 1983 surveys the forms of folklore in which these more benign arguments are located.)

Insofar as it enters into a number of specially coded environments, there is wide disparity between the usage of the term in different discourses:

— in bureaucratic life, where it is used to refer to the unique features of individuals as they are subject to official identification
— in political science, where it becomes involved in arguments on localism, nationalism, and chauvinism
— in social and political history, in which class, caste, status, standing, locale, or nation are used synonymously with identity
— in cultural history, where it is used as a synonym for national formation or in the discussion of patterns of domination and resistance as they are spelled out in particular practices, such as local and national festivals, Carnival, shivaree, or guerilla warfare and social banditry
— in ethnic studies, where it becomes synonymous with a group developing a greater sense of common history and set of cultural practices
— in the discourse on gender and the body, in which sexual orientation comes to the fore, often in parallel with ethnic identities as a way of focusing arguments concerned with historical conditions of invisibility—political and social erasure or discrimination
— in discussions of cosmopolitanism and the consumer economy, in which it tends to be deployed in Romantic terms as a descriptor of personal development by individuals making radical choices, as an artist, a consumer, a member of the "counterculture," and so on
— in cultural studies, that strange hybrid discipline, where it has been turned into a shibboleth in contrast to *subject* (McRobbie 1992:730; Hall 1996:1–36)[4]
— in the realm of the religious, where *spiritual identity* has inherited the meaning of *belief* and *soul,* a secularization and liberalization of the spiritual dimension of life that is much discussed in both the popular literature on social change and the literature on individual development of spirit

— in theories of personal development, where it is implicated in descriptions of the construction of self within a community's psychosocial resources.

A Folklore of Identity?

As a folklorist, I have been specially concerned with the idea of individual and cultural wholeness within our disciplinary discussions. The study of folklore, once singularly focused on shared and inherited beliefs and traditional practices, now has come to study the production and uses of the stories that a group or its individuals tell on themselves. Often, these stories are invoked by festive celebrations, in which both individual and group experiences are encouraged to be coordinated. Representative anecdotes evoked in friendly conversations as well as in times of reminiscence emerge as badges of both individuality and group membership. The broadscale introduction of identity into this discussion represents our unexamined attempt to maintain the importance of communities, even if the group under examination may come together only to tell these stories. The role of voluntary associations has not received a great deal of critical attention from students of expressive culture.

Coupled with the commodification of cultural forms as part of the entertainment sector of the service economy, local and regional styles and hand-crafted products attract a great deal of attention and personal investment. As representations of past practices they carry much of the burden of nostalgia, including the on-going dramatization of the experience of loss. Cultural study has been deeply affected by the bourgeois disease of nostalgia. We have all been engaged in creating and consuming objects and performances whose attractions arise from their internal sense of ephemerality and insubstantiality. In an attempt to reject the excesses of the commercial economy, we have been drawn into creating equally consuming passions, but for things and moments that celebrate a sense of pastness, that represent life before the commercial revolution.

My task, then, is to reveal some of this trace-work that lies just beneath the surface of the meanings of *identity* and its predecessors. I will rehearse some of the patterns of Renaissance and Enlightenment habits of mind as they enter into discussions of social identification processes and how these have been maintained in the present usages of the term. I will dwell on the changes that occurred in the 1960s throughout the West as they are reflected in broad alteration of vocabulary and sensibility. My objective will be not only to parse this semantic shift but to consider it in relation to the more flexible and heterogeneous ways of approaching cultural representations. In contrast to the implicit theory of integrated (or integratable) identities, I will suggest the greater usefulness of the play among and between identities amid cultural terrains subject to constant readjustments.

Identity and Difference

The multiple uses of the term *identity* developed from Renaissance and Enlightenment notions of how to give order to a world of increasing diversity. As commerce, travel, and entrepreneurialism developed, different ways of marking identity in the public realm emerged. Not only was *identity* used as a synonym for *name* or for *means of identification* in the emerging bureaucracies of the nation-state, but as a pointer to the social, political, and spiritual *place* of individuals and types in the order of things. Thus was humanity, and representative individuals, located in relation to God. Perhaps more important for the present argument, that ordering involved depicting the many types of humans by nation, locale, or occupation.

The encounter with heterogeneous populations engendered problems of surveillance and governance for expansionist regimes. Techniques for surveying diverse populations were a felt necessity; in this environment, inventories of subject populations were developed, censuses and collections, surveys of regional and local lifeways, all placed in a central archive for the use of those serving one or another imperial ruler. Hegemony might then be established by what today would be called databases. Which is not to argue that these devices were successful in achieving bureaucratic surveillance and control, only that they were developed as a scheme to do so.

At fairs and markets and in travels arising from the enlargement of material exchange, cosmopolitans throughout Europe developed an eye and an ear for difference. In fact, judging by the literature of the streets, colportage, the visual rendering of the various orders, native and exotic, became a fad throughout Europe by the late seventeenth century.[5] Reflecting the variety of costumes found at cosmopolitan markets and in popular festivities, these comic-strip map- or chart-like renderings conveyed the color and texture of street life in the centers of emporium culture.

Not only were these nationalities and their diverse styles commoditized in this published format. They were also available for purposes of travesty in these liberated environs. For here theaters and other places of illusion emerged as well where the various types became conventional stage roles identified through costume and carried objects. And in Carnival and other festivities that involved dressing up, they became part and parcel of the festive roles available to the celebrants.

This was an environment in which all roles become accessible to those who would so array themselves. This is also the arena in which other kinds of illusionist trickery were carried out. In fact, the street literature concerned with types also spawned a plethora of reports of the thieving technique of all sorts, of types of crimes and criminals, and of explorations of the variety of hoaxes.

The growth of the public sphere encouraged the development of street literature in which social and stylistic differences were given a visual and orderly—if also playful—accounting. When Jaques declaims on the Seven Stages of Man he is evoking the cliches of the Renaissance moment and putting it in conventional stage terms. Describing life in theatrical terms had already come to be one of the most common tropes, and one man in his time would play many parts.

The often-contradictory history of identity formation is suffused with the possibilities of upward mobility inherent in self-fashioning. While high-status dignitaries could parade themselves on state occasions dressed in their official garb, the playful and the ambitious could cobble together equally elevated identities through personal initiative. Dressing up ceremonially, moreover, opened up the possibilities of travesty. For under festive conditions, the high might dress as a stranger or an outcast, while the lowly might become prince or queen for the day.

In the main, discussions of identity are still strongly affected by the panoply of discrete public roles. Insofar as students of expressive culture have looked for texts, objects, and figures that represent such larger wholes, *identity* has been used more to refer to groups than individuals. But unlike other such keywords as *tradition* or *authenticity*, the semantic domain of *identity* is not tied to styles but to (apparent) matters of substance, states of being, or existence in its display.

Raising the place of openness, freedom, liberty, and other such concepts for exercising options, the emporium economy values choice-making above all else. Choice-making relies on observations of difference within the setting of public exchange. Folklorists and other students of expressive culture have entered into the discourse of difference in our acceptance of the principles of cultural relativity and pluralism. The special professional claim that we have staked out commonly focuses on observations of stylistic differences in material and expressive realms; to this extent we operate within the enterprise zone of ever-freer trade.

From this perspective, identity formation is a naturalized and presumably common element of all cultures. That this perspective must be resisted will become evident in my discussion. By not openly encountering the term, ethnographers of all persuasions have been able to assume the mantle of the invisible participant-observer, a role inherited in great part from the *flaneur* of early modernism, the cosmopolitan stroller in the city who follows Baudelaire in celebrating "the ephemeral, the fugitive, the contingent." Here the wanderer paints himself at the edge of pictures, responding to the varieties of life as it comes together in especially energetic places. Playing the role of the observer makes claims for invisibility—that is, without a recognizable identity, at least within the environment in which happenings are experienced and then reported.

Whiting Out

In his presidential address to the American Folklore Society, John Roberts points out some of the ironies that arise because of this unexamined and ambivalent professional stance. The field of folklore, Roberts argues, has a special take on the literature on identity. Like Ralph Ellison's eponymous hero in *Invisible Man*, folklore has benefited from the anonymity of operating without an identity recognized by the outside world (Roberts 1999). A lack of clearly stated purpose, while it raises embarrassing questions among other disciplinarians, has nonetheless proven to be something of a conceptual strength, freeing us from the necessity to develop fully shared understandings of the basic terms of the discipline, much less arrive at a common theoretical perspective. Roberts suggests that historically this has placed us in the social position of the protagonist of Ellison's novel, largely invisible to those around us, and therefore given the mobility to shape-shift and adapt ourselves to developing conditions.

This is a self-conscious move on our parts, an assumed invisibility, which has provided a useful rationale for pursuing and celebrating vernacular creativity wherever we encounter it. The appearance of engaged disengagement has proven seductive, not only to folklorists but cultural observers in general. When folklore was primarily the study of fragments of the constructed past, a poetic congruence between subject and scholar provided comfort to both scholar and collector. Both the folklore and the folklorist were presumed to engage with the most transparent, if mysterious, side of human expressive capabilities. Our objective was not only to discuss lore in terms of its origin and distribution but to assign meanings to the stuff of tradition, even the hidden meanings buried in historical reference or in the unconscious.

More recently we have pursued vernacular vigor wherever we encounter it. The sense of wonder with which antiquarian folklore study began is being revived in a new form. New theaters of memory and cabinets of curiosity are revealed wherever peoples congregate.

There is a shadow-identity here, or at least a historical identification on our part with marginal and often neglected peoples. Not only have we rescued the peasantry and their expressive forms from anonymity, we have also been drawn by the outcasts of the roads and the cities.

Across the Tracks, beyond the Pale

Identity also resides within another set of terms that are less positive and even less useful in developing a critique of postmodern culture. These terms are most commonly employed by the intelligentsia to describe the problems associated with questions of cultural equity: *inferiority, subordination, dispossession, disempowerment, marginalization, postcolonial*, even *counterhegemonic*. All are null terms defined in terms of loss and displacement, and all presume the existence of groups who have come into being as epiphenomena of imperialism through the deployment of negative stereotyping. How much do students of expressive culture attain our own sense of being by setting ourselves out as intermediaries or representatives of the dispossessed?

As with so many key terms, *identity* contains contrary meanings within its semantic field. When used to refer to self or group of identification, the word seems to emancipate, yet when used to refer to others it too often imprisons. Recent national political usage of this complex of terms takes away the element of choice from the process of self-identification.

In parts of the world embroiled in ethnic conflict, identity formation is not optional. You are what you are born into or what you are designated to be by the state or dominant group. The belligerent employment of identity has resuscitated the very idea of Balkanization, extending this concept to include many of the republics of the ex-Soviet sphere of influence. Here self-identification is accompanied by racial stereotyping and is deployed to justify the dispersal or murder of those regarded as enemies or outsiders.

Here, attributions of savagery and barbarism arising from a "resurgence of tribalization" and the intrusion of warlords into everyday life has provided the shorthand used by media pundits to explain local conflagrations—sometimes as an introduction for rationales for outside police intervention. Recent examples from Somalia and the Sudan, to say nothing of Afghanistan, were weighted with "objective reporting" in these terms.

An example: during the wars between various Balkan peoples, the popular press reported the awful displacements and massacres as evidence of the continuing "backwardness" of essentially "uncivilized" and "tribalized" peoples who are governed by crazy and despotic warlords.

I am especially attracted to the insights of Hermann Bausinger on these identity questions as they play themselves out in the modern world. Folklore and ethnicity, he points out, become implicated in dangerous political operations. In discussing identity in terms of ethnicity, "there is an inclination not to accept people just as human beings and neighbours but to look at them as members of another ethnic group with a clear tendency towards fencing off and demarcation. The only way out often seems to be the homogenization of political and ethnic frontiers. Thus, the autonomy of ethnic groups is extended from cultural to political goals—and quite often this attempt exposes minority groups to grave deprivations if not deportation and war" (Bausinger 1992:75).

Slovenian cultural commentator Slavoj Žižek points out the intensity of this stereotyping as it affects the politics of the region. The Balkans, he notes, "are portrayed in the liberal Western media as a vortex of ethnic passion—a multiculturalist dream turned into a nightmare." But this modality of thinking is not restricted to those living elsewhere. Slovenes themselves "say 'yes, this is how it is in the Balkans, but Slovenia is not in the Balkans; it is part of Mitteleuropa; the Balkans begin in Croatia or in Bosnia; we Slovenes are the last bulwark of European civilization against the Balkan madness'" (Žižek 1999:3). Others in the area adjust their response along the same axis of relative civility or barbarism.

It is not difficult for those on this side of the Atlantic to call all Balkan peoples barbarians, throwbacks to those times in which control over land provided the primary impetus for the nationality. Why, we ask implicitly, would anybody give themselves over to such thinking when all too clearly it undermines the achievement of individual potential? It seems self-evident that in the United States, at least, identity lies at the heart of how each of us may find a way to confront the equally slippery concepts of individuality and community. That neither individuality nor community are fixed states of being but contingent on the historical moment in which they are invoked seems self-evident in the late-twentieth-century environment of deep skepticism. For these concepts are employed as if they embodied "God-given" rights, yet this is patently not so. Both individual and group identities are contingent on the construction of the power relations that characterize liberal representative democracy. Or as philosopher Richard Rorty notices in *Achieving Our Country,* "We raise questions about our individual or national identity as part

of the process of deciding what we will do next, what we will try to become" (Rorty 1997:11).

Identity, in such a formulation, seems to mean the sum of the self-
classifications taken by an individual who recognizes alternatives. But,
as David Hollinger has forcefully suggested, is this process of choice-
making not better referred to as a process of affiliation? Writing in his
work of special social pleading, *Postethnic America*, this eminent historian attempts to recuperate the promises of social and cultural pluralism
without falling into the pit of the present multiculturalism debate. Says
Hollinger, "The concept of identity . . . can hide the extent to which the
achievement of identity is a social process by which a person becomes
affiliated with one or more acculturating cohorts"(Hollinger 1995:6–7).
Here, he is building on the distinction made by sociologists between
"achieved" and "ascribed" techniques of role allocation.

Surveying the varieties of usage of *identity* in the early 1980s, historian Philip Gleason locates the development of the present uses of the word
in the 1950s, between the publication of Oscar Handlin's *The Uprooted*
in 1951, in which it was not yet the reigning term for perceptions of diversity, and Will Herberg's *Protestant, Catholic, and Jew* of 1955. Herberg
argued that religion, by that time, had become "the most satisfactory vehicle of locating oneself in society and thereby answering the aching question of 'identity' (Herberg quoted in Gleason 1983:462). Yet this way of coming at religion has little to do with traditional and inherited churchly
practices; rather, by the time Herberg made his argument, belonging to a
religious community had already become a matter of individual choice.

Which discipline in the academy will control the discussion of cultural alternatives and changes? The growth of the materials and processes
of the production of popular culture scholarship is paralleled by the more
heavily theorized cultural studies literature. While folklorists and cultural anthropologists had attempted to assert their place in this negotiation, the claims of morally elevated and semiotically intensified "high"
theorists seems to have stolen the march on ethnographers.

Stuart Hall, the eminent cultural studies maven, calls attention to
these issues by asking "Who Needs Identity?" His response, not unchar-
acteristic of members of this cohort, surveys the work of Jacques Derrida, Louis Althusser, Michel Foucault, and Judith Butler, trolling for possible answers, and proceeds in this direction: "Since the deconstruction
of the subject is not the destruction of the subject, and since the 'cen-
tring' (sic) of discursive practice cannot work without the constitution
of subjects, the theoretical work cannot be fully accomplished without
complementing the account of discursive and disciplinary regulation with

an account of the practices of self-constitution" (Hall 1996:13). That should allow us to begin to solve the questions of Israel and Palestine, the Kurdish dilemma, and any other flare-ups that may arise.

Ethnic Politics, American Style

The introduction of the idea of identity was a part of the reassessment of the biases contained within previous models of society and culture. The mid-1960s witnessed a social upheaval that was paralleled by a shift in the central words and metaphors of public discourse. The increased political activism and the enlarged social concerns of that era were part of an expansion of educational opportunity, knowledge, and the ironic disposition that has dominated our lives until today. To prove one's humanity, one wanted to demonstrate the existence and the uniqueness of one's culture and one's folklore. Every group came to be designated in terms of its distinct lifeways, a habit of argument that is still very much with us in popular discussions of everyday life.

While the New Left proclaimed the New Politics, in the cultural science the New Ethnography was proclaimed, along with the New Perspectives in folklore (Paredes and Bauman 1972; Limon and Young 1986; Shuman and Briggs 1993). The various cultural and historical disciplines were adjusting their research agendas to give historical depth and geographical range to the traditional modes of resistance that were being displayed on the streets and the roads, where marches and sit-ins were taking place. Using a reinterpretation of the idea of types, the pluralistic idea of alternative "lifestyles" was brought to high visibility in those volatile times. Stylistic difference was articulated by self-consciously taking on the appearance of "the Other" by dressing as a peasant, farmer, or working-class stiff. That this was an extension of the archaic idea of travesty was forgotten for the moment; upending official structures was too potent a way of operating to relegate it to a historical process. It had to be reinvented as rites of inversion, processes of cultural reversibility, as evidences of resistance and counterhegemonic behaviors.

The idea of the folk had been substantially set in twentieth-century America primarily with reference to socially or geographically marginalized groups. But the term also continued to contain ideas of technological and educational backwardness. In resisting the system, the military-industrial complex, and an insensitive government, there was a broadscale inclination to identify with these marginalized folks—identity being achieved through altered patterns of dress and hair style, through organized social (the new equal-opportunity eating, which stressed peasant foods) and political action (demonstrations, marches, and other working-class techniques of resistance), and even through economic activity (selling on the streets, from blankets thrown down in front of the major emporia of a community). It became important to many people involved in countercultural work to identify as a member of a folk community. In this manner, the term *folklore* itself was democratized, removed from its earlier nationalistic deployment (Abrahams 1999).

In redefining the term *folklore* in the 1960s, the number and range of groups considered to be folk and to produce and practice lore was greatly extended. Certainly, the most significant change in the concept of identity has been its employment as a shibboleth in the discourse of difference—that is, in the apprehension of self and other[6]—especially as individuals cobble together personal identifications.[7] As it has moved to the center of public discussions of society and values, "getting it all together" has seemed not only a desirable state of being but one endowed by nature, a human right, if you will, or at least an entitlement in the truly civil polity. Personal choice becomes the buried concept in this praxis of self-identification.

From this liberal democratic perspective, not only is an identity a sociopolitical entitlement, it has replaced both pride of place and of station as a civic duty. Having an identity and using it as a way of creating a sense of self-worth becomes an obligation.

Unlike discussions of personal vocation, choices are no longer regarded as irreversible. Each choice seems to be arrived at for the sense of possibility it brings to one's life, one which heightens and deepens experience or well-being. "Never to have felt deeply is never to have lived at all" is the bromide of the moment. We have a duty to have an identity and to be happy with it, or at least to feel fulfilled by it.

Being unhappy or feeling unfulfilled becomes the bugbear of contemporary existence; a sense that not achieving these elevated states means that somehow we have individually and collectively lost our way. Thus the need to step out of life from time to time to "find oneself." In this environment of life-meanings, each time a life-choice is made (or is made for us), it is attended by a sense of loss, even a sense of being victimized by historical circumstance.

That this position is not necessarily found in other parts of the world is clear. In those systems in which one's identity arises from tribal, family, national, linguistic, or religious obligation, the achievement of an identity is not presumed. What could be more threatening to those of the West than "fundamentalists" or "dictators" who would make choices for others?

In the politically energized environment of the late 1960s and early 1970s, exiting from "the system" was symbolically enacted by self-consciously imitating previously despised or disempowered peoples. Not only African Americans and Native Americans provided the models for such imitation—that was already in the American grain before the beginning of the nineteenth century—but other excluded or outsider peoples became the models for serious or comic emulation. In response to such forces, the very character of folkness was self-consciously altered in the teaching of folklore and culture.

This folklore came to be taken as the constitutive elements of the group; knowing, performing, and participating in group activities conferred membership. By extension, individuals could be members of a number of such groups—indeed, one's life story could be conceived of as a record of taking on such allegiances. Historically distinctive groups, those who shared specific conditions, achieved high status in the national dialogue on cultural equities.

In a commercial economy, playing different roles and learning a variety of lines becomes a way of life for those in trade. As bourgeois values emerge from the growth of market activity, duplicity and mutability become second nature to those working in the marketplace. The traditional practices developed under these conditions would surely be as relevant to the study of expressive culture engagement as are the longer, more authoritative genres. In the postindustrial economy, moreover, entertainment is the sector of the economy receiving the greatest elaboration.

The massive displacement of peoples in the wake of the promises that the market economy makes to wage labor has been in the ascendancy throughout the West since the sixteenth and seventeenth centuries. But this kind of constant dislocation is little noticed in the literature on cultural production—especially that branch of the study concerned with the maintenance and refabrication of traditions.

Dealing with traditionally nonlanded peoples dramatizes folklorists' historical focus on small communities in particular places: the land-language-lore equation that emerged in the wake of Herderian thought. And now, the global economy questions the usefulness of the Romantic nationalist paradigm even more, especially as media of communication break down local, regional, and national boundaries. Not only has world music and dance drawn on the practices of traditional peoples, making them generally available all over the world, but rumor mills and gossip networks that used to be local and personal have now been extended to anyone in the world who has access to CNN, Internet, or any other 'mediascapes,' as Arjun Appadurai has called them.

The drift of immigrant-driven bourgeois cosmopolitanism resulted in profound changes of attitude toward expressive culture of all sorts. Clothing styles, body decoration, food choices provide a panoply of choices that underscores the centrality of choice-making in the achievement of personal identity. In such an environment, certain dimensions of traditional practices are seized upon and used in extralocal surroundings, bringing with them the aura of authenticity but gathering momentum as they are redeployed for New Age health, spiritual, or touristic entertainments.

This marketing has compromised the critical use of terms such as *identity, heritage, culture, authenticity,* and *folklore.* The result: an ironic interplay of meanings whenever these terms are employed, for now they always raise the specter of being bogus cultural inventions produced in the service of commerce.

Yet in everyday vernacular usage, all of these terms continue to be highly valued—and none more highly than *identity*—as they continue to embody the possible maintenance of a connection with the past and the promise of individual integrity. Nostalgia is at the center of such an enterprise, but that is not to undervalue the experience itself.

The promise of wholeness emerges out of those rare times when a feeling of flow descends on the individual, to use Mihalyi Csikczentmihalyi's term (Csikczentmihalyi 1975; Turner 1974), or when, as deep players like to say, they enter into the zone. Such evanescent occurrences carry promise of real and deep experiences—religious or secular times out of time when only the presence of the moment seems to matter. But they also involve being carried away, losing one's focus on the money- and power-seeking taking place under the guise of having fun.[8]

In such extraordinary moments, life is practiced in carrying out rules and exchanges that differ from those officially sanctioned and taken for granted. Just as in discussions of the law, both custom (or common law) and legislation (or written law) are a part of negotiations for civil rights.

The spaces and times set aside for such negotiations carried out at a high pitch have been usefully designated as *liminal,* or betwixt and between worlds, by Turner and his colleagues (Turner 1969; Turner 1974). Theory of ritual carried out in this mode has underscored the possibilities of renegotiating such basic matters as personal and social identity. At that point in the development of his ideas, Turner was most concerned with sacred ritual experiences; but as he confronted the altered cultural conditions of the late twentieth century, he devised the term *liminoid* to refer to other repeatable experiences not tied to notions of the sacred.

In zones of play, fun, even commerce, the customs and rules of everyday life are displaced for the ritual or festival moment. New rules, new roles, new ways of articulating time and space emerge in these moments. And it is precisely here, in this area of free exchange, that identities are most subject to being tested and changed or reconfirmed. Play and fun are invoked as ways of articulating these liberated states of mind.

In such worlds apart, dizziness and chance-taking, contests and even fights, and the entire range of imitations occur. Here Susan Stewart's descriptions of the worlds of nonsense and nostalgia assist greatly in understanding the nature of the rule renegotiation taking place; and Robert Cantwell's discussion of "ethnomimesis" details the many ways in which cross-cultural identification and imitation take place (Stewart 1979, 1984; Cantwell 1993). Within these worlds of play, fun, spectacle, even war and other kinds of high-intensity display, the very concept of identity implicitly comes under question.

Practices and objects that carry the patina of tradition, custom, and especially cultural memory are manipulated by those most deeply engaged in the exchange. Ethnomimetic acts question, confront, and undermine everyday techniques of asserting the uniqueness of local vernacular productions. Various imitations dominate contemporary expressive life while cultural rehearsals continue, and feelings of nostalgia adhere to both the experience as it takes place and the now-alienated objects that are carried away from the exchange—as souvenirs maintain the memory even as they assist in dissolving and redirecting it. This dissolving, this sense of loss in the concept of nostalgia, especially needs spelling out.

Dolorism

Lost lands and lost causes are among the basic elements of the deep story of westering peoples, in both the Old World and the New. Running in counterpoint to the stories of success in war or farming or commerce are stories and songs of failure. In their particularly American formulation, I call this story the American Dread, in contrast of course to the American Dream. Americans have been surrounded by these fictions, ventriloquized in blackface through the figure of the enslaved Africans or in Wild West shows by the Last of the Tribe. The family stories that arise at reunions remind one and all of the forced abandonment of the family farm or the family fortune; they all narrate the need for resilience in an emporium economy and the necessity of moving wherever the jobs take you. The sense of betrayal in this loss, the perils of living on the go, find their way into every facet of American entertainments.

Our popular entertainment forms in the nineteenth and early twentieth centuries took on these blue notes. In the figures of Old Black Joe,

Zorro, or the Last of the Mohicans, Americans found useful metaphors for the deep nostalgia of a restless people. These projections of nostalgia become politically potent when the story of loss is converted into narratives of victimization.

The argument from historical victimhood was unimaginable until the creation of the concept of the Holocaust in the 1960s and the subsequent reinvention of the idea of reparations. As Ian Buruma reports, albeit anecdotally, "it is as if everyone wants to compete with the Jewish tragedy, in what an Israeli friend . . . called the Olympics of suffering" (Buruma 1999:4). I think it is no coincidence that it was not until payment for deaths suffered during the Nazi era were made by Germany to Israel that ethnic pride movements throughout the West began taking on the rhetoric of victimhood as the rationale for their calls for other equities. Perhaps more felicitously, French historians, following the usage of Alain Corbin, designate this style as *dolorism,* pointing out that it affects not only the emerging literature of complaint but the research priorities and productions of the most visible scholars in many disciplines. Dolorism: "the constant dwelling on the awfulness, suffering and injustice of past lives, as if that were the only significant thing about them," as commentator Robert Tombs has noted, reviewing the Corbin oeuvre. "The retrospective conscription of long dead people into our own causes" then becomes an ever-present possibility, and worse, "our pharisaical self-satisfaction at always being historically on the right side" (Tombs 1999, citing Corbin 1994).

This habit of mind has been a very real problem in all the humanistic and social science disciplines since the decline of the civil rights movement in the United States in the late 1960s. At that point a new rhetoric of historically generated grievance was manifested. With the development of fair employment and equal-opportunity legislation, an environment was established in the United States in which historical and social grievances of the past were regarded as subject to redress in the present. Whole populations could identify themselves not only as being the descendants of an oppressed people but as continuing to experience the after-effects of this condition. The logical next step was to put forward individual claims to cultural identity based on the horrors of this shared past.

This line of argument—to argue a primordial origin for a cultural group passed on through a mystified process of cultural maintenance in the agency of mother's milk—gets ugly. It leads directly to twin evils: racism based on an exclusivist argument that a people should study only themselves and others of the same color or sexual orientation; and essentialized cultural forms and practices.

In Sum

Enlightened acceptance of cultural difference has become a core principle of commercial democracies. The most valued life-strategies arise from the equation between political and religious liberty and the marketplace notion of freedom of choice. The Marxian insight that these most important choices in bourgeois society are based on fetishizing commodities has become such a commonplace that it no longer carries much intellectual weight. Even students of situated expressive culture who have entered the field searching for alternatives to a consumer mentality find themselves not questioning this worldview except by taking notice of how local traditions have been adapted into products or productions aimed primarily at tourists and other cosmopolitan consumers.

In a tourist economy everything in culture can be recycled, everything is susceptible to being reused to produce moments of nostalgia without the pain of dislocation. Even the process of rehearsing and repeating significant experiences becomes useful to commerce. The Big Narratives can be revised and made to have, or to promise, a peaceable ending.

We must ask ourselves how much we really want to be involved in assisting peoples who perceive themselves to be oppressed by history to rewrite their own stories. How much do we want to aid those of the present who extend dolorism to include legal and financial reparations?

Identity discussions contribute, patently, to rationalizing losses of liberty and life. Here students of expressive culture have a lot of insights to offer, though little apparent inclination to do so, except to point to the existence of a lore of stereotyping and cultural cooptation. The lure of "taking sides" and of attempting to adequately represent the under-represented is too great. Being attuned to recognizing representative narratives and giving them their proper names is our professional business, is it not?

The new millennium will surely witness the imagining of new metaphors by which vernacular culture might better be understood. Certainly, if the pace of displacement of populations holds, while the rest of the world is bound together by technological means, we will have to forego any claims for critical understandings of culture by focusing exclusively on small-group aesthetic engagements. What will happen when questions of identity actively take into account the many diasporas? Diaspora itself has come to be naturalized, used in a neutral sense to describe whole groups of people on the move who carry extensive cultural equipment with them wherever they go. As the opprobrium regarding these populations on the move begins to be seen, not only as a display of difference but as a cultural resource, discussions of identity will be altered. This alteration is being felt already at those points in which cultural differences are subject to commoditization in the global economy. The association of vernacular creativity with the equation between land, language, and lore is questioned by those with an investment in the commercial movement of goods and services. Ethnic identities under such conditions become subject to being put to use in the culturally and socially plural environment, where they become imbricated in tourist economies and the heritage industry in general. Under such conditions, processes of hybridization and creolization achieve a more positive status in nationalist cultural theory. It is surely time to reexamine the concepts of culture emerging with the embrace of cosmopolitanism and the culturally plural character of the city and the market. Peoples involved in the import-export business of ethnically marked products and practices now choose to underscore their stylistically marked national identities.

While our task will certainly remain a matter of identifying and showing the widespread character of narrative typing of self and other, realistically such a discussion must be carried out by recognizing the contingent character of this lore and the rhetorical contexts in which typological attributions are made. We must examine how folklore enters into the characterizations of self and whether it is useful to regard selfhood as being the same as identity.

Identity will simply not hold up as a container of meaning under the conditions of the postindustrial world in which people move or are moved at a moment's notice. At these points will be discovered the conditions of vernacular creativity under adverse conditions that now provide the public with creative sustenance even as we of the middle class continue to fear and segregate the very people who consistently produce these marketable forms. The process of engaging consumers' fears and desires, especially with public entertainments, also maintains the social derogation of subject populations even as the subordinated continue to produce marketable vernacular styles. Questions of truth, justice, and authenticity have little place in this discourse except as they serve the fluidity of the market. A critical folkloristics and ethnology, now beginning to emerge, may provide insights into our role as commentators on the process and the directions in which the subject of our discipline should be expanded.

Notes

This article has been in the oven for so long that simply remembering all of those who helped me think through the question of identity and keyword articles in general are impossible to recapture. My apologies to those I leave out. My concern with the subject began in Texas, where Dick Bauman, Américo Paredes, and our students (especially Beverly Stoeltje and Susan Kalcik) talked through the subject ad nauseam. After a twenty-year hiatus, Burt Feintuch talked me into resuscitating the subject, persuaded me to carry out the writing, and then talked me through it as well. My good wife Janet Anderson, as always, has also been involved in developing both the argument and the ways in which it is couched. My colleagues Regina Bendix, Bob St. George, Dan Ben-Amos, Barbie Zelizer, John Roberts, Margaret Mills, Bob Cantwell, and John Szwed have talked through the subject so often that I know they have to be tired of it. The original issue of *Common Ground* focused the subject of keyword study so well that the participants in that project gave me the impetus to join in the discussion.

1. The European popular publications illustrating this anatomy of the world include the *Book of Trade*, the *Dance of Death*, the *Ship of Fools*, and the various modes of describing the "World Turned Upside Down." This colportage literature, variously referred to as anatomies or cosmographies, give voice to wonder and to social satire at the same time, ironically pointing to the vanity implicit in making such orders (Massin 1978). Moreover, these orders are celebrated in their fragmentation in cultural manifestations such as the Cabinets of Curiosity or Wunderkammern. The process of assembling these anatomies is brilliantly analyzed in Elizabethan terms as "the rehearsal of cultures" in Mullaney 1988; see also Daston and Park 1998; Stagl 1995.

2. Ben-Amos 1984; Bendix 1997; Abrahams 1992, 1993b. Dundes 1983 represents an early discussion of the folklore forms deployed in such arguments; see also Feintuch 1995.

3. I take up the reaction of folklore study to political and social developments in the wake of the 1960s in Abrahams 1992; 1993a; 1993b.

4. McRobbie makes an interesting plea to others following that field of interest. "Identity could be seen as dragging cultural studies into the 1990s by acting as a kind of guide to how people see themselves, not as class subjects, not as psychoanalytic subjects, not as subjects of ideology, not as textual subjects but as agents whose sense of self is projected onto and expressed by an expansive range of cultural practices, including texts, images and commodities" (McRobbie 1992:730).

5. This street literature has been mined heavily for traditional texts for purposes of annotation by folklorists and literary historians. But the colportage production has not been drawn upon by folklorists. Its relevance for an understanding of vernacular life and performance is patent, especially in the realm of festive displays.

6. This frame of reference emerges out of American Pragmatic philosophy as initiated by William James and pursued by George Herbert Mead; indeed, the very idea of reflexivity so current in cultural theorizing emerges from the same point. This position holds that the "self" is a human capacity for reflection upon actual situated practices. The achievement of self arises from a dynamic of interaction between the "I"—the subjective, creative, emergent

dimensions—and the "Me,"—the more known, outer, determined, social phase. Using the term *identification* as a name for this process, those writing from this perspective argue that humans are involved in a constant process of naming and renaming self. Sociologists pursuing role-theory and symbolic interactionism have approached this process in terms of a fit between selves and socially constructed categories.

7. Erikson in his later more political writings called attention to this troubling problem. Calling it the development of a "pseudo-species" in which ethnic or national differentiation became more important than common human concerns, he called attention to the process by which "one nation or group feels that it has the right, the power, even the obligation to denigrate those who look or act differently" (Erikson 1969, quoted in Gardner 1999).

8. Bendix (1997:176–87) surveys the literature in the United States, Germany and elsewhere. For recent studies building on such interventions, see, among others, Becker 1998; Neustadt 1992; Slyomovics 1998; Cantwell 1993.

References Cited

Abrahams, Roger D. 1992. "The Past in the Presence: An Overview of Folkloristics in the Late Twentieth Century." In *Folklore Processed: In Honour of Lauri Honko on His Sixtieth Birthday, 6 March 1992*. Ed. Reimund Kvideland et al. 32–51. Helsinki: Finnish Academy of Sciences and Letters.

———. 1993a. "After New Perspectives: Folklore Study in the Late Twentieth Century." In *Theorizing Folklore: Toward New Perspectives in the Politics of Culture*. Ed. Charles Briggs and Amy Shuman. 379–400. Special issue of *Western Folklore* 52.

———. 1993b. "Phantoms of Romantic Nationalism in Folkloristics." *Journal of American Folklore* 106:3–37.

———. 1999. "Academic Folklore and Public Folklore: Late Twentieth-Century Musings." In *Cultural Brokerage: Forms of Intellectual Practice in Society*. Ed. Regina Bendix and Gisela Welz. 127–37. Special issue of *Journal of Folklore Research* 36.

Amman, Jost, and Hans Sachs. 1973. *The Book of Trades (Ständebuch)*. New York: Dover.

Baron, Robert, and Ana Cara, eds. 2002. *Creolization*. Special issue of *Journal of American Folklore* 113.

Bausinger, Hermann. 1990 [1972]. *Folk Culture in a World of Technology*. Trans. Elke Dettmer. Bloomington: Indiana University Press.

———. 1992. "Change of Paradigms? Comments on the Crisis of Ethnicity." In *Folklore Processed: In Honour of Lauri Honko on His Sixtieth Birthday, 6 March 1992*. Ed. Reimund Kvideland et al. 73–77. Helsinki: Finnish Academy of Sciences and Letters.

Becker, Jane. 1998. *Selling Tradition: Appalachia and the Construction of the American Folk*. Chapel Hill: University of North Carolina Press.

Ben-Amos, Dan. 1984. "The Seven Strands of *Tradition:* Varieties of Its Meanings in American Folklore Studies." *Journal of Folklore Research* 21:97–131.

Bendix, Regina. 1997. *In Search of Authenticity: The Formation of Folklore Studies.* Madison: University of Wisconsin Press.

Bressler, Sandra Gross. 1995. *Culture and Politics: A Legislative Chronicle of the American Folklife Preservation Act.* Ann Arbor, Mich.: University Microfilms.

Briggs, Charles, and Amy Shuman, eds. 1993. *Theorizing Folklore: Toward New Perspectives in the Politics of Culture.* Special issue of *Western Folklore* 52.

Buruma, Ian. 1999. "The Joys and Perils of Victimhood." *New York Review of Books*, April 8, pp. 4–9.

Canclini, Nestor Garcia. 1995. *Hybrid Cultures: Strategizing for Entering and Leaving Modernity.* Minneapolis: University of Minnesota Press.

Cantwell, Robert. 1993. *Ethnomimesis: Folklife and the Representation of Culture.* Chapel Hill: University of North Carolina Press.

Cohen, Abner. 1971. "Cultural Strategies of Trading Diasporas." In *The Development of Indigenous Trade and Markets in West Africa.* Ed. Claude Meillassoux. 266–81. London: Oxford University Press for the International African Institute.

Corbin, Alain. 1994. *The Lure of the Sea: The Discovery of the Seaside in the Western World, 1750–1840.* Berkeley: University of California Press.

Curtin, Philip. 1984. *Cross-Cultural Trade in World History.* Cambridge: Cambridge University Press.

Csikczentmihalyi, Mihalyi. 1975. *Beyond Boredom and Anxiety.* San Francisco: Jossey-Bass.

Daston, Lenore, and Katherine Park. 1998. *Wonders and the Order of Nature, 1150–1750.* London: Zone Books.

Dorst, John. 1999. *Looking West: Excursions in a Landscape of Vision and Display.* Philadelphia: University of Pennsylvania Press.

Dundes, Alan. 1983. "Defining Identity through Folklore." In *Identity: Personal and Socio-Cultural—A Symposium.* Ed. Anita Jacobson-Widding. 235–60. Upsala: Upsala Studies in Cultural Anthropology.

Erikson, Erik H. 1964. *Childhood and Society.* New York: Norton.

———. 1969. "Letter to Ghandi." *New York Review of Books*, July 31, pp. 12–23.

Feintuch, Burt, ed. 1995. *Common Ground.* Special issue of *Journal of American Folklore* 107.

Friedman, Lawrence J. 1999. *Identity's Architect: A Biography of Erik H. Erikson.* New York: Scribner.

Gardner, Howard. 1999. "The Enigma of Erik Erikson." *New York Review of Books*, June 24, pp. 51–56.

Gleason, Philip. 1983. "Identifying Identity: A Semantic History." *Journal of American History* 69:910–31.

Grossberg, Larry, Cary Nelson, and Paula Treichler, eds. 1992. *Cultural Studies.* London: Routledge.

Hall, Stuart. 1996. "Who Needs Identity?" In *Questions of Cultural Identity.* Ed. Stuart Hall and Paul de Gay. 1–36. London: Sage.

Hannerz, Ulf. 1992. *Cultural Complexity: Studies in the Social Organization of Meaning.* Berkeley: University of California Press.

Hollinger, David A. 1995. *Postethnic America: Beyond Multiculturalism.* New York: Basic Books.

Hufford, Mary, ed. 1994. *Conserving Culture: A New Discourse on Heritage.* Urbana: University of Illinois Press.

Jacobson-Widding, Anita. 1983. *Identity: Personal and Socio-Cultural—A Symposium.* Upsala: Upsala Studies in Cultural Anthropology.

Kapchan, Deborah A., and Pauline Turner Strong, eds. 1999. *Theorizing the Hybrid.* Special issue of *Journal of American Folklore* 112.

Köstlin, Konrad. 1997. "The Passion for the Whole: Interpreted Modernity or Modernity as Interpretation." *Journal of American Folklore* 110:261–66.

Kvideland, Reimund, et al. 1992. *Folklore Processed: In Honour of Lauri Honko on His Sixtieth Birthday, 6 March 1992.* Helsinki: Finnish Academy of Sciences and Letters.

Lears, Jackson. 1981. *No Place of Grace.* New York: Pantheon.

Limon, Jose, and M. Jane Young. 1986. "Frontiers, Settlements, and Developments in Folklore Study, 1972–1985." *Annual Review of Anthropology* 15:437–60.

Massin. 1978. *Les cris de la ville: Commerce ambulants et petits metiers de la rue.* Paris: Gallimard.

———. 1981. *Les celebrites de la rue.* Paris: Gallimard.

McRobbie, Andrew. 1992. "Post-Marxism and Cultural Studies: A Post-Script." In *Cultural Studies.* Ed. Larry Grossberg, Cary Nelson, and Paula Treichler. 719–30. London: Routledge.

Meillassoux, Claude, ed. 1971. *The Development of Indigenous Trade and Markets in West Africa: Studies Presented and Discussed at the Tenth International African Seminar at Fourah Bay College, Freetown, December 1969.* London: Oxford University Press.

Mullaney, Steven. 1988. *The Place of the Stage: License, Play, and Power in Renaissance England.* Chicago: University of Chicago Press.

Neustadt, Kathy. 1992. *Clambake: A History of an American Tradition.* Amherst: University of Massachusetts Press.

Norbeck, Edward. 1974. *The Anthropological Study of Human Play.* Houston: Rice University Studies.

Paredes, Américo, and Richard Bauman, eds. 1972. *New Perspectives in Folklore.* Austin: University of Texas Press.

Price, Richard, and Sally Price. 1995. *On the Mall: Presenting Maroon Tradition-Bearers at the 1992 FAF.* Bloomington: Indiana University Press.

Roberts, John W. 1999. "'. . . Hidden Right Out in the Open': The Field of Folklore and the Problem of Invisibility." *Journal of American Folklore* 112:119–40.

Rorty, Richard. 1989. *Contingency, Irony, and Solidarity.* Cambridge: Cambridge University Press.

————. 1997. *Achieving Our Country: Leftist Thought in Twentieth-Century America*. Cambridge, Mass.: Harvard University Press.

Shuman, Amy, and Charles Briggs, eds. 1993. *Beyond New Perspectives*. Special issue of *Western Folklore* 52.

Slyomovics, Susan. 1998. *The Object of Memory: Arab and Jew Narrate the Palestinian Village*. Philadelphia: University of Pennsylvania Press.

Stagl, Justin. 1995. *A History of Curiosity: The Theory of Travel, 1550–1800*. London: Harwood Academic.

Stewart, Susan. 1979. *Nonsense: Aspects of Intertexuality in Folklore and Literature*. Baltimore: Johns Hopkins University Press.

————. 1984. *On Longing: Narratives of the Miniature, the Gigantic, the Souvenir, the Collection*. Baltimore: Johns Hopkins University Press.

Tombs, Robert. 1999. "Dolorism." *London Review of Books*, Mar. 28.

Turner, Victor W. 1969. *The Ritual Process: Structure and Anti-Structure*. Ithaca: Cornell University Press.

————. 1974. "Liminal to Liminoid, in Play, Flow, and Ritual: An Essay in Comparative Symbology." In *The Anthropological Study of Human Play*. Ed. Edward Norbeck. 53–92. Houston: Rice University Studies.

Žižek, Slavoj. 1999. "You May!" *London Review of Books*, Feb. 17, pp. 3–6.

Contributors

ROGER D. ABRAHAMS recently retired as the Hum Rosen professor of folklore and folklife and as the first director of the Center for Folklore and Ethnography at the University of Pennsylvania. As of late, he has been writing articles, published in diverse places, on festive gatherings in Early America and on the history of folklore studies.

BURT FEINTUCH is a professor of folklore and English at the University of New Hampshire, where he directs the Center for the Humanities. He has done fieldwork in musical communities in Great Britain, the United States, and Canada, and he has published books, articles, and sound recordings on music and dance, cultural conservation, and other subjects. With David H. Watters, he is the editor of the *Encyclopedia of New England Culture*, forthcoming from Yale University Press. From 1990 to 1995 he edited the *Journal of American Folklore*.

HENRY GLASSIE, College Professor of Folklore at Indiana University, received the Ph.D. in folklore from the University of Pennsylvania. He has served as the president of the American Folklore Society. Glassie is the author of *Pattern in the Material Folk Culture of the Eastern United States, Folk Housing in Middle Virginia, Passing the Time in Ballymenone, Irish Folktales, The Spirit of Folk Art, Turkish Traditional Art Today, Art and Life in Bangladesh, Material Culture,* and other books. He has received awards for his work from the governments of Turkey and Bangladesh.

TRUDIER HARRIS-LOPEZ is J. Carlyle Sitterson Professor of English at the University of North Carolina at Chapel Hill, where she teaches courses in African American literature and folklore. She has lectured throughout the United States, as well as in Jamaica, Canada, France, Germany, Poland, Spain, and Italy. Her authored books include *From Mammies to Militants: Domestics in Black American Literature*, *Exorcising Blackness: Historical and Literary Lynching and Burning Rituals*, *Black Women in the Fiction of James Baldwin* (for which she won the 1987 College Language Association Creative Scholarship Award), *Fiction and Folklore: The Novels of Toni Morrison*, and *The Power of the Porch: The Storyteller's Craft in Zora Neale Hurston, Gloria Naylor, and Randall Kenan*. She edited *New Essays on Baldwin's Go Tell It on the Mountain* and co-edited *The Oxford Companion to African American Literature*, *Call and Response: The Riverside Anthology of the African American Literary Tradition*, and *The Literature of the American South: A Norton Anthology*. During 1996–97, she was a resident fellow at the National Humanities Center, where she worked on her latest book manuscript, which is a study of legendary strong black female characters in African American literature. In 2000, she was awarded the William C. Friday/Class of 1986 Award for Excellence in Teaching.

MARY HUFFORD is the director of the University of Pennsylvania's Center for Folklore and Ethnography. She worked for many years as a folklife specialist at the American Folklife Center in the Library of Congress. She has published widely on folklore, cultural policy, and ecological crisis, including an edited volume, *Conserving Culture: A New Discourse on Heritage*. Her regional studies in central Appalachia and in southern New Jersey include her book *Chaseworld: Foxhunting and Storytelling in New Jersey's Pine Barrens*, and they reflect her broader interest in discourses on nature, environment, and the body, and the production of social imaginaries.

DEBORAH A. KAPCHAN is an associate professor of anthropology at the University of Texas at Austin and is the former director of the Center for Intercultural Studies in Folklore and Ethnology. She is the author of *Gender on the Market: Moroccan Women and the Revoicing of Tradition* and is currently completing a book on the musical and aesthetic dimensions of the Gnawa culture. She has written extensively on gender, genre, expressive culture, and social transformation in Morocco.

DOROTHY NOYES is an assistant professor of folklore in the Department of English at Ohio State University. She is interested in performance and public space in plural societies and has published articles, edited journal issues, and published an exhibition catalog on expressive genres ranging from riddle to suicide in various Romance-speaking cultures. Her forthcoming book *Fire in the Plaça* is an ethnography of a Catalan Corpus Christi festival during and after the Spanish transition to democracy.

GERALD L. POCIUS is a professor of folklore, a member of the Archaeology Unit, and director of the Centre for Material Culture Studies at Memorial University of Newfoundland. He has been an NEH Fellow at Winterthur Museum, a guest curator at the Newfoundland Museum, and the recipient of three SSHRC Research Grants from the Government of Canada. He has published widely on Newfoundland culture, and his current research interests include the world of professional wrestling and the vernacular architecture of St-Pierre et Miquelon. His book *A Place to Belong* received the Chicago Folklore Prize and the Cummings Prize of the Vernacular Architecture Forum. He is working on a manuscript on domestic interiors and concepts of heritage.

JEFF TODD TITON is a professor of music and director of the Ph.D. program in ethnomusicology at Brown University. Previously he held a joint appointment at Tufts University in the departments of English and music. He is best known to folklorists for his *Journal of American Folklore* article "The Life Story," which theorized personal narratives as self-contained fictions; for his books on blues *(Early Downhome Blues, Downhome Blues Lyrics)*, religious folklife *(Powerhouse for God, Give Me This Mountain)*, and southern Appalachian music *(Old Time Kentucky Fiddle Tunes)*; and for albums made from his field recordings, one featuring the fiddler and NEA Heritage Award winner Clyde Davenport *(Puncheon Camps)* and most recently *Songs of the Old Regular Baptists*. A portfolio of his documentary photographs was featured in *Time and Temperature*, one of the American Folklore Society's centennial publications, and he has also been involved in the theory and practice of documentary folklore films and multimedia computer programs. He is a fellow of the American Folklore Society, an old-time fiddler and banjo player, and an organic gardener and orchardist.

INDEX

Abrahams, Roger D., 14, 77, 130
Abrams, James, 159, 169
Adorno, Theodor, 151
Aesthetics. *See* Art
"Affecting presences" (Armstrong), 1–2, 51
American Folklore Society, 100, 106, 206
Anderson, Benedict, 15, 27, 33
Andersson, Lars, 186
Anthropology: approach to folk art in, 51; critique of representation in, 82–83; evolutionary, 152–53; of human movement, 127; interpretive (Geertz), 80–83, 87; tradition as concept in, 180–81
Appadurai, Arjun, 212
Appalachia, 158–68, 171n3
Armstrong, Robert Plant, 1–2
Art: "affecting presences" (Armstrong) and, 1–2, 51; as behavior, 54–55; as component of folklore, 42–44, 183; craft vs., 45–46, 50–51, 108–9; critical function of, 135, 162–64, 171n11, 171n14; cultural economy of, 22–23; "emotional core" of, 51–52; emotional impact of, 59; everyday life aesthetics and, 4, 54–55; "expressive culture" concept and, 2–3; "folk" as qualifier for, 49–51, 57–58, 61n2; folklore exhibition of, 21–22, 159–64; history of concept, 44–48, 55; individual vs. collective, 44, 55–60, 61n4; landscape gardens as, 160–62; outsider, 57; as performance, 52–53, 131; secularization of, 45–46; skill and, 44,

55–60; style and, 49–51, 61n1; symmetry/asymmetry in, 170n3; verbal vs. material, 50. *See also* Material culture
Artaud, Antonin, 123, 133
Audience: absence of, 185; as evangelical object, 79; impact on genre, 185–86; performance and, 10, 21–22, 29–33, 76, 113, 126, 133–34; responsibility of, 133–37. *See also* Performance
Authenticity: as adherence of text to source, 70, 111–12; blues performance and, 107–8; conservatism within networks and, 23–24; *hava* (Turkish concept of tradition) and, 192; marketplace distortion of, 213, 217; oral vs. literary ballads and, 107; scholarly disciplines and, 101–4, 109–10; social mobility and, 20; theatricality and, 78; tradition and, 182–84, 188–89; of "triumphant objects" (Klusen), 22. *See also* Tourism
Author, 70, 71, 89, 94, 117n4

"Backtalking," 164–69
Bahloul, Joelle, 20
Bakhtin, M. M.: on "chronotopes," 150–51; on dialogism in social networks, 26; on double grounding of events, 147–48, 161; on hybrid construction, 115; marketplace metaphor of, 21, 35
Balkanization, 207–8
Ballads, 90–91, 107, 185, 189–90
Baraka, Imamu Amiri, 3

Marxism, 35, 74–75, 216. *See also*
Class; Hegemony
Material culture: calligraphy, 186–87;
craft vs. art, 45–46, 50–51, 108–9;
"decorated palms," 21; as emblem
of community, 34–35; foodways,
20; photocopy lore, 110–11, 118n11;
pottery, 186; quilting, 108–9, 167;
recontextualization of, 23, 159–64;
as status symbol, 19, 42, 45–46. *See
also* Art
McCannell, Dean, 162–63
McDowell, John H., 30
McRobbie, Andrew, 218n4
Mead, George Herbert, 218–19n6
Mead, Margaret, 201
Meaning: authorial intention and, 71,
94; consensus and, 13, 30–31, 160;
contextual leakage of, 160, 166–67;
effect of frames on, 5, 148–49;
emergence in performance, 136–37;
postmodern irony and, 213
Mediation: anonymity and, 35, 90,
93–94; consensus and, 13, 30–31,
160; embodiment and, 93–94, 126–
28; graphics lore and, 114; hypertext and, 69, 90–95; media lore and,
114; "mediascapes" and, 212; photocopy lore and, 110–11, 118n11;
postmodernism and, 35, 114, 212;
small-scale technology and, 18,
108–9; in social networks, 18–19,
22–23, 35; textuality and, 90, 93–
94; virtual reality and, 30–31. *See
also* Representation
Medvedev, P. N., 115
Memory, 167, 189–91
Metatexts, 79, 95
Michaelangelo, 45
Milroy, Leslie, 19
Mimesis, 128, 214. *See also* Repetition; Theatricality
Modernism, 151–53, 161–62, 170n5
Morris, William, 55, 59–60, 188
Museums, 159–63, 167
Musharaf, Rashida (Bangladeshi
sculptor), 187–88
Music: ballads, 107; blues, 73–74,
107–8; folksong classification, 102;

isicathamiya (South African choir
singing), 132; musical notation,
126–27; spirituals, 106–7
Myth, 74, 104, 118n6

Naming, 12, 27, 29
Narrative: classification of, 102–3,
158; of context of commodities, 23;
doubly grounded communication
(Bakhtin) and, 147–48, 161, 169–
70n1; entextualization of, 122–23;
"folk literature" vs., 102–3, 117n4;
hypertext and, 90; ideology of fairy
tales (Zipes), 75; life stories, 73–74,
79, 168; lying, 164–68; myth, 74,
104, 118n6; narratology, 117n4;
oicotypes (von Sydow), 14–15; of
personal experience, 103, 118n5,
203; of religious conversion, 73;
storytellers and, 18; as verbal art,
50. *See also* Literature
Nationalism. *See* Romantic nationalism
Neighborhoods, 18–19
Network: community conflict with,
10–11, 33–34; density of, 17–19, 23–
24, 29; encapsulation of, 19, 23–26;
features of, 16–17; folk groups as,
13–14, 26; as "global ecumene"
(Hannerz), 18; homogeneity of, 18;
integrativity of, 19, 21–23; riddling
in, 14; segregativity of, 19–21; tradition in, 23. *See also* Group
New Deal folklore, 153–54, 158
New River Gorge National River,
161–64
Nolan, Hugh (Irish storyteller), 189–
90
Nostalgia, 179, 203, 214–15
Noyes, Dorothy, 134

Objectivity: art and, 48; commodification and, 22–23, 133–34, 162–63,
204–5, 216–17; constructed by culture brokers, 13; of cultural identity, 199–200, 204–5, 212–13, 215;
embodiment of performance and,
126–28, 133–34; of groups, 7, 10–11;
prime objects (Kubler) and, 189;

The University of Illinois Press
is a founding member of the
Association of American University Presses.

University of Illinois Press
1325 South Oak Street
Champaign, IL 61820-6903
www.press.uillinois.edu